010446 8
22713

Appearance Bias and Crime

Relying on experts in criminology and sociology, Appearance Bias and Crime describes the role of bias against citizens based on their physical appearance. From the point of suspicion to the decisions to arrest, convict, sentence, and apply the death penalty, crime control agents are influenced by the appearance of offenders; moreover, victims of crime are held blameworthy depending on their physical appearance. The editor and contributing authors discuss such timely topics such as Black Lives Matter, terrorism, LGBTQ appearance, human trafficking, Indigenous appearance, the disabled, and the attractive versus unattractive among us. Demographic traits such as race, gender, age, and social class influence physical appearance and, thus, judgments about criminal involvement and victimization. This volume describes the social movements relevant to appearance bias, recommends legislative and policy changes, offers practical advice to social control agencies on how to reduce appearance bias, and proposes a new sub-discipline of Appearance Criminology.

BONNIE BERRY, PhD, is the Director of the Social Problems Research Group and formerly university faculty. Her research interests include criminology, appearance bias, animal rights, academic misconduct and ethical violations, and all measures of social inequality. She is the author of several books and numerous scholarly journal articles. She has been awarded, among other prizes, the Inconvenient Woman of the Year Award from the American Society of Criminology's Women and Crime Division.

Appearance Bias and Crime

Edited by
BONNIE BERRY
Social Problems Research Group

CAMBRIDGE
UNIVERSITY PRESS

CAMBRIDGE
UNIVERSITY PRESS

University Printing House, Cambridge CB2 8BS, United Kingdom

One Liberty Plaza, 20th Floor, New York, NY 10006, USA

477 Williamstown Road, Port Melbourne, VIC 3207, Australia

314–321, 3rd Floor, Plot 3, Splendor Forum, Jasola District Centre,
New Delhi – 110025, India

79 Anson Road, #06–04/06, Singapore 079906

Cambridge University Press is part of the University of Cambridge.

It furthers the University's mission by disseminating knowledge in the pursuit of
education, learning, and research at the highest international levels of excellence.

www.cambridge.org
Information on this title: www.cambridge.org/9781108422314
DOI: 10.1017/9781108377683

First published 2019

Printed in the United Kingdom by TJ International Ltd, Padstow Cornwall

A catalogue record for this publication is available from the British Library.

Library of Congress Cataloging-in-Publication Data
NAMES: Berry, Bonnie, author.
TITLE: Appearance bias and crime / edited by Bonnie Berry, Social Problems
Research Group.
DESCRIPTION: Cambridge, United Kingdom ; New York, NY :
Cambridge University Press, 2019.
IDENTIFIERS: LCCN 2018043661 | ISBN 9781108422314 (hardback) |
ISBN 9781108432016 (pbk.)
SUBJECTS: LCSH: Criminal anthropology. | Physical-appearance based bias. |
Criminal behavior, Prediction of. | Discrimination in criminal justice administration.
CLASSIFICATION: LCC HV6035 .A67 2019 | DDC 364.2/4–dc23
LC record available at https://lccn.loc.gov/2018043661

ISBN 978-1-108-42231-4 Hardback
ISBN 978-1-108-43201-6 Paperback

Dedicated to the Memory of Bob Bursik

1951–2017

The arc of the moral universe is long but it bends toward justice.
Reverend Dr. Martin Luther King, Jr.

Contents

Biographical Sketches of Contributors

Robert Agnew, PhD, is Samuel Candler Dobbs Professor of Sociology at Emory University. He has published seven books and approximately 150 articles and chapters on the causes of crime and delinquency, with his books including *Toward a Unified Criminology: Assumptions about Crime, People, and Society*; *Criminological Theory: Past to Present*; *Juvenile Delinquency: Causes and Control*; *Why Do They Do It? A General Theory of Crime and Delinquency*; and *Pressured into Crime: An Overview of General Strain Theory*. He is best known for his development of general strain theory, one of the leading theories of crime and delinquency. He has served as President of the American Society of Criminology and is Fellow of that organization.

Bonnie Berry, PhD, is Director of the Social Problems Research Group and formerly university faculty. Her areas of research interest include appearance bias, animal rights, academic misconduct and ethical violations, and all measures of social inequality. She is the author of *Social Rage: Emotion and Cultural Conflict*; *Beauty Bias: Discrimination and Social Power*; *The Power of Looks: Social Stratification of Physical Appearance*; (coauthor) *Scholarly Crimes and Misdemeanors: Violations of Fairness and Trust in the Academic* World, and numerous research articles on a range of social problems topics. She is the recipient of the Inconvenient Woman of the Year Award (Division of Women and Crime, American Society of Criminology), the Herbert Bloch Award, and the Mentor of Mentors Award (the latter two from the American Society of Criminology).

Stephen A. Bishopp, PhD, is Associate Director for Research at the Caruth Police Institute in the Dallas Police Department in Dallas, Texas. He received his MS (2009) and PhD (2013) in Criminology from the University of Texas at Dallas. He is a 26-year veteran and Sergeant with the Dallas Police Department. His current research interests include evidence-based policing, criminological theory, and criminal justice policy. Steve is also an adjunct professor at the University of Texas at Dallas, the University of North Texas at Dallas, and Collin College. He teaches a variety of undergraduate courses on a number of topics including policing, criminal investigations, introduction to forensics, public policy, and criminal law. His most recent peer-reviewed publications appear in *Policing, Criminal Justice Policy Review,* and *Journal of Public Health.*

Brenda Sims Blackwell, PhD, is Professor and Chair of the Department of Criminal Justice and Criminology and Affiliate Faculty member of the Women and Gender Studies program at Georgia Southern University. Her areas of specialization include women, crime, and criminal justice, criminological theory, with a particular focus on elaborating power control theory, and social differentiation. She has published numerous articles in journals such as *Criminology, Deviant Behavior,* and *Journal of Criminal Justice,* and several book chapters. She has served as an editorial board member for the *Journal of Criminal Justice, Feminist Criminology,* and *Women and Criminal Justice.*

Denise Paquette Boots, PhD, is Program Head and Professor of Criminology and Senior Research Fellow in the Institute for Urban Policy Research at the University of Texas at Dallas. She is a former US Border Patrol Agent trainee and Level 4 juvenile counselor for adjudicated youth. Her research agenda focuses on issues related to interpersonal violence, with a specific emphasis on domestic violence and homicide, child abuse and neglect, mental health, life-course criminology, neuropsychological vulnerabilities, capital punishment, gendered pathways to crime and victimization, parricide, and outcome and process evaluations of problem-solving courts and criminal justice programs. Her professional community service activities include serving as an Executive Committee and General Taskforce member of the City of Dallas Domestic Violence Taskforce, as an editorial board member for the respected journal *Violence against Women,* and as the senior executive counselor for the Division of Women and Crime of the American Society of Criminology. In 2010, she was awarded the University of Texas Board of Regents' Outstanding Teaching Award, one of the most selective and prestigious teaching awards in the country. In 2016, she was awarded the Evelyn Gilbert Unsung Hero Award for her contributions to scholarship and teaching from the Minorities and Women Section of the Academy of Criminal Justice Sciences. In May 2016 she was awarded the UT Dallas President's Teaching Excellence Award for tenured faculty. Dr. Boots is frequently called upon as a consultant to various non-profit organizations, is a court-certified expert on family violence, and is regularly sought out by national and local media outlets regarding topics related to interpersonal violence.

Lorenzo Boyd, PhD, served as President of the Academy of Criminal Justice Sciences (2016–2017) and is an Associate Professor of Criminal Justice and Director of the Center for Advanced Policing in the Henry C. Lee College of Criminal Justice and Forensic Sciences at the University of New Haven. He earned a PhD in Sociology from Northeastern University, specializing in urban policing. He spent over a decade as a Deputy Sheriff in Suffolk County (Boston), Massachusetts and currently serves as a police consultant and conducts police training and promotional assessments. Dr. Boyd also served as a Senior Researcher at the North Carolina Juvenile Justice Institute where he conducted program evaluations on local community-based juvenile justice intervention programs.

Brenda Chaney, PhD, is Senior Lecturer at The Ohio State University in the Department of Sociology. Her long-term interests include women's imprisonment. She runs an Inside-Out Program and leads a lifers' book discussion group, both at the Ohio Reformatory for Women.

Dean A. Dabney, PhD, is Professor of Criminal Justice and Criminology in the Andrew Young School of Policy Studies at Georgia State University. Dr. Dabney's research agenda is principally focused on the study of organizational cultures within a criminal justice context using qualitative methods. In this regard, he has studied the use of confidential informants in law enforcement, homicide investigation, theft and substance abuse behaviors occurring among practicing pharmacists and nurses, incompetence among prison doctors, as well as shoplifting and employee theft in the retail industry.

Kimberly Conway Dumpson, JD, Esq., CFRE, is the Vice President for College Advancement and External Relations at Rhode Island College. She is a passionate advocate devoted to issues of access and affordability for students from diverse racial, ethnic, and socio-economic backgrounds. She is actively engaged in community service, and was recognized as the Women of the Year in Maryland as well as a Hometown Hero by Maryland Governor Martin O'Malley.

Mark S. Hamm, PhD, is Professor of Criminology and Criminal Justice at Indiana State University. He has published a number of books, including *In Bad Company: America's Terrorist Underground*; *American Skinheads: The Criminology and Control of Hate Crime*; and *Apocalypse in Oklahoma: Waco and Ruby Ridge Revenged*.

John G. Hansen, PhD, is Member of the Opaskwayak Cree Nation in northern Manitoba. He has been a Correctional Officer, an elementary and high school teacher, and a faculty member in the Aboriginal and Northern Studies Department at the University College of the North, Manitoba. He is currently an assistant professor in the Sociology Department at the University of Saskatchewan, and his research and teaching specializations are in the fields of restorative justice, indigenous justice; crime and society, focusing on Indigenous knowledge and ways of healing. He now lives in Saskatoon and writes on Indigenous topics.

Daniela Pisoiu, PhD, is Senior Researcher at the Austrian Institute for International Affairs. Her fields of research are: terrorism, radicalization, extremism, comparative regional security, American and European foreign and security policy. She completed her PhD at the University of St. Andrews, Centre for the Study of Terrorism and Political Violence and has conducted fieldwork on the topic of radicalization in Austria, Germany, and France. She is the author of *Islamic Radicalisation in Europe: An Occupational Change Process* (2011), coauthor of *Theories of Terrorism: An Introduction* (2017), and editor of *Arguing Counterterrorism: New Perspectives* (2014).

Bradford W. Reyns, PhD, is Associate Professor in the Department of Criminal Justice at Weber State University. His research focuses on different dimensions of criminal victimization, particularly victimological theory, victim decision-making, and the relationship between technology use and victimization. Reyns' recent work on these topics has appeared in *Justice Quarterly*, *Journal of Criminal Justice*, and *Journal of Research in Crime and Delinquency*.

Heidi L. Scherer, PhD, is Associate Professor in the Department of Sociology and Criminal Justice at Kennesaw State University. She is currently working on research related to victimization risk among subsamples of the population including college students with disabilities and those under correctional supervision. Scherer has peer-reviewed publications that have appeared in the *Journal of Interpersonal Violence*, *Crime and Delinquency*, and the *Journal of School Violence*.

Ian Skinner is Research Assistant and Undergraduate Student in Anthropology and Criminal Justice at Appalachian State University.

Elicka Peterson Sparks, PhD, is Professor of Criminology and Criminal Justice and Director of the Honors Program in the Department of Government and Justice Studies at Appalachian State University. In addition to scholarly articles and contributions to textbooks in criminology, she is the author of *The Devil You Know: The Surprising Link between Conservative Christianity and Crime*, and the coauthor, with Kit Gruelle, of *Intimate Partner Violence: Effective Procedure, Response, and Policy*. Her work has been cited in media outlets such as the *New York Times* and she has consulted on several documentaries, including *Blind Spot: Murder by Women* for PBS and HBO's *Private Violence*.

Brent Teasdale, PhD, serves as Professor and Chair of the Criminal Justice Department at Illinois State University. Dr. Teasdale primarily writes about violence by and against people with mental illnesses. With Drs. Bonnie Berry and Dean Dabney, he has recently been working on issues of appearance bias in arrest and victimization experiences.

Billy J. Ulibarrí, PhD, is Lecturer in the Department of Sociology and Anthropology at the University of Texas Rio Grande Valley. He studies issues of gender, sexuality, and victimization in the areas of gender-based violence and social movements. He is currently working on a study of adult probation populations in communities at the United States/Mexico border. He earned his doctorate in sociology from the University of New Mexico.

Jennifer Wareham, PhD, is Associate Professor in the Department of Criminal Justice at Wayne State University. She earned her PhD from the University of South Florida. Her research interests include juvenile justice, program evaluation, interpersonal violence, and criminological theories.

Terry Wotherspoon, PhD, is Department Head and Professor of Sociology at the University of Saskatchewan and Past-President of the Canadian Sociological Association. His extensive research and publication activities focus on relations between schooling and work, education, and social policy, and social inequality with particular emphasis on conditions and experiences of immigration and Indigenous populations. His research and publications in the sociology of education have been recognized with awards from the Canadian Education Association and the Canadian Association for Foundations of Education.

Acknowledgments

Most of all, I thank the contributors to this volume, without whom this project would not have been possible. They were specifically chosen because they are expert in their various specializations. They were so patient with my endless questions and so gracious in granting their time and effort to this project. Besides these folks, I am grateful to other academic colleagues who gave generously of their time lending their insights to this unique study. They include: Joanne Belknap, Robert Bogdan, Rich Felson, Bonnie Fisher, Dr. Chris Heringlake (DDS), Joanne Kaufman, Gary LaFree, Sarah Esther Lageson, Eric Longabardi, Rick McGary, Doug Meyer, Stephen Muzzatti, Susan Schweik, and Susan Tiano. Among those who have offered knowledge that I would otherwise have had no way of knowing, I thank Heather Valdez Freeman of the Tribal Law and Policy Institute.

The staff at Cambridge University Press, its reviewers, copyeditor Matthew Seal, Jackie Grant (editorial assistant extraordinaire), Joshua Penney (unparalleled content manager), and of course my editor Robert Dreesen have all been indispensable. They made it happen.

My family and other friends have always been there to listen and show genuine interest; moreover, they offered reprieves from work when I needed it the most but was too darn stubborn to admit it.

Finally, I thank my best friend, Pete Lara, for his steadfast support and patience. He has never wavered in his faith in me and my work. That means everything to me.

Introduction

The Nature of Appearance Bias and Its Relevance to Crime

Bonnie Berry

This is a story of evolution, or at least I hope it is. In my previous work, I wondered whether appearance bias – the last and least considered form of discrimination – will go the way of other biases (sexism, racism, homophobia, anti-Semitism, ableism, etc.). True, none of these "isms" are completely gone and may never be. Movement toward social equality has been a slow and incremental process eventually culminating in a broadening recognition of equal rights. The same may be true of appearance bias.

The consequences of broad-based appearance bias as it occurs in general society are dire enough, yet perhaps more dire are the consequences of appearance bias in this more restricted setting of crime control and criminal victimization. This text hopes to bring into stark relief the manner in which justice is denied, lives are ruined, and people die because of the judgments made about offenders' and victims' physical appearance.

This book applies the same principles as my earlier publications on appearance bias (e.g., 2007, 2008a), which focused on how society discriminates for and against humans with particular physical features. In the present endeavor, however, my contributing authors and I are addressing appearance bias as it operates in the crime control context. In general and in crime control, appearance bias is strongly related to social power, particularly socioeconomic status, with its effects more keenly observed in matters of crime control.

GENERAL DISCUSSION

It is well known that humans respond to other humans' physical appearance, but this phenomenon is not intricately or broadly understood.

Indeed, we usually think of it, if we think of it at all, as a "given"; that, yes, we do judge people on their appearance but that this judgment is normal and acceptable.

I began researching appearance bias in 1999 as it is experienced in the United States and worldwide. Among the themes that emerged is vulner- ability to forces that make or break us in the course of our daily lives, be those events blocked social opportunities such as education, employment, romance and marriage, social networks, and health care or be those events decisions made about us by a crime control system.

Appearance bias is an important social force because major decisions are made about people depending on their appearance; we are employed or not, well-educated or not, invited into club memberships or not, married or not, and receive health care or not at least partly or entirely because of our appearance. These decisions affect our lives in irreversible ways to the point of determining how long we live and how well we live. Generally, attractive people are granted opportunities that unattractive and plain people are refused. Unattractive and plain people are at a disadvantage insofar as having some of life's doors automatically closed in the pursuit of well-being and happiness. This form of prejudice, as is true for other forms of prejudice, can happen overtly or subtly.

People, of course, vary in terms of their attractiveness; most people are plain or ordinary looking, some are distinctly attractive, and some are unattractive. One of the first questions raised when a discussion of appearance bias is brought forward is agreement about "beauty" and non-beauty. It is said that beauty is in the eye of the beholder. If so, beholders agree on what constitutes good looks. There is, in fact, quite a lot of consensus regarding beauty standards: attractiveness and unattract- iveness are agreed upon cross-culturally and across time. The standards of beauty are mainly White, Northern European standards (blonde hair, light features) with extra points given to the tall and slim. "Cross-cultural studies have been done with people in Australia, England, China, India, Japan, Korea, Scotland, and the United States. All show that there is significant agreement among people of different races, and different cul- tures about which faces they consider beautiful..." (Etcoff, 1999: 138; see also Berry, 2011). Not only is beauty racially informed, it is not objective or neutral. "Although the overt racial standards of beauty are often unspoken, people across ethnic groups and class levels tend to agree about who possesses beauty and who does not" (Hunter, 2004: 30). Margaret Hunter's bringing up class levels is supremely important to this text; race is of course significant to judgments about attractiveness *and* about criminality but so is the oft-overlooked trait of socioeconomic status (SES). SES determines more than we commonly realize about our appearance, partly because the financially better off attract and mate with attractive people but probably more so because, without financial support, we cannot afford good skin care, dental care, healthy diets, and expensive grooming practices.

In other words, our appearance is largely beyond our control due to economic status and genetics, yet we add insult to injury when we realize that we are judged by the same, often-unreachable standards as those with ideal looks. While cross-culturally, we agree on the definition of beauty with the standards being mostly the same across race/ethnicity and around the globe, this poses a problem for those who cannot meet such rigid standards to be tall, thin, blonde, White, with even features, and no sign of disability or health issues. It poses such a problem that some who cannot reach these agreed-upon social standards will go to extraordinary lengths to alter their appearance in order that they may become well-employed, gain an education, get suitably married, or be admitted to coveted social circles. Think surgery (eyelid surgery to round out the Asian eye, breast implants, leg-lengthening, etc.) and less dramatic alterations (skin lightening, hair straightening, etc.). Often these alterations are not for beautification but are race-denying practices. There is nothing inherently unattractive about nonwhite racial features but, because the standards are what they are and in order to be socially accepted and socially desired, some will engage in nose tipping, lip flattening, eyelid rounding, and the like (Berry, 2007, 2008a).

Subjectivity and the Meaning of Attractiveness

Some people have a less desirable or less socially acceptable appearance than others. But what do these terms (desirable and acceptable) mean? Some of the variables I address herein to describe attractiveness and unattractiveness have nothing to do with objective measures of attractiveness, to the extent that objective measures exist. Among the subjective features would be the aforementioned racialized features. (Note that the word "racialized" is understood to mean nonwhite. This is quizzical in itself since very White features, such as blonde hair and blue eyes, could be taken to mean "racialized" in a, for example, Nordic sense.) Yes, it is agreed upon even among racial minorities that the standard for beauty is White Northern European. Yet, at its very basis, the question remains as to what precisely is unacceptable about Asian features, Indigenous features, and Black features? I can, and anyone can, say that racialized features per se are not attractive or unattractive; they are just racialized features. However, these variables are nevertheless markers that tell the social audience something, falsely, about the people who possess these markers. It is important to bear in mind throughout this book that these immediately visual signs (physical appearance) are exactly that: *signs*. The interpretation of those signs is the significant factor in the phenomenon of appearance bias.

Agreement about attractiveness has increased as time progressed, with the best possible explanation for this growing consensus being globalization of visual images. Through television, movies, magazines, billboards, and other visual media, the world's standards of acceptable and unacceptable looks are homogenized because we, internationally, are presented with a restricted image of what is beautiful. Media of all types can firmly embed already held views; media can also change views by influencing what we think of as attractive.

Media depictions of various appearance traits as attractive or unattractive can serve as microaggressions and can thus perpetuate and solidify appearance bias, with microaggressions serving as subtle or unintentional forms of offense commonly aimed at minorities (see Sue, 2010; also see further comments below in this chapter). The worldwide media depiction of the ideal type of beauty as tall, thin, even-featured Caucasian is itself a microaggression since, by its exclusion of people who don't fit this appearance pattern, it is a rejection.

Appearance bias can be thought of and experienced as microaggressions, but appearance bias can also be obvious and intended aggressions as in the overt signals denigrating those with appearance challenges, such as license plate holders declaring "No Fat Chicks." These standards, against which we are all judged and which are perpetuated via media, are unlikely to change soon. This means that, for nonwhites in a world that prizes Caucasian features, socially desirable features are beyond reach. But no more beyond reach than other physical features that are mainly a matter of luck (genetic or socioeconomic), such as good dentition, clear complexions, thick hair, evenly placed facial features, significant height, moderate to low body fat, and an absence of obvious disabilities.

Facial symmetry is important, so important that even a small variation in symmetry is sufficient to make one's face deemed to be unattractive. There are mathematical formulae that describe how far apart facial features should be and how large each feature should be. Too much or too little space between the upper lip and the end of the nose, eyes spaced too far apart or too closely together, a forehead too broad or too narrow, or a jaw too jutting or too receding can make a person looks-challenged. Think about this. This issue of facial symmetry is very strict. And now, think about this question: what is meant by "too" narrow, broad, close-together, far-apart, large or small? Yet, oddly, these dimensions are agreed upon within cultures and across cultures.

In short, while we may hope for minutely defined designations of attractiveness, the plain fact is that attractiveness relies on the principles above. We know attractiveness when we see it.

Much of the literature on beauty standards really pertains to indicators of youth and health. Youth and health are interrelated albeit not entirely. Healthy, youthful specimens are sought after for mating, for friendship, for employment, and for all manner of social networking. Good teeth, good skin, a free-swinging gait, an upright posture, thick hair (etc.) all speak to fecundity and to physical capability (see, e.g., Etcoff, 1999 for her work on "survival of the prettiest"). Such a person is able to mate and will give us no trouble in whatever capacity we may need them regarding work or the simple and easy enjoyment of life. However, sometimes, perhaps usually, the attraction to healthy and youthful-looking people is sex (as in a desire for sexual encounters) rather than reproductive capabilities. In the non-crime world, gay men prefer young, good-looking men as their part-ners. Young, good-looking, slightly built gay men are also more desirable as sex crime targets and thus criminally victimized more commonly than older and larger gay men (Felson, Cundiff, & Painter-Davis, 2012).

Obviously, appearance is complicatedly related to a number of demo-graphic variables: gender, age, race/ethnicity, and socioeconomic status. For example, women are held to different standards than men, as clearly seen in the harsher treatment of obese women compared to obese men (Bordo, 1995; Braziel & LeBesco, 2001; Wann, 1998). Appearance is also related to nondemographic variables such as sexual orientation, as we will see in this text. Finally, advanced societies are beginning to recognize the disadvantages faced by the poor, the elderly, the disabled, the migrant, the ethnic minority, the non-heterosexual, and all others who share a disvalued trait. It would be helpful if and when societies recognize these disadvantages as interfacing with physical appearance.

THE NEW ANALYSIS: CRIME AND PHYSICAL APPEARANCE

The physical attributes that will be discussed in this text refer to vulner-ability to being targeted as criminal offenders and vulnerability to victimization; both forms of vulnerability can refer to bias against people because of their physical appearance. In the broader, noncrime world, for instance, disability reduces social opportunities (access to buildings, denial of employment, poor health care, romance, etc.); at the same time, disability can make us vulnerable to crime. These appearance vulnerabilities – be they racial, gender, age, attractiveness, LGBTQ identity, attire, a "terrorist" appearance, etc. – are the same or similar, in process and in experience, as appearance vulnerabilities occurring in the subset crime world for suspected offenders and for victims of crime. To say that these appearance vulnerabilities are "the same or similar" in both populations is likely true, but to say that these vulnerabilities are *amplified* for the subset crime world may also be true since the appearance-challenged are a disadvantaged population to begin with.

There is very little published on this phenomenon, but I will advance the notion that appearance plays a far more salient role in criminal suspicion, conviction, sentencing, and victimization than has previously been considered. Myths will be dispelled, as I situate the discussion of appearance bias in the centuries-old but limited historical context of criminological interest in physical appearance and crime.

There is much to be said and, hopefully, this text will not disappoint in our search for understanding of the place of physical appearance in the crime control process. There are a few twists and turns; for example, given that attractive people are ordinarily greatly advantaged, one would think that would apply in crime control also. Usually this is the case but, as the reader will see, it is not necessarily always the case.

What We Need to Know

At rock bottom, one of the main questions that we, as sociologists and criminologists, hope to answer is how to most effectively deal with crime and criminal victimization; we have long strived to know what works and what doesn't work in crime control. Important elements of effective crime control are apprehending people who have indeed committed crime and preventing crime from occurring in the first place. Thus we aim to reduce crime and criminal victimization.

To that end, over the centuries, our efforts have primarily centered on determining causality with an eye toward preventive measures. Neglected in this search have been misperceptions about the identity of criminals and crime victims based on their physical appearance.

The question of how physical appearance influences crime is *intricate* and *important* yet *under-studied*. It is *intricate* in that physical features vary infinitely (body size, skin color, hair texture, disabilities, facial feature organization, etc.) while social perception of these physical features varies little cross-culturally and intra-culturally (Berry, 2007, 2008). As a public, we attribute personality, attitudinal, and behavioral traits to others depending upon their appearance: those attributions are commonly applied in similar ways, such as attributing laziness to heavy people, niceness to pretty people, capability to tall people, and suspected criminality to nonwhite people.

It is fairly well-documented that attractive people are more likely to get away with criminal offenses while unattractive people are more likely to be arrested, convicted, and sentenced harshly (Etcoff, 1999; Katz, 1995; Waldman, 2013). It is less well-documented that unattractive people are more likely to be victimized, and there are caveats to this general finding. For instance, teenagers, particularly teen girls who are bullied are not always unattractive but rather can be quite attractive, and their attractiveness is the reason for their being bullied. Mainly, however, the bullied are picked on because of a socially undesirable physical appearance, such as obesity, or for a gender-nonconforming appearance (Pascoe, 2012). Nearly always the actual bullying is obvious, as evidenced by threats, verbal assaults, and physical abuse, but the reason (being nonwhite, disabled, obese, etc.) can vary.

The question is *important* because major decisions about employment, health care, educational opportunities, etc. are made about people depending on appearance; these decisions affect our lives in long-term if not permanent ways. Myriad judgments are made about us based on what we look like, including, and this is my argument here, judgments about criminal involvement.

The relationship between appearance and crime is relatively *unstudied*, and the reason for that is somewhat puzzling given the importance of appearance in our lives and upon our social opportunities. The absence of scientific attention to this topic might be explained as (1) we assume that appearance is a "given," randomly assigned by the whimsy of nature, unchangeable, and thus ineligible as a target for study; (2) some appearance traits are viewed as the negatively judged person's own fault (notably poor dentition, obesity), and thus the appearance-challenged and their "faults" are not worthy of scientific consideration; and (3) criminals and crime victims are often already considered to be second-class citizens, unattractive ones more so, thus they are unattended scientifically and popularly.

However, appearance is a highly significant factor in understanding crime and criminal victimization partly because it does not have a complete overlap with behavior. That is, while there is some evidence that physical appearance may influence a person's career choice, to engage in a legitimate career versus a criminal career (see Chapter 2 by Teasdale and Berry in this text), probably most people who are plain or unattractive do not choose to engage in crime. Like race, poverty, immigration status, and the usual variables we study in relation to crime, appearance does not necessarily channel a person into crime or victimization but it does, like race and other demographic factors, very much have to do with public and criminal justice *responses* to crime and victimization. In short, unattractive people, like people with racial minority characteristics, may be more likely to be arrested, convicted, and severely sentenced than attractive and White people. And unattractive people, like people with minority characteristics, may be more likely to be victimized, to be bullied, and to not receive fair treatment compared to attractive and majority people.

Let me state the obvious that criminal behavior officially means crime as defined by and acted upon by responders to the supposed crime. This seems simple enough, and we know that a range of characteristics of alleged offenders and their environments heavily influence whether and what type of law enforcement will result. An obvious example would be the recent tumult over racially targeted stopping-and-frisking, "driving while Black," and the "papers-please" policies that are leveled against ethnic minorities and suspected undocumented immigrants based on skin color, attire, and, less so, language.

Microaggression, mentioned earlier, refers to subtle and unintentional insulting behavior. In the case of appearance bias, these non-obvious insults might be experienced as negative remarks about one's looks as when remarking that an overweight person has "such a pretty face" or that a Black person would look better if she or he underwent hair-straightening or lip-thinning. Microaggressions, moreover, are associated with newly considered "victimhood cultures" in which victimization for belonging to a particular category (racial, gender, disability, LGBTQ status, etc.) occurs, with victimhood taking on a more severe meaning in the context of crime control. While there has been some question about the rigor of microaggression research (see, e.g., Sue, 2010), it is a viable concept and a well-known phenomenon and must be addressed here.

Its relevance to the appearance-and-crime context as it is discussed in this text requires some analysis; to wit, one might argue that racial and other profiling as evidenced in patrolling and other crime control activities can be defined as microaggressions since, one might argue, crime controllers are making biased but better-to-be-safe-than-sorry assumptions about categories of people. However, given the possible outcomes of such profiling, such as legally baseless detention of transvestites or police killings of unarmed Black citizens, one might question whether criminal justice interventions can ever be subtle or "micro." While microaggressions occur in classrooms, casual conversation, debates, and other non-crime contexts, aggressive appearance bias as it occurs in the crime context is often if not always overt aggression. At least to my mind, the question of whether offenses against subjects of appearance bias, as crime victims or as crime suspects, leans toward a macroaggression versus a microaggression interpretation.

Assuredly, a global preference for White European features is racist. Nonetheless, the public, even the minority public, make assumptions about people of color that are not made of Caucasians. We see it in a recent publication by Dabney, Teasdale, Ishoy, Gann, and Berry (2017), my comments to Part II, and we see it more pointedly in Lorenzo Boyd's and Kimberley Conway Dumpson's work on Black Lives Matter (Chapter 4). The work by Dabney et al. clearly demonstrates that police judgments are greatly influenced by racialized features, with Black-centric hairstyles resulting in disparate decisions to arrest. The chapter by Boyd and Dumpson shows that Black lives do not matter, at least not so much as White lives.

While it can be said that criminologists have attended to physical features of criminals, much of this earlier work is limited. For instance, in very early historical works, as I will describe below, criminologists focused on atavistic facial and bodily features as well as phrenology (the study of skull shape and smoothness). In the twentieth century, we paid little attention to offenders' appearance with a few notable exceptions such as studies of somatotypes (body types) and their relationship to juvenile delinquency, and as reanalyzed by Sampson and Laub (1997). While those findings were useful, they are restricted in utility since we have yet to understand the enormous array of physical appearance features that affect the probability of engaging in crime; the probability of being suspected, convicted, and sentenced in criminal cases; and the probability of being viewed as a blameless or a blameworthy victim. This text moves us toward that goal.

The Crime Control Process

This book illustrates the process by which people, victims and offenders, are judged by their looks as they journey through the crime control process. From the moment that the police or the public views a suspect as a suspect, to the next stage of arrest, to the following stage of the booking photo (mug shot), and on to the trial (where prospective jurors can be asked if they believe they can "tell by looking" if a defendant is guilty or innocent), conviction, and sentencing, we find that physical appearance plays a role.

Not unexpectedly, the victims, suspects, and known offenders described herein represent a wide range of criminally involved people. Importantly, victims and offenders often overlap as, for instance, in the case of women prisoners, most of whom have been assaulted in their pre-prison lives (see Chapter 6 by Brenda Chaney). Victims will be discussed throughout this book with special attention paid to their appearance as it reflects on judgments about their blameworthiness in Chapter 7 by Jennifer Wareham, Brenda Sims Blackwell, Denise Paquette Boots, and me.

Moreover, the criminal justice process itself can negatively affect the appearance of victims and offenders, as we will see in the editorial comments to Part III and in the Conclusion (Chapter 15). I have described this biased treatment of the looks-challenged as twice- (or thrice- or multiply-) victimized: they have had their appearance ruined by victimization and then are judged harshly because of their altered appearance. They may be held blameworthy as victims, and they may be more likely convicted and sentenced harshly because their features have been destroyed. To make things more complicated still, appearance can be damaged, such as by losing one's teeth due to abuse or poverty, and appearance can be regained, as when one's teeth are restored via dental care while incarcerated. In this unexpected way, people's appearance can improve with incarceration. The released prisoners' appearance can affect their post-release success.

This analysis also takes into account the range of crime control actors involved in making judgments about suspects and victims. They include the medical profession (who determine, through forensic medical examinations whether someone has been assaulted, with darker skin showing abrasions and bruising less than lighter skin), the public who report crime, police, the members of the courtroom (juries, judges, attorneys), university students, and others. Interestingly, the appearance traits of the judgers can and do affect the crime control process, as found in comparing a militaristic police presence versus a less-heavily-armed police presence (see Chapter 9 by Steve Bishopp). Yes, it is complicated. And that is why we need to understand it.

THE FOCUS ON THE VISUAL

Robert Bogdan (2012), an expert on the visual side of human oddities and disabilities, refers to *visual rhetoric* as the "patterns of conventions that have a distinct style that cast the subject in a particular way" (p. 2). Obviously, this text concentrates on visual cues as evidence of criminal involvement, as offenders or as victims. In Bogdan's terms, a "distinct style" can spell trouble.

Visibly Stand-Out Features

In terms of victimization, unusual physical appearance – positive or negative (very attractive or very unattractive, gender nonconforming, etc.) – can lead to bullying and victimization. Obesity is one of the most common reasons that children are bullied (Brody, 2017). Obvious disabilities such as unusual gait or Down Syndrome facial features clearly indicate a difference and can signal ripeness for victimization, and will be discussed in Chapter 13 by Heidi Scherer and Bradford Reyns.

Suspicion is the beginning of the process of blaming people as involved in crime, as victims or as offenders. Given that suspicion is often a snap judgment and nearly always visual, we have a beginning point that is not uncommonly erroneous. It is assumed that young Black men are more criminally suspicious than anyone not falling into that narrow category. It is assumed that the physically disabled are not criminally suspicious. All of the following chapters point to the significance of visual appearance cues such as those mentioned above, as well as the very visibly non-heterosexual (Chapter 12 by Elicka Peterson Sparks and Ian Skinner) and my chapter on "scary clowns" and human oddities (Chapter 14). The public as well as the criminal justice system has immediate reactions – sympathy, fear, distrust, etc. – to the visibly different. In other words, visual cues are paramount in understanding the crime control process, with extreme visual cues serving as a reason for intervention, as when cross-dressers are arrested as sex workers when they are merely cross-dressers.

Uncommon or noteworthy appearance can serve as an accelerant to the discrimination process, with unusually dark skin, unusual attire, notable unattractiveness, tattoos and other contrived appearance alterations, and unusual grooming styles (such as racialized hair styles or heavy cosmetic use) used as signals of criminality or victim blameworthiness. It is known from general-society studies of appearance bias that common or indistinguishable features are preferred over unusual ones (see Etcoff, 1999: 146). Common-appearing people are viewed as nonthreatening; they do not represent "The Other." "Terrorist" identity in the form of hijabs, burkas, and other Muslim attire or the camouflage clothing and weaponry demarking White US-born "terrorists" makes assumed "terrorists" stand out from nonterrorists (see Chapter 10 by Daniela Pisoiu and Chapter 11 by Mark Hamm).

Visible Behavior

It is impossible to overestimate the importance of the physical presentation of self in all of life's varied interactions. First of all, physical appearance is visual, thus making it the initial judgment cue that we use to determine attributes, long before we hear what the person we are viewing has to say, long before we know anything else about her or him. We are often wrong in our assessments of others (and ourselves) based on physical appearance but, nonetheless, these judgments are firm and lasting.

Behavior is also visible and, as such, signals something about the actor. I realized that behavior overlaps with appearance because, obviously, it is visible but, more significantly, behavior speaks to an important trait of the individual. Already mentioned is the example of the visibly physically disabled, as when an unusual gait or spastic movements can signify vulnerability to attack. Another example is offered by Dean Dabney et al. (2017) in their work on confrontational suspect behavior (acting like an "asshole") as influencing police reaction.

Demeanor, Facial Expressions, and Body Language

Billy Uribarrí's analysis on how to spot human trafficking and Brenda Chaney's work on female suspects on trial (Chapters 5 and 6) point to the importance of demeanor and facial expressions. If one's demeanor indicates not wanting to be noticed, for instance avoiding eye contact, that can be a clue that she or he is a trafficking victim. If one's courtroom demeanor is contrite, that would be helpful to avoiding conviction; however, a cold, detached demeanor is taken to mean that the suspect on trial is guilty. The catch with the last example is that a cold, detached demeanor is necessary for survival in neighborhoods where an innocent and contrite facial arrangement can invite victimization.

Facial expressions are more or less voluntary. We can arrange our features to look angry, scary, afraid, kind, and so on. What we offer the world in terms of our facial expressions can be interpreted as what we are trying to convey: leave me alone, I'm pissed so you'd better back off, you're scaring me, and I am a nice person so please don't hurt me.

A lack of facial expression can also speak volumes. As mentioned above about a detached expression, it is not uncommonly interpreted as not caring about what has happened or what may happen next. Relatedly, there is the variously called "one-thousand mile stare" and "one-thousand yard stare." The latter was first coined after World War II to refer to exhaustion, causing a person to stare blankly while deep in thought. The former is more commonly attributed to criminal offenders hoping to appear as though the world around them is unimportant.

Body language also conveys similar signals as facial expressions. Standing with feet wide apart, taking up as much space as possible, indicates dominance. Taking up as little space as possible may infer not wanting to be noticed or confronted. Walking briskly can mean the walker is trying to get away or maybe just in a hurry. Walking slowly with a casually swinging gait can mean feeling comfortable in one's surroundings. Clenching one's fists can mean a readiness to engage in fisticuffs.

Context

The context in which people and their behavior occur is another insight that came up during the course of this work. Context, the surroundings in which one finds oneself, can be a clue about offending or victimization. For example, Latino-appearing men standing in groups in the early morning are often thought to be illegal immigrants awaiting pick-up for day-labor jobs. This same group of men hanging around in the evening or late afternoon may be assumed differently. A shy-appearing, bruised, young woman avoiding eye contact, standing next to an older man, in a hotel registration area is a clue that the young woman is a trafficking victim (see Ulibarrí's work in Chapter 5).

Invisibility

Visibility is best addressed in terms of its corollary, invisibility. As I will remark in the editorial comments to Part II and as will be described in Chapter 3 by Terry Wotherspoon and John Hansen, some who are discriminated against in general society and by the crime control system specifically are sometimes intentionally invisible or hope to be invisible. Indigenous peoples in Canada, Australia, New Zealand, and the United States are not uncommonly segregated from the larger population; thus they are invisible and thus they are ignored by the crime control and social services systems. Their appearance is notable when they are not segregated and can result in biased treatment to be sure. Yet integration is often no more helpful to them than their segregation. Latinos/as in the United States need to be integrated for reasons of employment and other opportunities, yet their visible presence works against them, especially given the harsh US deportation strategies in recent years; their offense need only be the fact of noncitizenship.

Another group of invisible or less visible at-risk people are the homeless. They need public services and yet, if they are visible, they can be subject to public abuse or criminal justice intervention. Homelessness overlaps with appearance for reasons that are easy to figure out: they lack access to baths and showers as well as clean clothing and grooming supplies.

THE HISTORY OF APPEARANCE AND CRIME

In the 1770s, scientists searched for explanations of deviant behavior. One of the prominent explanations was biological, specifically evolutionary, with the lower or less evolved humans being determined as criminal (Rennie, 1978). For purposes of this analysis, what I find interesting is that these "lower ... forms of life" (Rennie, p. 60) could be differentiated from the more evolved and less criminally inclined humans by appearance. "One could tell, *just by looking at them*, which men were of the higher and which the lower order" (Rennie, p. 61, emphasis in original). A physiognomist, Johann Kaspar Lavatar, purported to demonstrate a correspondence between the external and internal man (criminologists in those days did not consider the female as criminal) by examining visible physical traits. Moreover, phrenologists of the late eighteenth and early nineteenth century, such as Franz Josef Gall, believed that we could determine what was inside of a person's mind by examining the external bumps of the skull (Hunter & Macalpine, 1963; Lauvergne, 1844). The appearance of skulls and faces, then, were thought to tell us much about human behavior, including criminal behavior.

In 1876, Cesare Lombroso published *Criminal Man*, an examination of, among other features, pathological anatomy and the evolutionary development of the criminal offender. Lombroso, based on his physical examination of soldiers, criminals, and patients in an insane asylum, concluded that crime is the result of biological differences between criminal offenders and nonoffenders. Referring to the criminal man as a "theromorph," he thought he saw anatomical oddities in the skeleton, brain, skull, and other body parts that set the criminal apart from noncriminals. The atavistic state of the criminal can be seen in many facial and skeletal anomalies that resembled primate features as we would find in apes, features "in fact a type resembling the Mongolian and sometimes the Negro" (1906; 1918: xviii–xix). Bear this in mind when reading this text and ask yourself how far we have come, or not come, in identifying criminals by racial features.

Lombroso also noted that incidental differences such as tattoos are more prevalent among criminals. Clearly, tattoos are the result of decisions that tattoo wearers make and are not an inherent trait of "born criminals." But see Silver, Silver, Siennick, and Farkas (2011) for a discussion of the impact of tattoos on academic achievement, which can then affect occupational choices, criminal and noncriminal. Tattoos, piercings, and other contrived alterations may serve as signals of deviance to some audiences and even lead to police suspicions of criminal suspicion (Jablonski, 2006).

Subsequent research showed little physiological difference between offenders and nonoffenders and, in fact, Lombroso's later research revealed that environmental variables can also influence criminal behavior. From this, we might suppose that *public reaction* to physical appearance, as one environmental variable, might explain the likelihood of being either involved in crime or being apprehended as an offender. Public and official reaction to physical appearance is of utmost importance since the reaction itself can make the argument that physical appearance is meaningless except for the reaction to it. This brings us to Susan Schweik's work.

Ugly Laws

One of the very few detailed histories of appearance bias resulting in criminal justice intervention is Schweik's (2009) account of "ugly laws," which were enacted after the US Civil War (1860–1865) and which will be described in the editorial comments to Part V. In essence, and to great disbelief, the United States once had laws against the unattractive being in public view. Unemployed, homeless wounded soldiers of startling appearance were reduced to begging or laboring in the streets, as were a wide range of other civilians who were disabled or diseased. In a paradoxical turn, these unfortunates were denied full employment and other social opportunities because of their appearance and were thus forced to beg or work the streets through entertainment or selling items (such as news-papers). Yet, they were unwelcome to the public eye because of their appearance. The ugly laws allowed law enforcement to detain such indi-viduals to keep them away from view. The laws were disbanded because they were vague (per the ambiguous definitions of "ugly") and because of a public outcry against the cruel nature of the laws.

Somatotypes

Fast forward to the 1940s, 1950s, and 1990s concern about juvenile delinquency and body types. Research from the 1940s and as recently reanalyzed shows that we continue to pair body types with criminal inclinations when, instead, what would a more fruitful examination would be examining the reaction to the visual cues of body types and the resulting assumptions about criminality.

Attending particularly to youthful offenders, somatotype theories sug-gest that we can tell juvenile delinquency by body type; specifically, mesomorphs, or muscular youngsters, are more likely to engage in delin-quency than ectomorphs (thin children) or endomorphs (soft, fleshy chil-dren). The body structure, the thinking goes, aids in our understanding of the temperament and psychological composition of the individual. In essence, according to the well-known constitutionalists Sheldon Glueck and Eleanor Glueck (1950), endomorphs are inclined to physical comfort, are amiable and even-tempered; ectomorphs are cerebral, restrained, and sensitive; and mesomorphs are aggressive, dominant, high-energy, and ruthless. Glueck and Glueck found that 60 percent of juvenile offenders are mesomorphs (see also Glueck & Glueck, 1956).

The Gluecks began their study in 1939 and compared 500 institutional-ized delinquent boys to a matched sample of 500 nondelinquent boys in the same low-income environment (raised during 1928–1940 in Boston, Massachusetts), noting an interplay between somatic (physique) and other factors such as sociocultural, temperamental, and intellectual factors that could explain delinquency (see also Cullen & Agnew, 2011: 465). Using William Sheldon's classification schema (Sheldon, 1954; Sheldon, Stevens, & Tucker, 1940), they found that delinquent boys were disproportionately mesomorphic; they were temperamentally more aggressive and thus at a greater propensity for delinquency compared to thin and plump boys. Later studies found much the same:

mesomorphic somatotypes were more common among delinquents than nondelinquents (Cortes & Gatti, 1972; Gibbons, 1963; Hartl, Monnelly, & Elderkin, 1982).

Sampson and Laub (1997; 1993) reanalyzed these data and found support for some of the propositions and nonsupport for others. In the 1997 analysis, Sampson and Laub confirmed that social bonds (employment, marriage, etc.) inhibit crime and deviance throughout life, including adulthood, and that mesomorphy plays no role in criminal behavior or, importantly, criminal justice reaction in adulthood. Interviewing the same delinquent and nondelinquent boys from the Glueck and Glueck study as they became adults, Sampson and Laub found that the control group remained uninvolved in crime and that the delinquents accounted for most of the arrests after age 18.

Was it the mesomorphy itself, which psychiatric examinations determine to be associated with aggressiveness, or was it police and court reaction to mesomorphic boys presumed to be engaged in crime? Mesomorphy was found to be directly linked to *official* delinquency, which may mean, as Sampson and Laub suggest, that "mesomorphy's (relatively) stronger relationship with official delinquency stems in part from how juvenile justice officials reacted to large, stout and, muscular boys compared to non-mesomorphic e.g., weak or plump boys" (p. 183). Items such as family processes, school attachment, previous misconduct, and personality (in other words, nonvisible traits) were less indicative of official delinquency than mesomorphy. The focus on official delinquency is important because, it was found, *official bias* seems to be operating. Put in terms of this present volume, appearance bias operates in decisions made about criminal suspects. As Sampson and Laub stated, "Perhaps the juvenile court was more likely to institutionalize boys with mesomorphic body types because they were perceived to be bigger, more dangerous, and more culpable" (p. 184). There may also have been an ethnic component to the court's decision-making: extreme mesomorphs were more likely to be Italians (37% versus 18%), thus introducing ethnic bias into appearance bias and criminal bias.

All this makes sense in light of what is known about appearance bias. Body mass and ethnicity, both of which can affect appearance, influence social perceptions of the subjects. Yet, when these mesomorphic boys grew up, they are no more likely to be engaged in official crime than nonmesomorphic boys; that is, mesomorphy has "no predictive power whatsoever, whether it be for violent arrests, property arrests, official charges in the military, or excessive drinking . . . No matter what the later age..." (p. 184). While mesomorphy may differentiate official delinquents from nondelinquents in adolescence, per official reaction which may be biased, it has no bearing on later criminal involvement.

The Present

Though we no longer examine bumps on the skulls as indicators of criminality, we do and perhaps always will link appearance to behavior, be that behavior criminal behavior or vulnerability to criminal victimization. These judgments apply to adults as well as young children, with these judgments assuming that attractive adults and children are "good" and those with less desirable appearance are not good, as several of the contributing authors herein discuss.

Size continues to matter in many ways, affecting social opportunities, as has been argued in a number of treatments on the topic of appearance bias against obesity (e.g., Bordo, 1995; Braziel & LeBesco, 2001; Stearns, 1997). Obesity can be a factor in bullying behavior as when children are picked on and abused for being heavy (Brody, 2017; Olweus, 1978). When we consider adult victims' size and gender, we discover that stocky rape victims are considered less credible as witnesses to their assault than slender rape victims especially if the victims are good-looking (Katz, 1995).

Small women do not fare well compared to larger women in domestic assault cases, as found by Richard Felson in his "big people hit little people" study. Here, size matters in adult crime as documented by larger-sized men being more likely to be perpetrators in cases of domestic assault (Felson, 1996). This makes perfect sense as larger people are more capable of intimidation and carrying out physical threats against smaller people; often, we see this played out in cases of men (who are larger) assaulting women (who are smaller).

We have little or no control over our age, size, gender, race, and overall attractiveness. Sure, we can undergo gender reassignment but that process itself is noticeable and can lead to suspicion and exclusion. We can alter our racial features, mostly to appear more Caucasian, and plenty of nonwhites engage in race-denying strategies in order to be more socially acceptable and to gain the social opportunities otherwise denied them. As for overall attractiveness, we can, to some degree, make surgical and cosmetic changes to enhance our attractiveness. The old adage "beauty is as beauty does" implies that we can make ourselves more attractive if we try. This is true only in a limited fashion.

We can't stop time; thus we age. Nor can we accelerate time and mature faster than nature allows. We have less control over our body size than much of our society is willing to admit. My first book on the topic of appearance bias (2007) gives detail about the lack of success in controlling weight and, since that publication, science has learned more about the futility of common weight loss practices. And we have no control over height, short of growth hormones, which are very limited in effect.

Attractiveness matters... a lot. Attractive people are less likely to be reported for their offenses; if reported, they are less likely to be formally accused or convicted. This pattern is especially true for attractive women (Etcoff, 1999; Katz, 1995).

Research demonstrates the effects of attractiveness on judgments made about attractive and unattractive people hypothetically and actually involved in crime. When adult research subjects are asked to decide whether children depicted in photos were capable of offenses, such as stepping on dogs' tails or throwing icy snowballs at other children's heads, adults gave good-looking children the benefit of the doubt, presuming, for instance that the child was having a bad day or was a victim of circumstance. The subjects did not believe the attractive child had engaged in this behavior before or would do it again. The unattractive children were more likely to be viewed suspiciously and were predicted to be future delinquents. The opinions of the subjects, it was clear, were markedly influenced by the appearance of the children (Dion, 1972).

Physically attractive adults are less likely to be judged or punished for all manner of social transgressions from cheating on exams to minor thefts like shoplifting to committing serious crimes. Criminal justice decision-makers such as police, judges, and juries consider the current offenses and past behavior but additionally focus on the alleged perpetrators' level of attractiveness, asking the question, could this person who looks like this (attractive or unattractive) be guilty of committing a crime? Appearance bias even happens in traffic court. Observing cases in traffic court, one study found that "pleasant and neat-looking defendants" were fined less than those who were "messy." The same was found in simulated court cases: "Physically appealing defendants were given prison terms almost three years less than those meted out to unattractive ones for precisely the same offense" (Katz, 1995: 303). In short, all societal members make judgments and predictions about people's behavior based on their appearance, as do judges and juries.

So do police officers in the course of issuing traffic citations or not, as we see in Chapter 8 by Teasdale, Gann, and Dabney. In their observations of police ride-alongs, they discovered that there is evidence of discretion in ticketing male and female citizens of varying levels of attractiveness. But here's where the story gets interesting and the conclusions are unexpected: Teasdale et al. find that attractive male citizens are less likely to be ticketed than attractive female citizens. The officers were mostly male and mostly Black. Most of the citizens were nonwhite, which is reflective of the local population. It was found that the gender and the race of the officers did not matter in ticketing behavior; nor did the gender of the drivers. The one factor that had a discriminatory effect in citation issuance was the attractiveness of the male drivers: the more attractive the male citizens, the less likely they were to receive a citation. A similar process did not work to get female citizens off the hook; their level of attractiveness had no effect on ticketing.

While good looks usually work in the suspects' favor, they don't always. Good looks can backfire, telling us something about the expectations we have for good-looking people. In cases of swindling, or defrauding a person of money or property, we picture the stereotyped swindler as a smooth talker (usually male) offering get-rich-quick schemes, or a femme fatale of many a film noir whose mercenary motives are opaque (or irrelevant) to her besotted target. If accused of this type of crime, the good-looking fare worse than the less attractive. They look good enough to pull it off, and they are punished for abusing the power of their beauty (Etcoff, 1999: 49).

Except for the unique circumstance mentioned above, the "beautiful are assumed innocent" and the unattractive are presumed guilty (Katz, 1995: 303). Criminal lawyers have commented that when a beautiful woman is on trial, it is very difficult to convince the judge or jury that she is a criminal and should be convicted. Criminal lawyers also find it difficult to defend a man of assault if he is a brutish-looking hulk (p. 307).

So, in the present, we focus on an array of appearance variables that influence crime control intervention and our chances of being victimized. These variables include traits over which we have no control, such as race, or limited control such as unattractiveness.

In a way, we are going back to Schweik's address of ugly laws but with a far broader reach. Yes, there is a distinct difference between the way that criminal suspects and victims are dealt with depending on their level of unattractiveness. Attractiveness and unattractiveness are very important in understanding how the crime control system works. But there is more to the story: the variables that define criminal justice personnel, the public, physical and material objects that represent crime control, attire that signifies terrorism, lifestyle choices such as tattoos or piercings, disability, and many other human traits all work separately or together to constitute the phenomenon of appearance bias as it occurs in the crime control context.

THEORETICAL EXPLANATIONS

In my second book on the topic of appearance bias (2008a), I offer a range of theoretical explanations for the phenomenon of appearance bias, notably structuralism, functionalism, constructionism, critical (or conflict) theory, social exchange, dramaturgy, and symbolic interactionism, among others. To recap so that the reader has a foundation in how social science explains the meaning of physical appearance in general society, allow me a few paragraphs to set the stage.

Structural functionalism refers to how social phenomena aids society, with one of the best-known and controversial examples being the function of poverty (Davis & Moore, 1945), showing that even a major social problem like poverty can serve society as when poor people provide a market for the US military, day-old food, and used cars. Using this argument physical attractiveness serves as an indicator of health and fecundity, and in this way attractive people function to repopulate the world with healthy people. On a more minute and measurable scale, functionalism can explain the employment of people based on their appearance, a disparaged appearance or a socially valued one, as functional for the employees and for society, as can be interpreted in Chapter 14 herein and in my 2007 book. Or, consider that private prisons profit, literally, from prisons stocked with prisoners, commonly minority prisoners.

Constructionism refers to the fact that standards for beauty are merely that, constructs. They have no real meaning outside of what we as a society assign to them. This theory is best illustrated in Chapter 5 on how human trafficking has been constructed, deconstructed, and reconstructed.

Social exchange theory is an obvious explanation for the utility of beauty as something to be exchanged for marriage proposals, employment, educational opportunities, and so on. Old, unattractive men find young, beautiful women to marry them in exchange for money and a comfortable life. Beauty is a form of social capital. An attractive appearance can be exchanged for relief from criminal justice intervention.

Dramaturgy is better known through the common understanding of impression management and presentation-of-self; naturally, we hope to present ourselves well (be as attractive as possible) to manage our impression to others so that we may be as successful as possible (see, for example, Goffman, 1959). Or we may present ourselves as dangerous if it works in our favor.

Closely aligned with presentation of self, consider symbolic interactionism. Abercrombie and Fitch, among other high-end retailers, employ good-looking young people as their sales staff because it makes them, the retailers, look good (Berry, 2007; see also Mead, 1934 on the topic of the "social mirror" as when we use society as a reflector of ourselves). Humans choose attractive, exotic, or expensive nonhuman animal companions to represent themselves in a positive light. Applying the symbolic interactionist perspective, I have shown that humans deliberately select nonhumans who reflect what the humans hope others will see in them as humans. Humans who want to seem privileged, deadly, well-bred, wealthy, virile, unusual, etc. will select their nonhuman representatives accordingly (Berry, 2008b). Prisoners who want to be feared manage their appearance and behavior to do just that, with displays of weapons and gang membership.

Attribution theory, as expected, is a foundational theory that examines bias of any kind. Members of society, making observations and evaluations of others based on their physical appearance, commonly attribute traits to people that are often inaccurate but applied nonetheless. We have been socialized through many outlets such as movies (think Dr. Jekyll and Mr. Hyde) to think that good-looking people are good people and are not criminals, while weird-looking or ugly people are bad and are criminals. Other obvious examples of the association made between ethnicity and criminal behavior show that the public and social control agents attribute criminality to dark-skinned people. Still other examples include viewing the disabled as disvalued humans and thus more vulnerable to victimization, and gender-denying gays and transvestites are assumed to be either worthy targets of assault or sex workers.

Richard Felson has applied the routine activities approach to explain crime committed by those with appearance challenges as well as by those with the social control power bestowed upon them by their appearance, as discussed in my editorial comments to Part III. The Felson studies describe victimization in terms of opportunity: opportunities are presented in everyday life and some people will take advantage of those opportunities. Young, attractive sexual assault victims are ripe for victimization because of their availability for contact, smaller size, naïvete, and lower credibility (Felson & Cundiff, 2014). Large people (men) view small people (women) as vulnerable targets of physical abuse (Felson, 1996), and older prisoners violate younger and more susceptible prisoners in the already coerced environment of prison (Felson et al., 2012).

Strain theory is explained by its originator, Robert Agnew, in Chapter 1 in which he partially accounts for juvenile delinquency dependent upon the appearance of the delinquents. Social strain, to put it simply, refers to the uncomfortable feeling resulting from being pulled in more than one direction, for example, to commit juvenile delinquency or not. Agnew applies strain theory, labeling, and social control variables as mediators for the relationship between appearance and delinquency. Unattractive individuals are denied access to goals and opportunities, making them angry and frustrated. Thus they relieve this strain through illegitimate channels of goal attainment such as criminal activity. Agnew's chapter measures the interaction of physical appearance not only with strain but additionally measures the effects of appearance as interpreted by labeling theory and social control theory, demonstrating how the label of delinquency and the social bonds that delinquents possess (or don't possess) influences delinquency, compared to the role of appearance bias itself.

Focal concerns and the culpable control model are best explained in Chapter 7 by Wareham, Berry, Blackwell, and Boots on the topic of victim appearance and assigned blameworthiness. There are legal factors in blame assessment, such as intoxication and degree of force, and extra-legal factors, such as victim appearance, that impact criminal justice decisions, such as blameworthiness. Blame attribution can be due to extralegal factors that serve as proxies used by decision-makers regarding culpability.

Moral time theory, as proposed by Donald Black (2011), addresses appearance in much the same fashion as I do, in terms of inequality and appearance as a form of social capital. More to the point, Black's thesis is one centrally focused on social conflict. Social conflict can be examined along a number of axes such as superiority–inferiority, obviously a stratification issue, which makes it easy to see how appearance bias, as a means of ordering society unfairly, can lead to conflict. For the purpose of interpreting the relationship between appearance and crime, I would look to Black's thesis on realignment of power and status with its attention to oversuperiority and undersuperiority. As illustrated in cases of domestic abuse (as one example), the abuser who batters the victim to the point of worsening her appearance may be engaging in power restructuring, reducing the power differential and putting things back in the order that the abuser prefers. Even if the abuser does not worsen the appearance of the victim, the fact of abuse is an attempt to reorder stratification such that the victim is now in a less powerful position than the abuser. This same principle could explain old and unattractive prisoners assaulting young attractive prisoners: the young attractive men, usually in a superior social position to the older unattractive men in general society, find themselves ranked lower by the assaults that they suffer (Felson et al., 2012). Moreover, unconventional-appearing members of the LGBTQ community and transvestites are placed in a position lower than their already less-than-equal social stratum by unfair arrests and by assaults.

PROPOSED MODEL

So far, I have addressed the physical features over which we have limited or no control. Socioeconomic status (SES, a measure combining education, occupation, and income) is another feature over which we have limited control. This is not something that members of advanced societies like to admit, but it is increasingly obvious that our ability to change our SES is highly restricted. Some citizens of the United States may continue to adhere to the American Dream that if one works hard enough, one can acquire wealth. In recent times, it is an inescapable conclusion that this was never true. This one variable, SES, is well-known to be an important one in any discussion of crime. Low SES is related to the neighborhood in which one resides, the degree of suspicion aimed at a person, the availability of good legal representation, bail bond decisions, conviction and sentencing. Low SES is related to other crime-relevant variables all speaking to social disadvantages (race, particularly). It is also strongly related to appearance. Just to take one example of a three-way intersection between socioeconomic status, race, and appearance, consider that untreated tooth decay causes disfigurement and that it is an especially weighty burden for Blacks, Indigenous Americans, and Hispanics. In 2013, it was reported that half of Blacks and nearly all Indigenous Americans and Hispanics have no dental insurance (Otto, 2017: 195). Connecting socioeconomic status to appearance, we may have a multiplicative effect on how initial responders (citizens, police) view a victim or a suspect as well as what happens next. And that, dear readers, is the crux of this analysis: social inequality.

I had not intended to include an emphasis on socioeconomic status as an exogenous variable in this study of appearance and crime. However, the more I looked at the phenomenon, the more I could not escape the obvious that, although the main point is that appearance affects criminal involvement, crime control, and criminal victimization, SES affects the entire process.

It has long been known that crime, crime control, and victimization are affected by the socioeconomic status of offenders and victims. For example, the classic book *The Rich get Richer and the Poor get Prison* (Reiman & Leighton, 2016) is a key treatise on this occurrence, although there are many other indispensable sources that tell us the same basic story (e.g., Cole, 1999; Morris & Rothman, 1998; Tonry, 1998). Of all the other variables involved – community setting, gender, race, type of offense, and a host of other crime-relevant variables – socioeconomic status cannot be dismissed. If apprehended, the wealthy get off more easily and the poor are nailed from the point of suspicion onward (bail setting, legal representation, etc.). Yet it is also known that looks matter, and to make things clearer or more complicated, faces indicate one's socioeconomic status (Delistraty, 2017): judging from their smiling eyes, smiling mouths, and expression of overall happiness, one can guess that such faces belong to the financially stable. And the financially stable are not commonly viewed as criminally involved.

We can point to unsubtle traits, such as missing or rotting teeth, as indicative of low SES and which are judged as unattractive (Otto, 2017): poor dentition is strongly related to poor or absent dental care (Hudson, Stockard, & Ramberg, 2007). Conversely, higher socioeconomic status is related to attractiveness, as supported by Agnew's research (1984) as well as many other studies (e.g., Blum, 2003; Gilman, 1999; Gimlin, 2002). Those with greater financial security can afford health care, cosmetic treatments (hair color, skin care, plastic surgery, etc.), and body sculpting that create good looks.

The impact of socioeconomic status on physical appearance struck me full-on while reading the important recent book *Teeth* by Mary Otto (2017). The author examines the appearance of good dentition in several ways, but the bottom line is the ability to pay for dental care; indeed, she refers to the quality of teeth as an indicator of "visual personality" (p. 20). The cost of bad teeth is not only pain and dysfunction, it also entails stigma and a charge of moral failure. We hold people accountable for their dental appearance.

A "Hollywood smile" is not possible for much of the population my contributors and I are writing about here. BDD (body dysmorphic disorder), of which others and I have written, is the fear of being unattractive to the point that we view ourselves as unattractive when we are not unattractive and we undergo major expense and discomfort to make ourselves as attractive as possible. BDD would be an unimaginable luxury to the population described herein and is probably not a consideration in this crime-appearance context, but the concept does provide an interesting contrast to the general society's need for beauty and is a measurement against we are all compared. Because they are not financially well-endowed, most criminal suspects' and criminal victims' needs are closer to mere acceptance.

So now the reader has an idea of the many parts of the appearance-and-crime picture. The following chapters fill in the blanks of what I have discussed above and enlighten the reader as to the exact nature of the process of justice being affected by physical appearance. A path (or causal) model can be imagined, hypothetical yet grounded in scientific fact. By saying that the model is hypothetical, I mean that the values of the paths between variables are not empirically measured. We do know, as the contributing authors and I will show, that the paths exist but the weights of the variables and the values assigned to the paths are not yet numerically known, with the exception of the causal model in Wareham et al.'s chapter.

Basically, the IVs (independent or casual variables) are of two types: demographic variables (age, gender, race, socioeconomic status) and appearance traits (disability, body size, attractive, unattractive, etc.). These two types of IVs are certainly correlated and may be causal to each other such that demographic traits affect appearance traits and vice versa (appearance traits affect demographic traits). In other words, demographic variables (socioeconomic status, race, etc.) affects and is affected by appearance variables.

These two types of IVs affect the DV (dependent variable or effect), justice outcome. Justice outcome refers not only to suspected criminal offending but also to criminal victimization. For example, a less attractive appearance is related to an increased chance of criminal injustice. More minutely, having an appearance deficit such as unattractiveness or minority membership leads to a different justice outcome than being attractive and of majority membership. You get the idea.

CONTENTS, SOURCES, AND FORMAT FOR THE BOOK

As to sources of material, there is even less scientific literature to rely upon for this study than there was for the more generic appearance-bias work I have published, partly because, of course, the topic of appearance bias and crime is more specific than general societal-level appearance bias.

I have been fortunate, however, to attract work by social scientists who have investigated crime, crime control, and criminal victimization and who have been able to reframe their work in terms of appearance bias. These authors offer not only their own novel approach to this new topic, they offer extensive literature reviews of their topics, thereby grounding their work in the best scientific literature available. Additionally, the reader will notice that I rely on media sources. While media sources may not be the usual foundation for scientific works, they are useful here because (a) the ones I use are factually based and factually presented, and (b) they fill in the blanks for the dearth of scientific literature that does not exist. My hope is that this text will cause an eruption of new empirical work on this fascinating and troubling topic.

As to content and format, a range of methodologies will be applied and a range of theories will be advanced to explain the phenomenon of appearance bias in the crime and crime control context. Some of the chapters use qualitative analyses while others use advanced quantitative methodology. Some chapters attend little to theoretical explanations while others are squarely centered on theory. My objective in choosing the chapters and the contributors is to reveal a broad representation of the types of appearance bias that can take place, the kinds of people against whom these biases intrude, and the ways in which we may be able to lessen this form of social inequality. There are topics that will not be given intense treatment in this book such as parole decisions and jury selection, although they will be discussed. But the main points show appearance bias as it operates in the crime control context. Since I have a large reserve of work on the topic of appearance bias, I have plenty to say. But the greater insight comes from the contributing authors, not only in the research that they offer but the highly unusual interpretations that they proffer to this topic.

After these introductory remarks, the book is divided into five sections, with two or more chapters describing the topics of those sections. My editorial comments at the beginning of each section will explain and expand the contributing chapters. At the end of each section's editorial comments, I list questions to be considered by the readers as areas for further research. These questions may be useful for student readers as a form of instruction and creative inquiry.

Ending the book is, naturally, a conclusion that offers very little summary but instead concentrates on ways to ameliorate appearance bias in this context of crime and crime control. Some of these proposed solutions are practical, involving policy and legislative changes, but also even more fundamental changes such as voluntary and health-enhancing appearance alterations. As to legislative measures, think of anti-bullying policies enacted in schools, on the internet, and wherever bullying takes place. Policies that disallow disability discrimination have been effective, at least somewhat, but require enhancement. The same would be true for policy improvements to appearance-biased criminal justice against the LGBTQ, misjudged "terrorists," ethnic minorities, immigrants, and others. There is always more social-change work to be done, yet we recognize that these changes are evolutionary and incremental.

Some recommended social changes are, one might say, unrealistic since they involved changing engrained attitudes and behavior. However, judging from observations, social movements centered on appearance bias are not so unrealistic since we have seen some successes; plus, comparing them to social movements that are now long-established – such as civil rights – we might say that this new area of social change is only anticipatory. It is essential to raise social consciousness about the problem of appearance bias, overall, and its operation in the crime context is no exception.

A final proposed solution is a call for scholarly involvement, which can aid in policy changes and in raising awareness. The scientific community, of which I am a member, has not, to date, engaged in studies of appearance bias to the extent necessary. We are in the beginning stages of understanding appearance bias and there are an increasing number of analyses being conducted and published. We, the global community, need more.

References

Berry, B. (2007). *Beauty bias: Discrimination and social power.* Westport, CT: Praeger.

(2008a). *The power of looks: Social stratification of physical appearance.* Hampshire, UK: Ashgate.

(2008b). Interactionism and animal aesthetics: A theory of reflected social power. *Society and Animals*, 16 (1), 75–89.

(2011). Cross-cultural beauty standards. In M. Z. Stange, C. K. Oyster, & J. G. Golson (Eds.), *The multimedia encyclopedia of women in today's world* (pp. 139–144). Thousand Oaks, CA: Sage.

Black, D. (2011). *Moral time.* New York, NY: Oxford University Press.

Blum, V. L. (2003). *Flesh wounds: The culture of cosmetic surgery.* Berkeley, CA: University of California Press.

Bogdan, R. (2012). *Picturing disability: Beggar, freak, citizen, and other photographic rhetoric.* Syracuse, NY: Syracuse University Press.

Bordo, S. (1995). *Unbearable weight: Feminism, western culture, and the body.* Berkeley, CA: University of California Press.

Braziel, J. E. & LeBesco, K. (Eds.). (2001). *Bodies out of bounds: Fatness and transgression.* Berkeley, CA: University of California Press.

Brehm, H. N., Uggen, C., & Gasanabo, J. D. (2016). Age, gender, and the crime of crimes: Toward a life-course theory of genocide participation. *Criminology*, 54, 713–743.

Brody, J. E. (2017, August 22). Fat bias starts early and takes a serious toll. New York Times (Science Times section), p. 5D.

Cole, D. (1999). *No equal justice: Race and class in the American criminal justice system*. New York, NY: The New Press.

Cortes, J. B. & Gatti, F. M. (1972). *Delinquency and crime: A biopsychological approach*. New York, NY: Seminar Press.

Cullen, F. T. & Agnew, R. (Eds.). (2011). *Criminological theory: Past to present* (4th ed.). New York, NY: Oxford University Press.

Dabney, D., Teasdale, B., Ishoy, G., Gann, T., & Berry, B. (2017). Policing in a largely minority jurisdiction: The influence of appearance characteristics associated with contemporary hip-hop culture on police decision-making. *Justice Quarterly*, 34 (7), 1310–1338.

Davis, K. & Moore, W. E. (1945). Some principles of stratification. *American Sociological Review*, 10, 242–249.

Delistraty, C. (2017, July 25). Rich or poor? Your face might give it away. Retrieved from www.cnn.com.

Dion, K. K. (1972). Physical attractiveness and evaluation of children's transgressions. *Journal of Personality and Social Psychology*, 24, 207–213.

Etcoff, N. (1999). *Survival of the prettiest: The science of beauty*. New York, NY: Anchor Books.

Felson, R. B. (1996). Big people hit little people: Sex differences in physical power and interpersonal violence. *Criminology*, 34, 433–452.

Felson, R. B. & Cundiff, P. R. (2014). Sexual assaults as a crime against young people. *Archives of Sexual Behavior*, 43, 273–284.

Felson, R. B., Cundiff, P., & Painter-Davis, N. (2012). Age and sexual assault in correctional facilities: A blocked opportunity approach. *Criminology*, 50, 887–912.

Gibbons, T. C. N. (1963). *Psychiatric studies of borstal lads*. London, UK: Oxford University Press.

Gilman, S. L. (1999). *Making the body beautiful: A cultural history of aesthetic surgery*. Princeton, NJ: Princeton University Press.

Gimlin, D. L. (2002). *Body work: Beauty and self-image in American culture*. Berkeley, CA: University of California Press.

Glueck, S. & Glueck, E. (1950). *Unraveling juvenile delinquency*. New York, NY: Commonwealth Fund.

(1956). *Physique and delinquency*. New York, NY: Harper.

Goffman, E. (1959). *The presentation of self in everyday life*. Garden City, NY: Doubleday.

Hartl, E., Monnelly, E., & Elderkin, R. (1982). *Physique and delinquent behavior: A thirty-year follow-up of William H. Sheldon's Varieties of delinquent youth*. New York, NY: Academic Press.

Hudson, K., Stockard, J., & Ramberg, Z. (2007). The impact of socioeconomic status and race-ethnicity on dental health. *Sociological Perspectives*, 50, 7–25.

Hunter, M. (2004). Light, bright, and almost white: The advantages and disadvantages of light skin. In C. Herring, V. Keith, & H. D. Horton (Eds.), *Skin deep: How race and complexion matter in the "color-blind" era* (pp. 22–44). Chicago, IL: University of Illinois Press.

Hunter, R. & Macalpine, I. (1963). *Three hundred years of psychiatry, 1535–1860.* New York, NY: Oxford University Press.

Jablonski, N. (2006). *Skin: A natural history.* Berkeley, CA: University of California Press.

Katz, S. (1995). The importance of being beautiful. In J. M. Henslin (Ed.), *Down to earth sociology*, 8th ed. (pp. 301–307). New York, NY: Free Press.

Lauvergne, H. (1844) (1912). Quoted in Constancio Bernaldo de Quiros, *Modern theories of criminality.* Boston, MA: Little Brown.

Lombroso, C. (1906, 1918). *Crime: Its causes and remedies.* Boston, MA: Little Brown.

Mead, G. H. (1934). *Mind, self, and society.* Chicago, IL: University of Chicago Press.

Morris, N. & Rothman, D. J. (Eds.). (1998). *The Oxford history of the prison: The practice of punishment in western society.* New York, NY: Oxford University Press.

Olweus, D. (1978). *Aggression in the schools: Bullies and whipping boys.* Washington, DC: Hemisphere.

Otto, M. (2017). *Teeth: The story of beauty, inequality, and the struggle for oral health in America.* New York, NY: The New Press.

Pascoe, C. J. (2012). *Dude, you're a fag: Masculinity and sexuality in high school.* Berkeley, CA: University of California Press.

Reiman, J. & Leighton, P. (2016). *The rich get richer and the poor get prison.* New York, NY: Routledge.

Rennie, Y. (1978). *The search for criminal man: A conceptual history of the dangerous offender.* Lexington, MA: D. C. Health.

Sampson, R. J. & Laub, J. H. (1993). *Crime in the making.* Cambridge, MA: Harvard University Press.

(1997). Unraveling the social context of physique and delinquency. In A. Raine, P. Brennan, D. Farrington, & S. Mednick (Eds.), *Biosocial bases of violence* (pp. 175–188). New York, NY: Plenum Press.

Schweik, S. M. (2009). *The ugly laws: Disability in public.* New York, NY: New York University Press.

Sheldon, W. (1954). *Atlas of men: A guide for somatotyping the adult male of all ages.* New York, NY: Gramercy Publishing Company.

Sheldon, W., Stevens, S., & Tucker, W. (1940). *The varieties of human physique.* New York, NY: Harper and Row.

Silver, E., Silver, S. J., Siennick, S., & Farkas, G. (2011). Bodily signs of academic success: An empirical examination of tattoos and grooming. *Social Problems,* 58, 538–564.

Stearns, Peter N. (1992). *Fat history: Bodies and beauty in the modern west.* New York, NY: New York University Press.

Sue, D. W. (Ed.). (2010). *Microaggressions and marginality: Manifestation, dynamics, and impact.* Hoboken, NJ: John Wiley & Sons, Inc.

Tonry, M. (Ed.). (1998). *The handbook of crime and punishment.* New York, NY: Oxford University Press.

Waldman, K. (2013). Fat women, please stay away from crime scenes, male jurors are biased against you. Retrieved from: www.slate.com/blogs/xx_factr/2013/01/10/no_justice_for_fat_women.

Wann, M. (1998). *Fat!So?* Berkeley, CA: Ten Speed Press.

PART I

UNATTRACTIVENESS, CRIMINALITY, AND VICTIMIZATION

EDITORIAL COMMENTS

Chapters 1 and 2 explain the manner in which unattractive people are victimized as well as prone to be involved (or suspected to be involved) in crime. Unattractive features can include poor dentition, poor skin conditions, etc. Generally, with some caveats, those who are criminally involved as victims or as offenders have appearance deficits that the noncriminally involved don't have. These challenges may not be only unattractive appearance traits, such as poor complexions, but also challenges that come with being members of minority categories, as discussed in other sections of this text. As expected, other social forces invade this process and phenomenon, namely social power variables such as socioeconomic status, disability, age, orientation, gender, and race.

I covered the meaning of attractiveness and unattractiveness in the Introduction, but will review that meaning here in light of the two chapters in this section. Physical traits that run the gamut of "attractive" to "unattractive" pose enormous biases for and against those with good looks versus those without. We might assume, given what has been reported in limited scientific works on the topic, that unattractive people who face a number of social disadvantages from blocked avenues to education, romance and marriage, social networks, employment, and health care also face discrimination in the criminal justice system.

In a study of physical appearance and self-reported juvenile delinquency, Robert Agnew (1984) found that unattractive individuals are more often engaged in delinquency (reprinted here as Chapter 1). He hypothesized that strain, labeling, and social control mediated the relationship between appearance and delinquency, and his hypothesis was partially supported. Based on his then-current and previous research, Agnew illustrated that unattractive youngsters, compared to attractive ones, were more likely to be blamed for transgressions and their crimes were viewed as signs of deep-seated, long-term criminality. In Agnew's study, high school students were rated on physical appearance, dress, and grooming. It was determined that less attractive high schoolers are more involved in criminal activity than attractive ones, but the explanations for that relationship are very complex as Agnew explains.

This is indeed a complicated matter. For instance, in an earlier study (Cavior & Howard, 1973), photographs of institutionalized male delinquents were compared to male high school students, the incarcerated youths were assessed to be more unattractive. Agnew wondered whether the incarcerated youths had been judged more unattractive because (1) unattractive delinquents are more likely to be officially processed than attractive delinquents or whether (2) institutional life results in a decline in physical attractiveness. These chicken-and-egg questions will be revisited throughout this text: (1) whether the unattractive (by whatever measures) are more likely to be involved in crime control as victims or as offenders or (2) whether involvement in the crime control system causes a decline in physical attractiveness.

Similarly to Agnew, I have hypothesized that there is a social control response to appearance itself; for example, whether being unattractive *causes* or *influences* the likelihood of being apprehended, arrested, convicted, and harshly sentenced. I further wonder about the degree to which events rooted in lower socioeconomic status, such as drug and alcohol use, absent dental care, and histories of physical abuse, result in unattractiveness. This question comes up repeatedly in this book. It is known, for instance, that socioeconomic status is strongly related to dental care (Hudson, Stockard, & Ramberg, 2007; Otto, 2017). Conversely, higher socioeconomic status is related to attractiveness as supported in Agnew's research as well as other studies (e.g., Blum, 2003; Etcoff, 1999).

Agnew's overall conclusion matches what Teasdale and I find in Chapter 2: appearance has a statistically significant and relatively large effect on delinquency. Whether this has to do with association, as Agnew, a strain theorist, proposes, is not solidly determined. Unattractive people may be alienated from nondelinquents and drawn to delinquents; in other words, unattractive individuals are more likely to be seen as delinquent and, thus, conventional adolescents may not want to associate with them. Moreover, unattractive youngsters may associate with delinquents and may, as a consequence, turn to delinquency.

In Chapter 2, Brent Teasdale and I update Agnew's work but show that physically unattractive adolescents are more likely to be offenders *and* to be criminally victimized. Related to lifestyle and socioeconomic status, and relying on previous work by Mocan and Tekin (2010), we see that unattractiveness increases the probability of criminal involvement, ranging from burglary to selling drugs but also that "human capital development" plays a role. Human capital, or what I have called "social capital" in earlier works (2007, 2008), refers to the resources one has to "sell" to employers or to society at large. Unattractive people are less likely to be employed and far less likely to be employed well. That is, those with appearance deficits not uncommonly have lower-status jobs if they have jobs, and they don't make a lot of money. Since that is the case, one alternative is to engage in crime, especially crime that pays, such as property offenses or selling drugs. In sum, blocked opportunities may lead to criminal behavior as an occupation, to restricted association with other criminal offenders, and to being criminally victimized.

Throughout this section and the text as a whole, one conclusion reached is that it would be helpful to change social attitudes toward acceptance of a wide variety of levels of attractiveness. A related main point is one raised by Agnew, that of the relationship between a poor environment, replete with bad experiences based upon one's physical appearance and, thus, criminal behavior. People who are poor and who have been physically abused are affected in their appearance. They may have broken bones that are not repaired or are poorly repaired, their hair may be in poor condition, they may suffer the physical ravages of alcoholism and drug abuse (such as dehydration), and they cannot afford the expensive and time-consuming hygiene and grooming practices that the better-off can afford.

QUESTIONS

The assumption being made in both chapters is that physical appearance can serve as a channel into a life of crime or a noncriminal life. Obviously, the appearance-and-crime nexus is not foreordained since there is not a complete overlap: some attractive people live criminal lives and some unattractive people, probably most of them, do not become criminal offenders. So, how can we measure the proportion of unattractive people who go into criminal careers?

Also, what can be done about the criminal victimization of appearance-challenged people? If people are victimized because they are physically less than optimal or because they are very attractive, what can be done?

References

Berry, B. (2007). *Beauty bias: Discrimination and social power.* Westport, CT: Praeger.

(2008). *The power of looks: Social stratification of physical appearance.* Hampshire, UK: Ashgate.

Blum, V. L. (2003). *Flesh wounds: The culture of cosmetic surgery.* Berkeley, CA: University of California Press.

Cavior, N. & Howard, C. (1973). Facial attractiveness and juvenile delinquency among black and white offenders. *Journal of Abnormal Child Psychology, 1,* 203–213.

Etcoff, N. (1999). *Survival of the prettiest: The science of beauty.* New York, NY: Anchor Books (Random House).

Hudson, K., Stockard, J., & Ramberg, Z. (2007). The impact of socioeconomic status and race-ethnicity on dental health. *Sociological Perspectives, 50,* 7–25.

Mocan, N. & Tekin, E. (2010). Ugly criminals. *The Review of Economics and Statistics, 92,* 15–30.

Otto, M. (2017). *Teeth: The story of beauty, inequality, and the struggle for oral health in America.* New York, NY: The New Press.

I

Appearance and Delinquency

Robert Agnew*

Data indicate that a major determinant of the way we view and treat people is their appearance. Most research has focused on physical appearance, with data indicating that unattractive people are viewed in a less positive light than attractive people (Dion, 1973; Dion, Berscheid, & Walster, 1972; Miller, 1970). Among other things, unattractive people are seen as less intelligent, less likely to continue their education and to obtain prestigious jobs, more aggressive and antisocial, and more dishonest (Clifford & Walster, 1973; Dion, 1973; Dion & Berscheid, 1974; Dion et al., 1972). There is also evidence that people act on these stereotypes. Unattractive people are liked less; their work is more likely to be judged inferior; they are more likely to be blamed for their transgressions; and their transgressions are more likely to be seen as indicative of a chronically antisocial character (Byrne, Ervin, & Lamberth, 1970; Dion, 1972; Dion & Berscheid, 1974; Efran, 1974; Landy & Sigall, 1974; Rich, 1975; Sigall & Ostrove, 1975; Stoebe, Insko, Thompson, & Layton, 1971).

Although data are limited, evidence also indicates that dress and grooming have a similar effect on how we view and treat people (Elder, 1969; Hoult, 1954; Lefkowitz, Blake, & Mouton, 1955; Mills & Aronson, 1965; Roach & Eicher, 1965; Sigall & Aronson, 1969; Silverman, 1945). There is some debate about whether appearance is an important variable in situations where there is a prior history of interaction between participants (Berscheid & Walster, 1974; Cavior & Dokecki, 1973; Felson & Bohrnstedt, 1979; Owens & Ford, 1978). As Berscheid and Walster (1974: 205) point out, however, appearance would still be an important variable even if it were relevant only in first impression situations. Such situations are common and can have a large effect on the individual. Examples might include police–juvenile contacts, teacher–student contacts, and student–student contacts.

Based on the above findings, we would expect appearance to be related to delinquency. In particular, we would expect delinquency to be highest among physically unattractive, poorly groomed, and poorly dressed individuals. Labeling theory would predict higher levels of delinquency among such people given that they are more likely to be viewed and treated as delinquents – which may, among other things, lead these people to develop a delinquent self-concept (Payne, 1973). Strain theory would also predict higher levels of delinquency among individuals with a poor appearance. Given that these individuals are more likely to be denied access to a wide variety of goals, they may become frustrated and angry. As a consequence, they may turn to illegitimate channels of goal achievement, or they may attack those who frustrate them (see Cavior & Howard, 1973, for a similar argument). Finally, social control theory (Hirschi, 1976) would predict lower levels of attachment and commitment among individuals with an unattractive appearance. Given that these individuals are not as well treated as attractive individuals, they may not form strong attachments to parents and other conventional individuals. Their poor treatment may also result in a lower commitment to conventional activities, such as school.

Although there are many reasons for expecting a relationship between appearance and delinquency, only one study has examined the relationship between these variables. Focusing on physical appearance, Cavior and Howard (1973) found that the photos of institutionalized delinquents were judged more unattractive than the photos of male high school students. This difference, however, does not demonstrate that unattractive individuals are more delinquent. The institutionalized delinquents may have been judged more unattractive because (1) unattractive delinquents are more likely to be officially processed than attractive delinquents – a possibility strongly supported by available data; (2) institutional life results in a decline in physical attractiveness; or (3) the photos of the institutionalized delinquents – taken in a photographic vending machine of the type found in amusement parks – were of lower quality than the high school yearbook photos of the comparison group. There have also been studies on the relationship between body build and delinquency, with limited data suggesting that mesomorphic or muscular boys are more delinquent (Glueck & Glueck, 1950). Body build, however, is a variable distinct from the quality of one's appearance. This is demonstrated by the fact that even though attractive individuals are more likely to have mesomorphic body builds (Berscheid & Walster, 1974; Staffieri, 1967), we would predict a negative relationship between attractiveness and delinquency.

THE CURRENT STUDY

This study will examine the relationship between appearance and delinquency among a national sample of high school students. The appearance of all students will be directly estimated by interviewers, and self-report measures of delinquency will be used to control for the possible bias against unattractive people in official data. The central hypothesis is that unattractive people will be more delinquent than attractive people. It is also predicted that the effect of appearance on delinquency will be mediated largely by strain, social control, and labeling variables.

Examining the effect of appearance on delinquency is important because it may shed light on a hitherto neglected cause of delinquency. Also, if appearance is related to delinquency, the finding will provide support for programs designed to improve the appearance of delinquents or to reduce the discrimination against unattractive people. Such programs might be as radical as plastic surgery for offenders, which has been tried with limited success (Kutzberg, Mondell, Lewin, Lipton, & Shuster, 1978). They might also involve efforts to teach delinquents good health and grooming skills. Such efforts have already been attempted with the mentally ill (Cavior, cited in Berscheid & Walster, 1974: 210). In addition, efforts might be made to reduce the discrimination against unattractive people by sensitizing individuals such as teachers and police to the stereotypes they hold.

DATA AND METHODS

Data are from the Youth in Transition survey, a national, longitudinal survey of adolescent boys conducted by the Institute for Social Research, University of Michigan (Bachman, O'Malley, & Johnston, 1978). The survey employed a panel design, and the first data collection took place in the fall of 1966, a time when the respondents in the sample were beginning the tenth grade of high school. A multistage sampling procedure was used to select 2,213 boys who, according to the researchers, constitute an "essentially unbiased representation of 10th grade boys in public high schools throughout the contiguous United States"

(Bachman et al., 1978: 3). The second data collection took place during the spring of 1968, near the end of the eleventh grade for the respondents. A total of 1,886 boys were surveyed, which is 85.2 percent of the time 1 sample. This study employs the time 2 data, although limited use of the time 1 data is made in constructing the attractiveness measure.

MEASURES

Appearance

Respondents were interviewed for approximately two hours by a trained interviewer from the Survey Research Center. Interviewers collected demographic data and asked respondents about their peers, family, and school life. They did not ask respondents about their delinquent behavior. This information was obtained from a questionnaire filled out by the respondents. At the end of the interview, the interviewers were instructed to rate the respondent's "general appearance" as excellent, good, fair, or poor. These ratings form the basis of the appearance measure.

In making the ratings, interviewers were told to pay attention to physical appearance, dress, and grooming. As indicated, most prior studies on appearance have focused only on physical appearance. It seems important, however, to consider dress and grooming as well. Certain data, for example, indicate that variations in dress can have a dramatic impact on how we rate the overall attractiveness of a given individual (Hoult, 1954).

Recent research indicates that ratings of attractiveness may be influenced by the personality and abilities of the individuals being rated (Felson & Bohrnstedt, 1979; Gross & Crofton, 1977). Because the interviewers interacted with the adolescents for two hours before making their attractiveness ratings, one might argue that the ratings are based more on the personality of the adolescents and less on their appearance. There are, however, reasons for doubting this argument. Gross and Crofton focused only on female subjects, and Felson and Bohrnstedt's study examined individuals who had a long history of interaction. The subjects in this study were males, and they interacted with the raters for only two hours in a relatively formal situation. Two separate studies by Owen and Ford (1978) found that short personality descriptions did not affect the attractiveness ratings given to photos of males. Nevertheless, steps were taken to ensure that the appearance measures were valid.

To increase the validity of the appearance measures, the sample was divided into two groups: those rated excellent at time 1 and time 2

(10 percent of the sample, N = 186) and those rated fair and/or poor at time 1 and time 2 (5.6 percent of the sample, N = 105). Individuals who were rated good or who received divergent ratings at the two time points were excluded. By focusing on extreme groups, we reduce the ambiguity of the attractiveness stimuli and thereby minimize the effect of personal knowledge on the attractiveness ratings (see Felson & Bohrnstedt, 1979: 390–391). Cavior and Dokecki (1973), for example, found that knowledge of the subject had a relatively small effect on attractiveness ratings when the subjects were at the extremes of the attractiveness scale. At the middle ranges of the attractiveness scale, however, personal knowledge had a relatively large effect on ratings. It should also be noted that by using two time points and eliminating those with divergent ratings, we ensure that the adolescents in the sample have been at the same level of attractiveness for at least a year and a half. As Berscheid and Walster (1974: 201–205) point out, the physical changes associated with adolescence may lead to sudden shifts in attractiveness – a fact that can confound the results of any study.

Certain data on the validity if the appearance measures are available. The interviewers in the study stated that the unattractive boys had worse complexions ($p < .01$) and were not as physically mature ($p < .01$) as the attractive boys. The unattractive boys in the study were also more likely to be at the extremes of the weight distribution ($p < .05$), even though there were no statistically significant differences between the unattractive and attractive boys in height. Reflecting this fact, the unattractive boys were more likely to say that they were overweight ($p < .01$). These data suggest that the attractiveness ratings were based on the appearance of the adolescent, and they attest to the validity of the attractiveness measure.

Delinquency Measures

Three self-reported measures of delinquency, adopted from Gold (1966), are employed. The first is a general scale called "seriousness of delinquency." The ten items in this scale deal with minor and serious theft, fighting, arson, robbery, etc. Response categories for each item range from 1 (never committed the act) to 5 (committed the act five or more times). Scale scores range from 1 (never committed any of the acts) to 5 (committed all acts five or more times), with a mean 1.28 and a standard deviation of .46. Variation in this scale is largely due to the minor theft (larceny under $50, shoplifting) and fighting items.

The other two scales are "trouble with parents" and "delinquent behavior in school." Given the argument that attractiveness is most important in first impression situations, we would expect bias against the unattractive to be greater at school than at home. For this reason, we predict that attractiveness will have a greater effect on school-related delinquency than on family-related delinquency. And if bias against the unattractive is greater at school, unattractive individuals should be more likely to direct their hostilities at the school and, whenever possible, to avoid school. Also, given that stereotyping and discrimination are greater at school, unattractive individuals may be more likely to conform to the delinquent label when at school. Finally, the attachment of unattractive individuals to teachers and fellow students should be lower than their attachment to parents. The delinquent behavior in school scale contains seven items and focuses on truancy, vandalism of school property, fighting at school, aggression against teachers, etc. This scale is scored in the same manner as the Seriousness of Delinquency scale. Scale scores range from 1 to 5, with a mean of 1.50 and a standard deviation of .66. Scale variation is due largely to the truancy and fighting items. Trouble with parents is a three-item scale that focuses on running away from home and aggression against mother and father. Scale scores range from 1 to 5, with a mean of 1.13 and a standard deviation of .47. The three items contribute about equally to scale variation.

Socioeconomic Status and Race

Data indicate that socioeconomic status (SES) and race may be associated with both appearance and delinquency (Cavior & Howard, 1973; Elder, 1969; Elliott & Ageton, 1979; Ryan, 1966). For this reason, it is necessary to control for these variables when examining the effect of appearance. A five-item measure of SES is employed, with equal weight being given to father's occupational status, mother and father's education, possessions in the home (19 specific possessions), number of books in home, and number of rooms per person in home. Race is treated as a dummy variable, with blacks being scored 1 and white 0 (see Kim & Kohout, 1975: 374–383, for a discussion of dummy variables).

Social Control, Strain, and Labeling Variables

Nine measures of social control are employed. These measures are quite similar to the major indices of social control employed by Hirschi (1969), and they include all of the scales that Wiatrowski, Griswold, and Roberts (1981) found to be significantly related to delinquency in their study of social control theory. The first eight scales are adopted from Wiatrowski et al., and a description of the factor-analytic procedures used to create these scales can be found in that study. High scorers on the five-item parental attachment scale state that they feel close to and want to be like their mother and father. High scorers on the 27-item school attachment scale state that school is enjoyable, that the information presented in school is interesting and of practical value, and that it is good to study hard and achieve academic honors. Commitment is measured by the student's occupational aspirations, educational aspirations, average school grades, and frequency of dating (three items). Involvement is measured by a three-item scale. High scorers state that they spend much time on homework, often discuss class ideas with friends, and often do extracurricular reading. Belief is measured by a seven-item scale indexing the value placed on honesty. An additional measure of belief was created by a factor analyzing five belief items in the survey. The four items in the resultant deviant beliefs scale all loaded at least .58 on the same factor. High scorers on this scale state that it is good to engage in such activities as charging bills without knowing how to pay for them, borrowing money without expecting to pay it back, and holding a library book needed by another student.

Measures of strain were created by performing two separate factor analyses, the first on seven items related to anger and the second on seven items related to frustration. High scorers on the seven-item anger scale state that they lose their temper easily, are irritated by small things, carry a chip on their shoulder, and feel like a powder keg ready to explode. All items load at least .35 on this scale, with most loadings in the .6 range. High scorers on the seven-item frustration scale state that they have gotten a raw deal out of life, have not got what is "coming to them," are jealous of others, feel cheated, and hold grudges. All items load at least .38 on this scale, with most loadings in the .6 to .7 range.

The data set does not contain a measure of delinquent self-concept. As a consequence, a general measure of self-concept is employed. The ten-item measure is similar to that used by Rosenberg (see Bachman et al., 1978: 96–98), and high scorers state that they are good people, have many good qualities, have much to be proud of, and are useful to have around. Although this is a rough surrogate for a measure of delinquent self-conception, it will allow us to determine whether unattractive individuals view themselves in a more negative light than attractive individuals. A complete list of all scales is available from the author.

METHODS

The data are analyzed in three steps. First, the delinquency scales are regressed on appearance, SES, and race. Appearance is treated as a dummy variable, with unattractive individuals scored 1 and attractive individuals scored 0. This step of the analysis allows us to determine whether unattractive individuals are, in fact, more delinquent than attractive individuals. Second, each social control, strain, and labeling variable is regressed on appearance, SES, and race. This allows us to determine whether unattractive individuals are lower in social control, higher in strain, and more likely to have a negative self-concept. Third, the delinquency scales are regressed on appearance, SES, and race and the social control, strain, and labeling variables. If these latter variables mediate the relationship between appearance and delinquency, then controlling for them in the regression analysis should eliminate the relationship between appearance and delinquency.

RESULTS

... Appearance has a significant effect on all scales, with the unattractive being more delinquent. After race and SES are controlled, appearance explains 4 percent of the variation in seriousness of delinquency, 4 percent of the variation in trouble with parents, and 9 percent of the variation in delinquent behavior in school. As predicted, appearance has a significantly greater effect on school-related delinquency than family-related delinquency ($p < .05$). The correlation coefficients indicate that appearance is not significantly related to race, although attractive people are significantly more likely to be high in SES ($r = .42$, $p < .01$).

Relationship between Appearance and the Intervening Variables

According to the second hypothesis, unattractive people are more likely to be delinquent because they are lower in social control, higher in strain, and more likely to have a delinquent self-concept. ...

Focusing on the social control variables, we find that unattractive adolescents are significantly lower in parental attachment, school attachment, and all but one of the measures of commitment. Unattractive individuals have lower occupational aspirations, educational aspirations, and grades than attractive individuals. In certain cases, the differences between attractive and unattractive individuals are quite large. Unattractive individuals, for example, aspire to occupations that, on average, are 15 Duncan prestige points lower than the occupations desired by attractive individuals. Unattractive individuals do not differ from attractive individuals in terms of the frequency of dating. There are also no significant differences between the two groups on the involvement scale. Other studies have found a weak or insignificant relationship between attractiveness and dating among males (Berscheid, Dion, Walster, & Walster, 1971; Krebs & Adinolfi, 1975; Walster, Aronson, Abrahams, & Rottman, 1966). It may be the case that unattractive males date and interact socially with unattractive females. Also, certain data suggest that the male's desirability as a dating partner is influenced by a number of variables besides appearance (Berscheid & Walster, 1974).

Given that unattractive individuals are lower in parental attachment, it is possible that they are also less committed to conventional beliefs (Hirschi, 1969: 29–30). The data provide partial support for this data. Unattractive individuals score slightly lower on the honesty scale and slightly higher on the deviant beliefs scale than attractive individuals. Overall, however, the biggest differences between attractive and unattractive adolescents are in the areas of attachment and commitment.

The data on strain theory indicate that appearance is not related to anger and only weakly related to frustration – with the unattractive being more frustrated. These findings are surprising when we consider the discriminatory manner in which unattractive individuals are treated. A possible explanation for the findings, however, is suggested by the data on aspirations. These data suggest that unattractive individuals do not want as much out of life as attractive individuals. Because unattractive individuals desire less, they may not become very frustrated or angry when they receive less. It may be the case that unattractive individuals were strained in the past and adapted by lowering their aspirations. A longitudinal study examining young children over their life course would be necessary to test this idea. The unattractive adolescents in this study, however, are currently no more angry and only slightly more frustrated than the attractive adolescents.

Finally, the data indicate that unattractive individuals have a lower self-concept than attractive individuals. This lower self-concept suggests that unattractive individuals have come to view themselves in the same way that they are viewed by others.

Overall, the data indicate that unattractive individuals are lower in many forms of social control, are slightly higher in frustration, and have a lower self-concept. These data should be interpreted cautiously because they do not prove that appearance *causes* low social control, frustration, and a negative self-concept. The data only demonstrate an *association* between these variables. The association may be due to the fact that both appearance and the intervening variables are caused by the same third variable. The possibility is reduced by the controls for SES and race, as well as the fact that everyone in the sample is of the same gender and age. It is difficult to think of another third variable that would have a substantial causal impact on both appearance and the intervening variables... The association may also arise from the fact that certain of the intervening variables have a causal impact on appearance. Adolescents with a low self-concept, for example, may devote less attention to their appearance. Aside from a few variables like self-concept, however, it is difficult to imagine that the intervening variables have a substantial causal impact on appearance. The relatively enduring nature of appearance, as measured in this study, also reduces the likelihood of such a causal impact. Further, there are strong theoretical reasons for believing that appearance has a substantial causal impact on intervening variables. Therefore, although the data do not demonstrate causality, there is good reason to believe that appearance is at least partly responsible for the variation in the intervening variables.

Controls for the Intervening Variables

If the effect of appearance on delinquency is mediated by the social control, strain, and self-concept variables, then controls for these variables should substantially reduce the effect of appearance. Therefore, the delinquency scales were regressed on appearance, SES, race, and all the intervening variables...

Controls for the intervening variables reduce the effect of appearance on delinquency from 9 percent (seriousness of delinquency) to 31 percent (trouble with parents). The most important mediating variables are grades, deviant beliefs, and school attachment. These data provide only limited support for the second hypothesis. Despite the controls, appearance continues to have a significant and, based on the standardized betas, relatively large effect on the delinquency scales.

CONCLUSION

Like Cavior and Howard's study (1973), this study indicates that there is an association between appearance and delinquency. This study, however, builds on the work of Cavior and Howard in four ways. First, the study employs difference measures of appearance and delinquency. These measures overcome possible sources of bias in Cavior and Howard, and thereby strengthen our confidence in the association between appearance and delinquency. Second, the data indicate that appearance has a stronger association with school-related delinquency than family-related delinquency. This suggests that unattractive individuals are most likely to be delinquent in situations where the stereotypes and discrimination against them are most prevalent. Third, the data indicate that appearance has a relatively large effect on delinquency. The relative effect of appearance may have been exaggerated, given that the study focused only on people who were at the extremes of the attractiveness scale. Nevertheless, the standardized betas suggest that appearance is not a trivial variable. Fourth, the data shed some light on why appearance is related to delinquency. In particular, the data suggest that a small part of the association between appearance and delinquency is explained by social control theory. Contrary to the argument of Cavior and Howard (1973), the data do not indicate that frustration or anger play an important role in mediating the association between appearance and delinquency.

A large part of the association between appearance and delinquency was left unexplained. There are a number of possible reasons for this. As indicated, it was not possible to determine if the adolescents in the sample had a delinquent self-concept. Had such a measure been available, it may have explained part of the association between appearance and delinquency. It is also possible that appearance is related to delinquency for reasons having to do with subcultural deviance theory. Because unattractive individuals are more likely to be seen as delinquent, conventional adolescents may not want to associate with them. Unattractive adolescents may associate with delinquents and may, as a result, turn to delinquency. Finally, the association between appearance and delinquency may be due to factors that are not related to the major sociological theories of delinquency. There may, for example, be personality differences between attractive and unattractive individuals (see Krebs & Adinolfi, 1975). Although there is some debate over the importance of personality traits in the explanation of delinquency (Hindelang, 1972; Tennenbaum, 1977), it is possible that such traits play a role in mediating the effect of appearance on delinquency. It has also been suggested that there may be genetic differences between physically attractive and unattractive people (Berscheid & Walster, 1974). If true, such differences may also partly explain the association between appearance and delinquency.

In addition to exploring these additional reasons for the association between appearance and delinquency, future research should build on this article in a number of ways. First, such research should employ measures of appearance that limit the interaction between rater and ratee. This will allow such research to examine those in the middle ranges of the attractiveness scale. Data (not shown) from this study indicate that moderately attractive individuals fall closer to attractive individuals in terms of delinquency and the intervening variables than to unattractive individuals. Second, such research should employ data that allow a more accurate determination of causal direction. Third, future research should examine adolescent females as well as males. Certain data suggest that attractiveness is more important for females than males (Berscheid & Walster, 1974), and for this reason we might expect an even stronger association between appearance and delinquency among females. Finally, future research should begin to explore the policy implications presented here. Such research, in particular, should explore the effectiveness of programs designed to reduce the discrimination against unattractive individuals or to improve the appearance of these individuals.

References

Bachman, J., Kahn, R., Mednick, M., Davidson, T., & Johnston, L. (1969). *Youth in transition, Vol. 1.* Ann Arbor, MI: Institute for Social Research.

Bachman, J., O'Malley, P., & Johnston, J. (1978). *Adolescent to adulthood.* Ann Arbor, MI: Institute for Social Research.

Berscheid, E. & Walster, E. (1974). Physical attractiveness. In L. Berkowitz (Ed.), *Advances in experimental social psychology, Vol. 7* (pp. 157–215). New York, NY: Academic Press.

Berscheid, E. K., Dion, K., Walster, E., & Walster, G. (1971). Physical attractiveness and dating choice: A test of the matching hypothesis. *Journal of Experimental Social Psychology, 4,* 508–516.

Byrne, D., Ervin, C., & Lamberth, J. (1970). Continuity between the experimental study of attraction and real-life computer dating. *Journal of Personality and Social Psychology, 16,* 157–165.

Cavior, N. & Dokecki, P. (1973). Physical attractiveness, perceived attitude similarity, and academic achievement as contributors to interpersonal attraction among adolescents. *Developmental Psychology, 9,* 44–54.

Cavior, N. & Howard, C. (1973). Facial attractiveness and juvenile delinquency among black and white offenders. *Journal of Abnormal Child Psychology, 1,* 203–213.

Clifford, M. & Walster, E. (1973). The effect of physical attractiveness on teacher expectation. *Sociology of Education, 46,* 248–258.

Cross, J. F. & Cross, J. (1971). Age, sex, race and the perception of facial beauty. *Developmental Psychology*, 5, 433–439.

Dion, K. (1972). Physical attractiveness and evaluations of children's transgressions. *Journal of Personality and Social Psychology*, 24, 207–213.

(1973). Young children's stereotyping of facial attractiveness. *Developmental Psychology*, 9, 183–188.

Dion, K. & Berscheid, E. (1974). Physical attractiveness and peer perception among children. *Sociometry*, 37, 1–12.

Dion, K., Berscheid, E., & Walster, E. (1972). What is beautiful is good. *Journal of Personality and Social Psychology*, 24, 285–290.

Efran, M. (1974). The effect of physical appearance on the judgment of guilt, interpersonal attraction, and severity of recommended punishment in a simulated jury task. *Journal of Research in Personality*, 8, 45–54.

Elder, G. (1969). Appearance and education in marriage mobility. *American Sociological Review*, 34, 519–533.

Elliott, D. & Ageton, S. (1979). Reconciling race and class differences in self-reported and official estimates of delinquency. *American Sociological Review*, 45, 95–110.

Felson, R. & Bohrnstedt, G. (1979). Are the good beautiful or the beautiful good? *Social Psychology Quarterly*, 42, 386–392.

Glueck, S. & Glueck, E. (1950). *Unraveling juvenile delinquency*. New York, NY: Commonwealth Fund.

Gold, M. (1966). Undetected delinquent behavior. *Journal of Research in Crime and Delinquency*, 3, 27–46.

Gross, A. & Crofton, C. (1977). What is good is beautiful. *Sociometry*, 40, 85–90.

Hindelang, M. (1972). The relationship of self-reported delinquency to the scales of the CPI and MMPI. *Journal of Criminal Law, Criminology, and Police Science*, 63, 75–81.

Hirschi, T. (1969). *Causes of delinquency*. Berkeley, CA: University of California Press.

Hoult, T. (1954). Experimental measurement of clothing as a factor in some social rankings of selected American men. *American Sociological Review*, 19, 324–328.

Johnson, R. (1979). *Juvenile delinquency and its origins*. Cambridge, UK: Cambridge University Press.

Kim, J. & Kohout, F. (1975). Special topics in general linear models. In N. Nie, C. Hull, J. Jenkins, K. Steinbrenner, & D. Dent (Eds.), *Statistical package for the social sciences: SPSS* (pp. 369–397). New York, NY: McGraw-Hill.

Krebs, D. & Adinolfi, A. (1975). Physical attractiveness, social relations and personality style. *Journal of Personality and Social Psychology*, 31, 245–253.

Kutzberg, R., Mondell, W., Lewin, M., Lipton, D. & Shuster, M. (1978). Plastic surgery on offenders. In N. Johnston & L. Savitz (Eds.), *Justice and corrections* (pp. 688–700). New York, NY: John Wiley.

Landy, D. & Sigall, H. (1974). Beauty is talent: Task evaluation as a function of the performer's physical attractiveness. *Journal of Personality and Social Psychology*, 29, 299–304.

Lefkowitz, M., Blake, R., & Mouton, J. (1955). Status factors in pedestrian violation of traffic signals. *Journal of Abnormal Social Psychology*, 51, 704–706.

Miller, A. (1970). Role of physical attractiveness in impression formation. *Psychonomic Science*, 19, 241–243.

Mills, J. & Aronson, E. (1965). Opinion change as a function of the communicator's attractiveness and desire to influence. *Journal of Personality and Social Psychology*, 1, 173–177.

Owens, G. & Ford, J. (1978). Further consideration of the "what is good is beautiful" finding. *Social Psychology*, 41, 73–75.

Payne, W. (1973). Negative labels: Passageways and prisons. *Crime and Delinquency*, 19, 33–40.

Rich, J. (1975). Effects of children's physical attractiveness on teacher's evaluations. *Journal of Educational Psychology*, 67, 599–609.

Roach, M. & Eicher, J. (1965). *Dress, adornment, and the social order.* New York, NY: John Wiley.

Ryan, M. (1966). *Clothing: A study in human behavior.* New York, NY: Holt, Rinehart, and Winston.

Sigall, H. & Aronson, E. (1969). Liking for an evaluator as a function of her physical attractiveness and nature of the evaluation. *Journal of Experimental Social Psychology*, 5, 93–100.

Sigall, H. & Ostrove, N. (1975). Beautiful but dangerous: Effects of offender attractiveness and nature of the crime on juridic judgment. *Journal of Personality and Social Psychology*, 31, 410–414.

Silverman, S. (1945). *Clothing and appearance.* New York, NY: Bureau of Publications, Teachers College, Columbia University.

Staffieri, J. (1967). A study of social stereotype of body image in children. *Journal of Personality and Social Psychology*, 7, 101–104.

Stoebe, W., Insko, C., Thompson, V., & Layton, B. (1971). Effects of physical attractiveness, attitude similarity, and sex on various aspects of interpersonal attraction. *Journal of Personality and Social Psychology*, 18, 79–91.

Tennenbaum, D. (1977). Personality and criminality: A summary of the literature. *Journal of Criminal Justice*, 5, 225–235.

Walster, E., Aronson, E., Abrahams, D. & Rottman, L. (1966). Importance of physical attractiveness in dating behavior. *Journal of Personality and Social Psychology*, 4, 508–516.

Wiatrowski, M., Griswold, D., & Roberts, M. (1981). Social control theory and delinquency. *American Sociological Review*, 46, 525–541.

Endnote

* Editor's note: This chapter is excerpted and reprinted, with permission, from an article published in *Criminology*, Vol. 22, No. 3, August 1984: 421–440. For statistics tables and appendix, please see original.

2

"Ugly" Criminals and "Ugly" Victims

A Quantitative Analysis of Add Health Data

Brent Teasdale and Bonnie Berry

There is a striking absence of academic research on the topic of physical appearance as it relates to criminal behavior and criminal victimization. Of the little that is known, the findings pertain to adult criminals and focus on criminal justice reactions to their crimes, such as the manner in which appearance affects judges' and juries' decisions on guilt determination and subsequent sentencing. Lacking is scientific information about the manner in which physical appearance affects reactions to juveniles, be they delinquents or victims of crime. That topic is the focus of this chapter.

One of the few studies of "ugly criminals" as substantiated by an analysis of Add Health data (to be described below) is conducted by Mocan and Tekin, (2010). Overall, Mocan and Tekin find that unattractive people are more likely to commit crime, average-looking people less so, and attractive people, least so. More importantly perhaps, they suggest that attractive people receive preferential, more lenient, treatment from the judicial system, reducing their likelihood of apprehension, arrest, detention, and conviction "as a function of the extent of beauty of the individual" (p. 7); however, they present no data to examine this assertion empirically. In sum, regardless of legal responses to physical appearance, the Add Health data show that being very attractive reduces the individual's engagement in criminal activity and being unattractive increases it for a number of crimes, ranging from burglary to drug offenses.

Our study is a bit broader. Using Add Health data, we examine the relationships between physical appearance and arrest and between physical appearance and physical assault victimization. We discover that, in both instances, appearance influences the incidence of arrest as well as the incidence of victimization. Logistic regression analyses demonstrated that the less attractive the subjects, the more likely they are to be arrested, holding constant offending behavior. We also find that attractiveness is a significant predictor of criminal victimization, with greater attractiveness being associated with lower odds of victimization.

What follows is a description of the data source, analysis, and results. Following that is a brief discussion of appearance and crime cross-referenced with social and economic capital, notably the relevance of employment (legitimate and illegitimate) to appearance and to crime.

DATA AND METHODS

In this analysis, we test the null hypothesis that appearance is not associated with arrest or victimization. In order to test the relationships between physical attractiveness and victimization and arrests, we utilize data from the National Longitudinal Study of Adolescent to Adult Health (Add Health). Add Health is a nationally representative study of adolescents who were in the seventh through twelfth grades in 1995. The study followed this cohort, reinterviewing them in 1996, 2001, and 2008. For our purposes we utilize data from waves 1 (1995) and 4 (2008). We measure attractiveness based on interviewer's responses in 1995 (wave 1), and self-reported victimization, offending, and arrest measures from adulthood (wave 4, 2008). The wave 1 data is representative of adolescents in schools from the United States with respect to region, urbanity, school type, and size (Harris, 2011).

The sampling plan for the Add Health data follows a multi-stage clustered random sample. In the primary sampling stage, 80 high schools and one feeder middle school (selected with probability proportional to contribution to the high school) were selected for inclusion in the study. Some schools (N = 28) spanned the developmental period from seventh through twelfth grades, so the result was 132 schools (80 high schools and 52 feeder middle schools) in the sample (Harris, 2011). Within schools, students were stratified by grade and sex, and approximately 17 students from each stratum were selected using random sampling techniques. This resulted in approximately 200 adolescents per school (6 grades × 2 sexes × 17 students = 204). Individuals with missing data on any of the study variables were excluded, resulting in an analysis sample of 15,482 respondents.

Measures

We have two dependent variables: arrest and victimization. Our primary dependent variable of interest is arrests. These were measured retrospectively in adulthood, based on the wave 4 item that asked respondents "Have you ever been arrested?" It was coded 1 = yes and 0 = no. Our second dependent variable of interest is whether an individual was victimized or not. Victimization items asked respondents how often over the past year they had experienced the following: (1) "someone pulled a knife or gun on you?" (2) "someone shot or stabbed you?" (3) "someone slapped, hit, choked, or kicked you?" and (4) "were you were beaten up?" These four items were summed and dichotomized to indicate whether the individual had experienced any violent victimization (1 = yes, 0 = no) over the past year.

Our primary independent variable of interest is physical attractiveness. This is measured based on the wave 1, in-home adolescent interview. The trained Add Health interviewers were asked to rate the physical attractiveness of the respondent on a 5-item Likert scale. Response options ranged from "Very Unattractive" (1) to "Very Attractive" (5) with "About Average" (3) serving as the midpoint.

In addition, our analyses control for sex (1 = female, 0 = male), race (Black, Hispanic, other nonwhite, and White), socioeconomic status (SES), and offending behavior. Our measure of offending is an attempt to control for the possibility that unattractive individuals offend at greater rates, compared with attractive individuals. Thus our measure of attractiveness truly represents differences in criminal justice responses to attractive and unattractive individuals, not differences in responses to offenders and nonoffenders. Offending behavior was coded as 1 if the respondent self-reported any of the following criminal behaviors: property damage, theft, burglary, assault, battery, drug sales, handling stolen goods, identity theft, and writing bad checks. If the respondent self-reported none of the above behaviors, they were coded 0 on the offender variable. The SES measure combined occupational prestige as determined by census occupational group codes and parents' educational attainment. These four items (two per parent, or two items if the adolescent only had one parent) were standardized and then averaged to create the SES measure.

Data Analysis

Because of the complex sampling design of the Add Health, we analyze the data using Stata (Version 13). The analyses take into account the complex nature of the sampling strategy by utilizing the svyset (complex survey estimation) suite of commands. Specifically, we model the nesting of students within study schools and the stratification of the primary sampling units by region. In addition, since both our arrest and victimization outcomes are dichotomous, we model them using design-adjusted logistic regression models. The results of these analysis steps are unbiased coefficients and standard errors that take into account the dichotomous distributions of the dependent variables and the complex nature of the sampling plan of the Add Health data.

RESULTS

Before we turn to the multivariate analyses, we present a data description in Table 2.1. As shown in Table 2.1, the sample is roughly evenly split between females (53.6 percent) and males (46.4 percent). Approximately 26 percent of the sample self-reported offending behaviors in the past year and approximately 22 percent of the respondents reported experiencing a violent victimization in the past year. About 28 percent of the respondents reported ever being arrested. Finally, the mean physical attractiveness rating was about 3.5, which is between "About Average" and "Somewhat Attractive" on the 5-point Likert scale.

Next, we turn to the question of whether individuals who are less attractive are more likely to be victimized than their more physically attractive counterparts. First, we present the bivariate relationship between attractiveness and violent victimization using a design-adjusted crosstab. Importantly, fewer individuals are rated as Very Unattractive

TABLE 2.1. *Descriptive Statistics*

	Mean	S.D.	Range
Arrested	.282	.450	0–1
Victim	.215	.411	0–1
Attractiveness	3.57	.871	1–5
Female	.536	.499	0–1
Black	.221	.415	0–1
Hispanic	.108	.311	0–1
Other	.149	.356	0–1
Age	16.16	1.72	11.4–21.4
SES	−.139	.908	−2.41–1.60
Offender	.259	.438	0–1

compared with Very Attractive. Also, most individuals are rated as About Average in physical attractiveness. With the exception of the Very Unattractive category, increases in physical attractiveness correspond with decreases in self-reported past-year violent victimization, confirming our hypothesis that more attractive individuals are less likely to be physically assaulted. Specifically, 25.4 percent of those respondents coded as Unattractive self-reported past-year victimization, while 20.4 percent of those respondents who were coded as Very Attractive self-reported victimization. The design-adjusted F-test of the linear association between attractiveness and victimization ($F_{3.81,487.89}$ = 4.69) is significant (p = .0012) This is confirmed in our multivariate analysis, where we adjust for sex, race, age, and SES when estimating the association between attractiveness and victimization. As shown in Table 2.3, we find that for each one unit increase in physical attractiveness, the odds of victimization are reduced by about 4.2 percent (OR = .958). This association remains significant, in spite of the controls for sex, race, age, and SES differences in the rate of victimization.

TABLE 2.2. *Bivariate Association between Attractiveness and Victimization*

	Not Victimized (%)	Victimized (%)
Very Unattractive	228 (78.1)	64 (21.9)
Unattractive	533 (74.6)	181 (25.4)
About Average	5,213 (77.3)	1,531 (22.7)
Attractive	4,273 (80.0)	1,068 (20.0)
Very Attractive	1,903 (79.6)	488 (20.4)

Design-Adjusted F (3.81, 487.89) = 4.69, p = .0012

TABLE 2.3. *Multivariate Logistic Regression Predicting Victimization*

	b (se)	OR
Intercept	−.286 (.196)	.75
Physical Attractiveness	−.043 (.021)	.96[*]
Female	−.306 (.044)	.74[***]
Black	.335 (.049)	1.40[***]
Hispanic	−.033 (.105)	.97
Other	.113 (.054)	1.12[*]
Age	−.030 (.011)	.97[**]
SES	−.116 (.027)	.89[***]

Design-Adjusted F (7, 122) = 16.72, p < .0000

Finally, we turn to the question of whether individuals who are less attractive are at greater risk of arrest. Paralleling our analysis of victimization, we begin with a bivariate test of the idea, using the design-adjusted crosstab in Stata. The results of this analysis are presented in Table 2.4. As shown in Table 2.4, with the exception of the Very Unattractive category, increasing attractiveness is associated with a lower risk of arrest, with the Unattractive individuals having the highest rate of arrest (33.2 percent) and the Very Attractive individuals having the lowest rate of arrest (22.3 percent). The linear association between attractiveness and arrest is highly significant (p < .0000) based on the design-adjusted F-test ($F_{3.49,446.91}$ = 19.75). This is confirmed in our multivariate analysis where we adjust for sex, race, age, and SES differences in the rate of arrest and differences in the rate of arrest for offenders and nonoffenders.

As shown in Table 2.5, when including controls, the effect of physical attractiveness on arrest remains significant (p = .020). Holding constant sex, race, age, SES, and offending behavior, for every one unit increase in physical attractiveness, the odds of an arrest are decreased by 5.8%

TABLE 2.4. *Bivariate Association between Attractiveness and Arrest*

	Not Arrested (%)	Arrested (%)
Very Unattractive	217 (74.3)	75 (25.7)
Unattractive	477 (66.8)	237 (33.2)
About Average	4,632 (68.7)	2,112 (31.3)
Attractive	3,929 (73.6)	1,412 (26.4)
Very Attractive	1,859 (77.7)	532 (22.3)

Design-Adjusted F (3.49, 446.91) = 19.75, p < .0000

TABLE 2.5. *Multivariate Logistic Regression Predicting Arrest*

	b (se)	OR
Intercept	1.011 (.319)	2.75**
Physical Attractiveness	−.059 (.025)	.94*
Female	−1.21 (.040)	.30***
Black	.300 (.065)	1.35***
Hispanic	−.221 (.107)	.80*
Other	−.295 (.125)	.74*
Age	−.014 (.016)	.99
SES	−.151 (.027)	.86***
Offender	.866 (.042)	2.38***

Design-Adjusted F (8, 121) = 168.66, p < .0000

(OR = .942). Note that being male, African American (as opposed to white), being White (as opposed to other) and offending also significantly correlate with an increased odds of arrest. Socioeconomic status correlates with a significantly decreased odds of arrest.

CONCLUSIONS

In this study, we analyze Add Health data (National Longitudinal Study of Adolescent to Adult Health) to examine whether violent victimization depends upon level of attractiveness. We find that 22 percent of the respondents reported experiencing a violent victimization in the past year (had a knife or gun pulled on them; were shot or stabbed; were slapped, hit, choked, or kicked; or were beaten up). With the exception of the Very Unattractive category, increases in physical attractiveness correspond with decreases in self-reported violent victimization in the past year, confirming the hypothesis that more attractive individuals are less likely to be physically assaulted. Specifically, 25.4 percent of those respondents coded as Unattractive self-reported past-year victimization, while 20.4 percent of those respondents who were coded as Very Attractive self-reported victimization. This finding is confirmed by our multivariate analysis, where we adjust for gender, race, and SES when estimating the association between attractiveness and victimization. Our results suggest that adolescents' physical attractiveness, as measured by independent raters, has long-term effects on the self-reported adulthood outcomes, both the likelihood of arrest and the likelihood of victimization.

That our results hold, given that the raters of the IV (attractiveness) are independent of the respondents who report on the DVs (arrest and victimization) and given that there is a 13-year time-lag between the measures of the IV and the measures of the DV, is impressive. It is all the more impressive that the results hold for arrest when we control for sex, race, SES, and offending behavior, bearing in mind that, as Mocan and Tekin have noted, attractiveness is correlated with offending.

It seems unlikely that the results of our study could be spurious due to unmeasured factors, since sources of spuriousness must cause both the IV and the DV. While it is likely that we could include third variables in our models that would predict our outcomes, it is unlikely that those variables would also cause variation in physical attractiveness, since that variation is likely due to genetic and biological factors. Of course, perceptions of attractiveness are influenced by culture and other socialization variables, but since the raters of the respondents' physical attractiveness were not also rating the subjects on the dependent variables, it seems unlikely that this would bias our results.

Although the present results seem unlikely to be biased by missing sources of spuriousness, it is still possible that we have missed a key (mediator) variable that may intervene in the relationship between physical attractiveness and outcomes (arrest and victimization). It is likely that a mediator is the result of physical attractiveness (labor market experiences, life stressors, etc.) and consequently leads to arrest and victimization. Importantly, we did adjust for offending in our analysis of arrest, since this is likely a key mediator of that association, with offending resulting from attractiveness and causing arrest. However, we did observe a significant direct effect of attractiveness on arrest, even when holding constant these offending behaviors. That is, there must be something else that links physical appearance to arrest, beyond simply offending behavior.

Our results point to the important and neglected role of physical attractiveness in criminological and criminal justice processes. Further, our results are suggestive of a social reaction perspective, where the role of the audience's response to those who are less attractive (both police officer responses and perpetrator responses) has strong impacts on individuals depending on their level of attractiveness. This is in line with much of the research on attractiveness. It also parallels early criminological research, where for example Steffensmeier and Terry (1979) found that citizen decisions to report shoplifting behavior varied by the appearance of the perpetrator (hippy versus conventional). These findings also support what is known about bullying of school children for their appearance, specifically obesity (Olweus, 1978), interpersonal violence against college students based on sexual orientation (Snyder, Scherer, & Fisher, 2018), and criminal victimization of the visibly disabled (Scherer, Snyder, & Fisher, 2016; Thorneycroft & Asquith, 2015; and Scherer and Reyns, Chapter 13 in this volume).

An Important Side Note: Appearance, Crime, and (Il)legitimate Employment

Unattractive people face a social deficit in terms of lawful employment and crime. As noted in the Introduction to this text, a labor market penalty is visited upon unattractive people and propels them toward criminal activity. Work has long been known to operate as an inhibitor of criminal involvement for two main reasons: (1) work takes up time and thus the employed has a goodly number of hours taken up during the day that cannot be devoted to criminal pursuits and (2) work provides money and thus there is less need to commit crime for financial gain. In Mocan and Tekin's 2010 discussion paper, "Ugly Criminals," we find a number of useful analyses pertaining to legitimate and illegitimate employment. Essentially, using Add Health data, Mocan and Tekin found that "being very attractive reduces a young adult's (ages 18–26) propensity for criminal activity and being unattractive increases it for a number of crimes, ranging from burglary to selling drugs" (p. 15). They argue that this is the result of human capital development. Specifically, they find lower IQ and lower wages among the unattractive, which they suggest then leads these individuals to criminality.[1] While we acknowledge the possibility that criminality results indirectly from physical appearance, perhaps a stronger proposition is that the level of attractiveness influences criminal justice intervention, from apprehension to arrest to conviction and sentencing.

As discussed in the Introduction to this volume and elsewhere (Berry, 2007, 2008), social opportunities dependent upon appearance include education, employment, romance and marriage, friendships, and club membership. These advantages have not been discussed as *intervening variables* in the path between appearance and crime, but perhaps they should be. However, employment may be such an intervening variable between appearance and criminality. Mocan and Tekin point out that appearance has a strong effect on employment, with the unattractive suffering a labor market penalty. This is well understood and well documented elsewhere. But they project further, saying that this labor market penalty "provides a direct incentive for unattractive individuals toward criminal activity" (p. 15). This direct line has not been remarked upon previously.

While the second author has argued that appearance matters less (but still does matter) in highly skilled, unionized jobs, Mocan and Tekin argue that "less attractive people sort themselves into the criminal sector" (p. 16). Specifically, "beauty commands a positive earnings premium in the legal market" and "criminal activity is a labor market choice of rational agents where the decision to engage in crime is made by comparing the financial rewards from crime to those obtained from legal work" (pp. 15–16). Based on self-reported criminal activity, (a) unattractive individuals commit more crime in comparison to average-looking ones, (b) very attractive individuals commit less crime in comparison to those who are average-looking, and (c) specifically, attractive females are less likely to be detained for suspicion of crime (p. 16).

Beauty is a form of social capital, as will be discussed in Chapter 7 by Wareham, Berry, Blackwell, and Boots. Simply put, attractiveness can be socially exchanged for all manner of other opportunities, such as jobs, dates, friendship, and so on. Attractiveness can instill trust, which would be particularly useful for crimes of financial fraud and other white-collar crimes requiring that victims not be suspicious of the offender. However, as we have seen clearly demonstrated here, good looks may operate across the range of crime, including street crime. Because apprehension and conviction is a reduced possibility for attractive people, they are less likely to be apprehended and convicted for all manner of crime. Since good-looking people have an advantage in both legal and criminal sectors, the net effect of beauty on crime is unambiguous. To differentiate appearance by type of employment by criminal involvement (appearance x employment type x criminality), we might say that since most criminals are self-employed, according to Mocan and Tekin, this would motivate unattractive people to join the criminal sector and attractive people to participate in the legal labor market. It follows, then, that the average level of beauty would be higher in the legitimate labor market compared to the criminal sector (Mocan & Tekin, 2010, p. 5). To summarize, looks matter. Looks can influence the type of employment we engage in (legitimate or illegitimate), in our criminal involvement apart from employment, and in our chances of criminal victimization.

References

Berry, B. (2007). *Beauty bias: Discrimination and social power.* Westport, CT: Praeger.
  (2008). *The power of looks: Social stratification of physical appearance.* Hampshire, UK: Ashgate.
Harris, K. M. (2011). *Design Features of Add Health.* Chapel Hill, NC: Carolina Population Center.
Mocan, N. & Tekin, E. (2010). Ugly criminals. *The Review of Economics and Statistics, 92,* 15–30.
Olweus, D. (1978). *Aggression in the schools: Bullies and whipping boys.* Washington, DC: Hemisphere.
Scherer, H. L., Snyder, J. A., & Fisher, B. S. (2016). Intimate partner victimization among college students with and without disabilities: Prevalence of and relationship to emotional well-being. *Journal of Interpersonal Violence, 31,* 49–80.
Snyder, J. A., Scherer, H. L., & Fisher, B. S. (2018). Interpersonal violence among college students: Does sexual orientation impact risk of victimization? *Journal of School Violence, 17* (1), 1–15.

Steffensmeier, D. J. & Terry, R. M. (1973). Deviance and respectability: An observational study of reactions to shoplifting. *Social Forces*, 51, 417–426.

Thorneycroft, R. & Asquith, N. L. (2015). The dark figure of disablist violence. *The Howard Journal of Criminal Justice*, 54, 489–507.

Endnote

1 The first wave of longitudinal data for the Mocan and Tekin study was gathered in 1994–1995; the second wave in 1996; and the third wave in 2001–2002. The first two waves were definitely pre-recession; probably the third also. We wonder if these same findings would hold up in our current economic conditions when even attractive, skilled, educated people cannot get legitimate jobs.

PART II

RACE, ETHNICITY, AND NATIONALITY AS TARGETED IDENTITIES

EDITORIAL COMMENTS

From the popular press, we know that people of color are more likely to be stopped and frisked, more likely to be flagged down and ticketed for traffic violations, and more likely to be asked to prove citizenship status (Carbado, Harris, & Crenshaw, 2013; Durose & Langton, 2013). A subtlety is offered by Drakulich and Crutchfield (2013) on this topic when they write that "residents of minority neighborhoods are more likely to *perceive* the police as biased..." (p. 402, emphasis added). This finding leaves the door open to questioning how much of the bias is *perceptual* on the part of minority citizens, but is at least partially answered by Drakulich and Crutchfield's finding that economically disadvantaged race/ethnicity minority communities are indeed "more likely to experience biased policing..." (p. 402). Again, we find that socioeconomic status is inseparable from race, ethnicity, and appearance.

Dabney, Teasdale, Ishoy, Gann, and Berry (2017), in a study of police activity in a largely minority jurisdiction, found that Blacks are more likely to be arrested than Whites, but the story doesn't end there. Black skin in combination with gender (being male) and clothing and hair style choices (specifically, a "hip-hop" appearance) enhance the probability of arrest. Such a racialized appearance is sufficient for police suspicion, but the question of the depth of skin color can get infinitely complex. Lykke (2016) cites research showing that, of the defendants who avoided imprisonment, White men with "darker skin and more Afrocentric features were apparently penalized for resembling Black men and were more likely than other White men to receive a prison sentence" (p. 4).

IMAGE 1. Being Black is not a crime (Getty Images)

This raises the question of whether it is racialized appearance or race itself that leads to crime control intervention. May (2015) examines US patterns of excluding Blacks from public venues, such as nightclubs, based on dress codes. Black men wearing the same clothes as White men, for instance baggy pants, are not allowed into these places of entertainment while the White men are. May finds that it is an "increasingly common experience for African-American men seeking access to popular nightclubs" to be denied access based on a dress code that does not apply to White men (p. 39). The dress codes are a means of racial profiling: "Around the U.S., in privately-owned but ostensibly public entertainment venues, dress codes have become an informal color line" (May, p. 39).

It has long been established in criminological literature that US Blacks are treated unfairly by the criminal justice system (for example, Cole, 1999; Lykke, 2016; Tonry, 1995). They are more commonly suspected of crime, the charges leveled at them are more serious, they are poorly represented in court, they are sentenced more harshly to longer prison sentences, and they are more likely to receive the death penalty than are Whites for the same suspected crimes. The evidence starts at the first sign of suspicion and follows the crime control process to the conclusion (see Image 1).

There is abundant and accumulating evidence that police, courts, and corrections respond in a biased manner to suspects and indicted perpetrators because of their physical appearance. These examples of differential intrusion all pertain to skin color, not crime. In other words, those who are targeted are assumed to be involved in crime while Whites engaging in the same behavior (walking, driving, running errands, working, and other everyday activities) are not confronted. Not surprisingly, the data from New York City on stopping and frisking (Francescani, Roberts, & Hicken, 2012) have shown that, in the great majority of cases, there was no wrongdoing to investigate. Francescani and colleagues report that only 12 percent of those stopped were arrested or ticketed, suggesting that those stopped had done nothing for which to be stopped. More than 85 percent of those stopped were Black or Hispanic, while they make up only 51 percent of the city's population. Likewise, Buettner and Glaberson (2017) find that over 80 percent of those stopped in New York are Black and Latino young men, and only a small percentage of the stops produced an arrest (see Gelman, Fagan, & Kiss, 2012, for an empirical examination of these issues, and see Herring, Keith, & Horton, 2004, for an analysis of broad social repercussions of skin color).

Black and Indigenous Lives Matter

Tragic endings such as we have seen in the Trayvon Martin case, in which an African-American teenager was shot and killed by a neighborhood watch officer in February 2012, *can* be avoided; they are *not* avoided because of biased reactions to skin color. Mr Martin was walking home, carrying a bag of candy and a can of iced tea. He had done nothing except be Black. Since that killing (and long before, although it was less discussed), the United States has experienced a large number of such killings, prompting the "Black Lives Matter" movement. Using case histories, legal analyses, and official statistics, Lorenzo Boyd and Kimberly Conway Dumpson (Chapter 4) offer a detailed study of the Black Lives Matter movement, where it came from and where it may be headed.

A timely topic, skin color matters greatly in the response to suspected crime and abuse of citizenry. The mattering (importance) of Black lives can refer not only to police killing people who are legally innocent; it refers to broader patterns that display a disregard for Blacks' lives because of their race. A prime example would be lead poisoning of the water supply in Flint, Michigan, which affects underprivileged Blacks. In 2016, it was discovered that Black citizens in Flint were being poisoned by lead in the water supply, while the Republican governor and his appointees repeatedly denied that the water was tainted and that the inhabitants were being permanently damaged (Smith, 2016). Finally, too late for most of the Flint inhabitants, emergency managers were charged with felonies over the tainted water (Davey & Smith, 2016). White, better-resourced inhabitants of the state of Michigan were not subjected to this horror. And the fact that the denial took so long to be recognized as a denial and then efforts to fix the water supply delayed can only be explained by the fact that poor Black inhabitants' lives were viewed as less valuable than those of better-off White lives. I mention this case here because poisoning people is a criminal act; singling out particular categories of people for poisoning is a form of bias crime.

Victims of color are also subject to bias, and not just from the crime control system. Skin color, as determined by medical examiners, can conflict with the reality of sexual assault. Examinations of female patients after having engaged in consensual sex shows varying evidence of abrasions and bruises, which are less evident with dark-skinned women than with light-skinned women. It doesn't take a huge inferential leap to wonder if, based on forensic examinations of sexual assault victims, Black women are less likely to be evaluated as having been assaulted compared to White women. These widely disparate interpretations by the medical staff examining anogenital injuries can lead to health care disparities as well as disparities in criminal justice outcomes (Sommers, Fargo, Baker, Fisher, Buschur, & Zink, 2009; Sommers et al., 2006; Sommers et al., 2008). This topic will be considered again in the Conclusion (Chapter 15) in which I recommend changes to the social control systems that can be made less discriminatory; specifically, I rely on Dayna Bowen Matthew's (2015) work on *Just Medicine: A Cure for Racial Inequality in American Health Care.*

Bias, in terms of prosecution and victimization, against Australian, Canadian, and US Indigenous peoples is also abundant. As Terry Wotherspoon and John Hansen show in Chapter 3, part of the problem is *invisibility* rather than *visibility* of the Canadian Indigenous. Because the Indigenous are corralled away from the broader public eye, they are vulnerable to the national criminal justice system but are also vulnerable to abuse by each other with very little or no restitution. Their lives are hardly optimal anyway in terms of poverty, disease, and the usual manifestations of racial discrimination, but add to that their criminal victimization by their fellow Indigenous members and formalized social control systems, and we have a very unjust situation. It has been this way since Indigenous people have had contact with White people as the dominating culture. Two recent books provide a view of the genocidal treatment and slavery practices against the American Indigenous people (Madley, 2016; Resendez, 2017). These practices, newly revealed, are referred to as hidden histories, matching my point about invisibility.

But back to the main point of this text about bias against visible physical appearance, with Indigenous peoples, we confront the question of identifiability. As Gabrielle Scrimshaw remarked recently, there is a strong rural–urban divide such that 80 percent of White Canadians live in cities and half of the Canadian Indigenous live in rural areas (2018). Combine that picture with the fact that, in the United States and Canada, the Indigenous live on reservations, separately from Whites, and we have invisibility factors in play. However, as Scrimshaw points out, when the Indigenous are identifiable by physical features, it does not go well for them. In a case of a White man killing an Indigenous man, Coulten Boushie, the White man was found not guilty by a jury. The jury selection excluded five potential jurors who were "visibly Indigenous" (p. 29).

The Indigenous can be misidentified. When I contacted the Tribal Law and Policy Institute's program director, Heather Valdez Freeman, about Indigenous people's representation in the US criminal justice system, she informed me that, during her time at the National Institute of Justice, she spoke with both tribal and state law enforcement as well as members of the Indigenous community. She learned that:

Native people are very often not identified as Native when arrested and when incarcerated. The process for racial/ethnic identification is the officer looking at the arrested and making their own assumptions. As a result, Native people are often identified as Hispanic. Last names can lead authorities to identify Native people as Hispanic, as well. One of the consequences of this misidentification [is that] statistics are out of whack and often undercount Native folks. It is also a good way [for the Indigenous] to get lost in the system.

Over-identification and false representation can occur when assuming that people with dark complexions living in certain parts of the country are Indigenous. Valdez Freeman went on to say:

There are also places in the US where anyone brown is considered Native – a judge in North Dakota described this situation in his state. In this case, the anti-Native sentiment is often conflated with historical animosities mixed with a good dose of racism. These negative views on the part of the non-Native community find their way into law enforcement and surface not just in police interactions with offenders, but also in their interactions with tribal police, which as you can imagine, has the potential to interfere with public safety.

                                        (Freeman, personal communication, May 30, 2017)

Like Heather Valdez Freeman, Cunneen and Tauri (2016) remark on the difficulty with measuring representation of the Indigenous in criminal and victim populations because Indigenous people are not uncommonly categorized as "other," as in White, Black, Hispanic, and other. That difficulty aside, we do know that the Indigenous are vastly overrepresented at every step of the criminal justice process. Moreover, their imprisonment rate is not only disproportionately large, it is increasing. In Canada, Indigenous offenders represent 20 percent of the total federal prison population compared to 3 percent of the Canadian adult population. In more remote areas of Canada, Aboriginal people make up 70 percent of the total prisoner population. In Australia, Indigenous people are imprisoned 13 times more than the non-Indigenous. Similar patterns are found in New Zealand and the United States.

As with Black lives, Indigenous lives are less valued than White lives by the criminal justice system. We know this by examining US Justice Department statistics showing that, while crime rates are higher among Indigenous people than for all but a few of the nation's most violent cities, the Justice Department (which is responsible for prosecuting the most serious crimes on reservations) files charges in only about half of the murder investigations and turns down almost two-thirds of the sexual assault cases (Williams, 2012). The 310 reservations in the US experience more than two and a half times the violent crime rate compared to the national average. US Indigenous women are 10 times more likely to be murdered than other citizens; and they are raped or sexually assaulted at a rate four times the national average, with more than one in three having either been raped or experienced an attempted rape.

Canadian and US Indigenous societies have a dual court system, the tribal court system and the dominant culture's court system. Tribal courts in the United States have the authority to prosecute tribal members but cannot sentence those convicted to more than three years in prison. Since that is the case, tribes frequently seek federal prosecution for serious crimes. But federal prosecutors decline to file charges for about half of the cases. For example, the US government did not pursue rape charges on reservations 65 percent of the time in 2016 and turned back 61 percent of the cases of sexual abuse of children. It also appears that Indigenous offenders in Australia (and perhaps elsewhere) received lighter sentences when their victims are also Indigenous (Black, 2017), which corresponds to the US situation in which Black offenders are punished less (for example, are less likely to receive the death penalty) when their victims are also Black.

But the key point for this analysis of appearance and crime is that Indigenous people are remotely located, thus they are invisible and forgotten. They are unknown and unattended not only by public citizens but by the social control systems that could aid (or harm) them.

When I asked Rick McGary, who is currently studying Indigenous peoples and crime in Australia, about appearance bias, he told me that, while it is unknown whether obviously identifiable Indigenous peoples are treated worse in the Australian crime control system, a not-so-subtle level of appearance bias does certainly take place. He is publishing "a photographic documentation and analysis of symbols in the criminal courtrooms (basically looking for signs of settler supremacy like photos of [England's Queen] or the complete absence of symbols of Indigenous people . . .)" (McGary, 2017, personal communication, July 13). Although, as his research has progressed, he reported to me in January 2018, that the courtrooms in Australia are displaying the Queen's portrait a lot less and that "more and more, courtrooms here are devoid of anything but the national seal – not even flags" (personal communication, January 21, 2018).

He also told me, when I asked if Indigenous people can be clearly identified by their racial traits, that Indigenous people in Melbourne intentionally wear headbands and other clothing signals that advertise their Indigenous status. Black-looking Indigenous people are viewed as the only true Indigenous people; Whites dressing as Indigenous are immediately suspect according to real and obvious Indigenous peoples (personal communication, July 15, 2017).

In a personal communication with Terry Wotherspoon and John Hansen (December 11, 2017), they told me that there is almost no literature on the issues of specific appearance traits of the Indigenous as they may pertain to crime. There "is such diversity in the Indigenous populations that many people cannot be readily identified," which works out well for those Indigenous people who can pass as White. They told me that there are a few general indicators of Indigenousness: they typically have brown eyes, dark hair, dark skin, and some pronounced facial characteristics. Moreover, the Indigenous display some stand-out dress and grooming styles, as when some of the men and women wear feathered jewelry or clothing items with beadwork or traditional Indigenous designs (see Image 2). But one cannot necessarily distinguish the Indigenous from the non-Indigenous, visually speaking. Living within a reservation, however, is something of a visual trait

IMAGE 2. Russell Means and Dennis Banks, leaders of the American Indian Movement, in federal district court, St Paul, Minnesota, for the occupation of Wounded Knee (South Dakota) 1974. Charges dismissed. (Getty Images)

in itself since the boundaries themselves are visible. And when the Indigenous venture into broader White society, they are visually targeted.

Shocking Cross-Cultural Comparisons

I learned many startling things in the course of this research on appearance bias and crime. Against my prejudgment, the United States is the least discriminatory of the nations I researched regarding their treatment of Indigenous people. Compared to Canada, New Zealand, and Australia, "the US is still statistically less awful than nations that like to declare the US is racist" (McGary, personal communication, January 21, 2018). While the incarceration rate for Blacks in the United States is approximately 4:1, and the incarceration rate of US Indigenous compared to Whites is 2:1, the incarceration rates for Indigenous in Canada is 10:1, and in New Zealand is 6:1, while Denmark's incarceration of Greenlandic Inuits is 3.5:1 (McGary, personal communication, January 21, 2018).

An Absence of Racial Identifiers

One of the more surprising things I learned from this project came from Billy Ulibarrí's analysis of human trafficking (Chapter 5), which showed an absence of appearance identifiers. Being untrained in the study of human trafficking, I had expected that human trafficking victims would be limited to those we read about in the news and that they are obviously physically identifiable from White people. Specifically, I had wrongly assumed that Ulibarrí would write about Mexicans, South Americans, Filipinos and other Pacific Islanders. Which he does, but as he expertly points out, the crusade to target White children and White women as victims and all of us as potential traffickers removes the racial and nationality appearance markers.

The ubiquitous ads on US milk cartons and in advertising flyers that we receive in the mail asking "have you seen me?" commonly show White children and White women as the alleged victims. Parents reminding their children to be cautious around strangers ("stranger danger"), as aimed at the most innocuous-appearing people, is another sign that we cannot, in the current social construction of trafficking, rely on appearance markers.

This is a complicated story, however, varying across time and, significantly, dependent upon moral crusades. While Ulibarrí does address Mexicans, Filipinos, et al. as willing or unwilling arrivals to the United States, the most amazing finding from his work is the absence of physical appearance traits and even nationality definers. This zero effect is equally significant to a non-zero effect since it tells us the opposite of what we might expect: appearance may have no influence on crime and victimization when we are encountering a moral panic telling us that we can all be victimized, regardless of age, race, color, nationality, or any other appearance-related traits; we can all be seen as potential victims. This is part of the false construction of the moral panic over human trafficking.

Yes, human trafficking exists and is personally and socially destructive in its outcomes. But to make it seem as though we are all equally vulnerable to trafficking results is a false picture of trafficking and, worse, an ineffective system of control of trafficking. In fact, as Ulibarrí explains, definitions of targeted human trafficking change over time depending on the social construction of human trafficking and the needs and desires of the population receiving the trafficked people. For instance, Ulibarrí discusses the limited-in-time "Natasha Trade" as a phenomenon speaking to the movement of Russian and Eastern European women brought to the United States at the behest of US men. Southeastern Asian women have been brought to the United States as domestic workers and kept under horrifying conditions. Presently, the social message is that any color and any nationality of women and children, especially children, are at risk. And the color of those children is seemingly unimportant since the overriding message is that danger is everywhere regardless of our appearance.

Other Colors and Other Nationalities as Victims

Neglected in the public discussion of racial targeting are the lesser-known public and official reactions to Latinos/as and Asian Americans. Asian Americans are thought to exhibit prosocial behavior more than other races in the United States, including Whites, but are also assumed to not be US citizens, refusing to fit in, and, for these reasons, are denigrated (Luo, 2016; Walsh & Yun, 2017). As noted in the Introduction, these assumptions can be forms of microaggression, the insults described by Derald Wing Sue (2010) as subtle (or not so subtle) and unintentional offenses. Latinos/as (or Latinx, the gender-neutral term contemporarily used in lieu of Latinos/as) are assumed to be in the US illegally and assumed to be criminally inclined. Unknown or unacknowledged by the public and as has been widely documented, "migrants" (which, in the United States, usually means "Mexicans") are *less* likely to commit crimes than non-migrants (Perez-Pena, 2017).

There are neglected and forgotten categories of victims in terms of their race, ethnicity, and nationality. One ethnic category that is isolated and has historically been associated with criminality is the Roma peoples of Europe (Gypsies). Like the Canadian, Australian, and US Indigenous peoples, they are isolated physically from the main populations, yet they are visibly different from most Europeans. The circumstances of this historically maligned group have not improved over the centuries, as was recently reported in the news media (Gladstone, 2017). Roma are being sickened in United Nations camps in, for example, Kosovo. There they were victimized by lead poisoning, much like the poisoned Black citizens in Flint, Michigan.

SUMMARY

As I researched the materials for this book and as I spoke with a range of people about the relationship between skin color (as a representation of race and ethnicity) and crime, the significant but humanly foolish tendency to react immediately to visual cues is immediately made apparent. The snap judgments we make, often incorrectly, about people's appearance and the relationship to crime as a suspect or as a victim can be so obvious and so inaccurate. More to the point about various racial traits and referring again to Heather Valdez Freeman's remarks about confusing Hispanics with Indigenous US citizens, I would point out that Black Americans are almost never confused with any group other than Blacks. This is not to say that Hispanics and Indigenous peoples are treated better in the criminal justice system than Blacks. They probably are not. My point is that immediate judgments are less mistakable in the case of Blacks. With Hispanics and Indigenous peoples, there can be vague and confusing judgments. Yet the outcomes are not good for any people of color if color determines judgments about criminal involvement.

QUESTIONS

Regarding Indigenous people, if assimilation is a bad idea, and all who study Indigenous people agree that it is, how can we resolve the invisibility problem alluded to above? If Indigenous people are isolated from mainstream society, and they are more likely to victimize each other without proper criminal justice oversight, how can we measure and effectively respond to this victimization? Yet, if they are assimilated into a mainstream society, they are victimized by the mainstream system. How can this be resolved?

Regarding Black people in the United States, how should we respond to those who say that "all lives matter"? Of course they do, but the sticking point is that not all lives are equally subjected to brutality.

Regarding Latinos/as in the United States, should they be more readily identifiable or should they melt among the background of US society (in other words, be unseen) and not be readily identifiable? At the present moment, it would seem invisibility would be the safer route.

Regarding refugees of various nationalities, how can we convince those who want to refuse them entry, safety, and social services that they are deserving? This situation exists not only in the United States but worldwide (most notably in Europe and the Middle East).

References

Ayres, I. (2015, February 24). When whites get a free pass. *New York Times*, p. A19.

Black, D. (2017, July 15). Personal communication.

Buettner, R. & Glaberson, W. (2012, July 11). Courts putting stop-and-frisk policy on trial. *New York Times*, pp. A1, A3.

Carbado, D. W., Harris, C. I., & Crenshaw, K. W. (2013, August 15). Racial profiling lives on. *New York Times*, p. A21.

Carbado, N. & Howard, C. (1973). Facial attractiveness and juvenile delinquency among black and white offenders. *Journal of Abnormal Child Psychology*, 1, 203–213.

Cole, D. (1999). *No equal justice: Race and class in the American criminal justice system*. New York, NY: The Free Press.

Cunneen, C. & Tauri, J. (2016). *Indigenous criminology*. Chicago, IL: Policy Press.

Dabney, D., Teasdale, B., Ishoy, G. A., Gann, T., & Berry, B. (2017). Policing in a largely minority jurisdiction: The influence of appearance characteristics associated with contemporary hip-hop culture on police decision-making. *Justice Quarterly*, 34, 1310–1338.

Davey, M. & Smith, M. (2016, December 21). Two former Flint emergency managers are charged over tainted water. *New York Times*, p. A12.

Drakulich, K. M. & Crutchfield, R. D. (2013). The role of perception of the police in informal social control: Implications for the racial stratification of crime and control. *Social Problems*, 60, 383–407.

Durose, M. & Langton, L. (2013, September 24). Police behavior during traffic and street stops. Bureau of Justice Statistics. Retrieved from www.bjs.gov.

Francescani, C., Roberts, J., & Hicken, M. (2012, July 3). Under siege: "Stop and frisk" polarizes New York. Retrieved from Reuters. www. Reuters.com.

Freeman, Heather Valdez. (2017, May 30). Personal communication.

Gelman, A., Fagan, J., & Kiss, A. (2012). An analysis of the New York City Police Department's "stop-and-frisk" policy in the context of claims of racial bias. *Journal of American Statistical Association*, 102, 813–823.

Gladstone, R. (2017, April 19). Roma sickened in U.N. camps are still waiting for redress. *New York Times*, p. A6.

Herring, C., Keith, V. M., & Horton, H. D. (Eds.). (2004). *Skin/deep: How race and complexion matter in the "color-blind" era.* Urbana, IL: University of Illinois Press.

Luo, M. (2016, October 11). An open letter to the woman who told us: Go back to China. *New York Times*, p. A1.

Lykke, L. (2016). Darker skin, harsher sentence. *Contexts*, 15, 4.

Madley, B. (2016). *An American genocide: The United States and the California Indian catastrophe, 1846–1873.* New Haven, CT: Yale University Press.

Matthew, D. B. (2015). *Just medicine: A cure for racial inequality in American health care.* New York, NY: New York University Press.

May, R. A. B. (2015). Discrimination and dress codes in urban life. *Contexts*, 14, 38–43.

McGary, R. (2017, July 13 and 15). Personal communication. (2018, January 21). Personal communication.

Otto, M. (2017). *Teeth: The story of beauty, inequality, and the struggle for oral health in America.* New York, NY: The New Press.

Perez-Pena, R. (2017, January 26). Migrants less likely to commit crimes. *New York Times*, p. A14.

Resendez, A. (2017). *The other slavery: The uncovered story of Indian enslavement in America.* Boston, MA: Houghton Mifflin Harcourt.

Scrimshaw, G. (2018, February 16). A killing in Saskatchewan. *New York Times*, p. A29.

Smith, M. (2016, October 29). State braces as inquiry into Flint crisis widens. *New York Times*, p. A11.

Sommers, M. S., Fargo, J. D., Baker, R. B., Fisher, B. S., Buschur, C., & Zink, T. M. (2009). Health disparities in the forensic sexual assault examination related to skin color. *Journal of Forensic Nursing*, 5, 191–200.

Sommers, M. S., Zink, T., Baker, R., Fargo, J., Porter, J., Weybright, D., & Shafer, J. (2006). Effects of age and ethnicity on physical injury from rape. *Journal of Obstetrics, Gynecology, and Neonatal Nursing*, 35, 199–207.

Sommers, M. S., Zink, T. M., Fargo, J. D., Baker, R. B., Buschur, C., Shambley-Ebron, D. Z., & Fisher, B. S. (2008). Forensic sexual assault examination and genital injury: Is skin color a source of health disparity? *American Journal of Emergency Medicine*, 26, 857–866.

Sue, D. W. (Ed.). (2010). *Microaggressions and marginality: Manifestation, dynamics, and impact.* Hoboken, NJ: John Wiley & Sons, Inc.

Tonry, M. (1995). *Malign neglect: Race, crime, and punishment in America.* New York, NY: Oxford University Press.

Walsh, A. & Yun, I. (2017). Examining the race, poverty, and crime nexus adding Asian Americans and biosocial processes. *Journal of Criminal Justice* (in press).

Williams, T. (2012). Higher crime, fewer charges on Indian land. Retrieved from *The New York Times.* www.nytimes.com/2012/02/21.

Wotherspoon, T. & Hansen, J. Personal communication, December 11, 2017.

3

Racial Profiling and Reconciliation

The Quest for Indigenous Justice in Canada

Terry Wotherspoon and John Hansen

INTRODUCTION

Canada tends to be highly regarded internationally for its progressive policies and perspectives on cultural diversity. In recent years the nation has been cited for its efforts to celebrate its diversity and welcome new immigrants and refugees even as many other nations are closing doors and building walls. Over the past four decades solid legal frameworks, including the introduction of a Charter of Rights and Freedoms, human rights provisions, and other constitutional and legislative measures, have ensured strong foundations to support these actions. Formal apologies for historical acts of exclusion or repression, including measures that banned or created barriers for entry of Asian immigrants, forcibly removed Canadians of Japanese and Ukrainian heritage from their homes and property, separated Indigenous children from their families in residential schools or removed them into foster homes or adoption, have reinforced perceptions that past grievances have been superseded by new realities of openness and inclusion.

Despite these advances, Canadian society is not immune to the kinds of politics, policies and practices associated with xenophobia and racism representing prominent barriers to minority populations in many contemporary Western societies. In the Canadian context political campaigns based on repression of racial groups and markers of racial status typically encounter substantial backlash, but this has not stopped their periodic recurrence in various guises. As public opinion polls reveal, perspectives on race relations and minority groups are generally favourable across the nation but there are significant exceptions to this pattern (Canadian Race

Relations Foundation, 2016). Newspaper and television reports and social media regularly convey incidences of racial discrimination, negative stereotyping and other forms of exclusion directed at members of racialized populations.

Looming prominently amid longstanding and complex forms of racialized oppression throughout Canada's history are the experiences of Indigenous peoples who have regularly encountered both interpersonal discrimination and systemic colonization. This chapter highlights some of these dynamics in a context in which the nation has committed itself to moving toward reconciliation and adoption of new relationships with Indigenous people. We focus on how racial profiling and social control exercised through policing practices and criminal justice systems represent deep contradictions in a White settler colonial society that has advanced what appear to be such progressive objectives.

Being Indigenous as a Crime

Three separate incidents in one small western province that gained media attention between late 2014 and mid-2017 illustrate encounters that are played out on a regular basis in many communities across the nation:

- Simon Ash-Moccasin, a First Nations playwright, actor and community activist, was stopped and questioned by police while walking near a casino parkade on his way to a Christmas party for the editorial board of a magazine on which he served in late 2014. Aware of police protocol and his rights, he did not respond to police inquiries as to where he was headed, following which he was injured as he was thrown against a wall, handcuffed, and thrown into a police vehicle. Police were later reprimanded for inappropriate actions related to a "crime" he described as "walking while Indigenous" (Ash-Moccasin, 2014; Saskatchewan Public Complaints Commission, 2016: 15–16).
- Coulten Boushie, a 22-year-old First Nations man, was fatally shot in the back of the head by a farmer who claimed he was protecting his property after four young Indigenous people had driven into his yard reportedly to seek assistance to repair a flat tire in the summer of 2016. Police officers were dispatched to report the death to his mother, who could not believe that her son had been killed. The officers then entered and began to search her house without permission, in the process questioning (accusingly, and wrongly) if she was drunk (Friesen, 2016).

– Bobby Cameron, the chief of the Federation of Sovereign Indigenous Nations, was stopped by police while driving on a well-travelled highway and asked if he had been drinking, in response to which he indicated the encounter was "sickening and disgusting," especially because it reinforced stereotypes that "Indians are drunks" (Grimard, 2017). The encounter occurred shortly after Cameron and others had spoken out about two other incidents in which an Indigenous man and woman, respectively, were detained by security personnel and accused of shoplifting while carrying items they were about to purchase in retail outlets in the same region.

These narratives are incomplete, demanding to be rounded out by participants and direct observers likely to offer diverse and sometimes conflicting accounts. Public discourses surrounding these events are also framed through alternative interpretations. Nonetheless, common to all of them are circumstances in which Indigenous people have been identified, victimized and detained through treatment that draws on and reinforces negative racialized stereotypes, becoming in turn the focus of reactions further characterized by a high degree of polarization as condemnation of the actions and the environment in which these occur themselves become the target of additional racially charged and stereotypical statements. Racial profiling is denounced or denied at the same time that it is reproduced and reinforced by daily circumstances with real consequences – both immediate and long-term – that are dangerous and sometimes even fatal. In order to understand the significance of such actions, it is necessary to have a sense of the historical and contemporary relationships in which they are embedded.

Indigenous People in the Canadian Context

Highly significant, often complicated relationships exist between Indigenous people and the Canadian state. Indigenous populations are diverse in nature, characterized by differences related to cultural, linguistic and geographical factors, legal status, treaty rights, identity, and socioeconomic circumstances. In accordance with the terms of the United Nations Declaration on the Rights of Indigenous Peoples, Indigenous peoples include all persons who are descendants of peoples who have occupied and established relationships with the land for several centuries. Under Canada's constitution and related legislation, Indigenous people (officially designated as Aboriginal) include First Nations, Métis, and Inuit populations; in addition, the population includes those of Indigenous heritage and identity who do not have official status. About 4.9 percent of the total Canadian population report Aboriginal identity, of whom nearly three out of five (58.4 percent) are First Nations (Statistics Canada, 2017: 1–2). About three-quarters of those with First Nations identity have registered or treaty Indian status, and among those with status close to half (44.2 percent) live on reserves (ibid., 2). Many Indigenous people – First Nations in particular – reside in some of Canada's poorest or badly underserviced communities and neighbourhoods, but many others are highly influential or occupy relatively favourable social or economic positions.

Canadians in general tend to have an incomplete understanding of these differences in status and circumstances and their significance for Indigenous–state relations (Angus Reid Institute, 2015; Environics Institute, 2016). The release in 2015 of the final report of the Truth and Reconciliation Commission of Canada (TRC) has provided impetus both to educate the public about, and to honour commitments associated with, these relationships (TRC, 2015). The commission's work, based on oral testimonies and documentary materials, concerns the role that a national system of residential schooling played in separating several generations of Indigenous children from their families and cultural heritage. The report situates residential schooling as part of a broader framework of government policies and related practices representing processes of cultural genocide, with devastating negative consequences for many Indigenous people and their communities (TRC, 2015: 1–3). The report includes a series of calls for action devoted to foster meaningful reconciliation, which the federal government has committed to implement in full (Trudeau, 2015); the government has also moved to compensate survivors of a "60s scoop" in which thousands of Indigenous children were placed for adoption after being taken from their families and communities.

These initiatives are promising, though they are not without contention given their association with deeply traumatic circumstances not fully comprehended by many Canadians. Tense dynamics are often played out, in part, through media and public discourses that tend to pose Indigenous people as an "other" (in relation to non-Indigenous people), whether represented sympathetically by those trying to gain an appreciation for Indigenous status and experiences or in more negative terms by those who frame Indigenous status as something accompanied by (possibly undeserved) rights and entitlements (Wotherspoon, 2014). There is no easy resolution to these issues insofar as they are grounded in contradictions associated with the affirmation of Indigenous rights and status within a nation-state committed to democratic principles but founded on colonialism marked by displacement of its Indigenous population.

The incidences cited offer stark manifestations of these contradictions enacted on a regular basis across different social venues. Where residential schooling and isolated reserves once separated Indigenous people from White society, today policing, sentencing and incarceration maintain, both overtly and in more subtle ways, similar delineations. Indigenous people in Canada, in common with experiences among racialized minority populations including many Black communities in the United States, are both more likely to be victimized by crime and overrepresented in detention and prison. This is in part a result of socioeconomic circumstances and related factors that contribute to significant forms of vulnerability. It is also a reflection of entry points through which Indigenous people are frequently singled out or detained based on visible markers of racialized identity. Racial profiling stands as a major gateway through which individual, systemic and structural characteristics intersect to open pathways toward these disproportionate outcomes.

Racial Profiling and Indigenous Populations

The phenomenon of racial profiling remains highly controversial and contested, despite extensive documentation of its practice. Throughout much of Canada's history various minority populations have been subjected to questioning, detention or arrest by police and other authorities based especially on racial markers, whether under the guise of nineteenth-century bylaws in which men wearing braids were subject to arrest (oriented to Chinese labourers in western Canada) or contemporary practices of "carding" (street checks and requests by police for identification without cause, experienced particularly by Black and Indigenous youth in urban areas). Although various racist and discriminatory policies and practices have been well-documented in scholarly, human rights and educational literature (Ontario Human Rights Commission, 2003 and 2017; Satzewich, 1998; Tator & Henry, 2006), the concept of racial profiling itself is of more recent vintage. Parallel with a focus on the preponderance of traffic stops and street checks experienced by African-Americans (Harris, 1997; Meehan & Ponder, 2002), the concept of racial profiling entered into Canadian vocabularies in the early part of the twenty-first century as media reports and human rights agencies highlighted similar problems in Ontario and Quebec (Wortley & Tanner, 2003). Frequent articulation of similar problems encountered by other minority groups, including Muslims and especially Indigenous populations, have made it clear that racial profiling is not an isolated phenomenon.

Despite profound concerns about what it represents as both a specific and a systemic issue (Brossard & Pedneault, 2012; Ethno-Cultural Council of Calgary, 2010; Ontario Human Rights Commission, 2017), there is extensive debate over the nature and significance of racial profiling in Canada. Some police forces deny that they practice racial profiling, others justify it as an important tool in their mandate to keep the peace, and still others have adopted prohibitions against it (Bahdi, Parsons, & Sandborn, 2010: 33–34; Gill, 2014). In some cases, notably after the 9/11 attacks or in areas where residents are concerned about high crime rates, there is even considerable public support for police to engage in racial profiling (Bahdi, 2003). Much of the criminological and legal analysis echoes these alternative perspectives while extending debate further to contest the definition and measurement of the phenomenon (Gabor, 2004; Hier & Walby, 2006; Melchers, 2003; Williams, 2006; Wortley & Tanner, 2003; Wortley & Tanner, 2005). In Canada, unlike many other nations, police do not maintain, and in many cases are prohibited from reporting, racial information in the collection of crime-related data (Owusu-Bempah & Millar, 2010). In response to these methodological and definitional issues, especially with respect to official police data, researchers, human rights organizations and community groups have paid greater attention to surveys focusing on self-reported incidences and perceptions of victimization. Regardless of one's perspective, it becomes clear that racial profiling is a significant political and social issue extending well beyond its technical and official dimensions.

Discourses associated with racial profiling have made it possible to name and openly discuss longstanding practices that often maintained a low profile beyond a few exceptional cases. However, for Indigenous people, racial profiling signifies a further chapter in an ongoing chain of experiences of formal exclusion and discrimination in core venues of Canadian society as well as more informal and personalized encounters with racism (Narine, 2012; Tator & Henry, 2006: 39–40). The notorious "starlight tours" – a practice long denied by police, in which intoxicated individuals, predominantly Indigenous youth, are driven to the outskirts of towns or cities and dropped off (frequently left with no outerwear in freezing temperatures) – have only recently been acknowledged after public inquiries into the deaths of individuals found much later were buttressed with accounts of numerous others who survived the process (Reber & Renaud, 2005). Although some police forces have taken action to prohibit the recurrence of such practices, others continue to deny the practice has ever existed (e.g., McLean, 2015). In the meantime, the periodic discovery of new bodies and mysterious disappearances continue to alarm Indigenous communities. Their broader concerns that police and other officials do not take their voices seriously have become especially pronounced not only in Prairie cities where reports of starlight tours have been widespread, but in other prominent cases including the "Highway of Tears" in northern British Columbia where the disappearance and murder of several mostly Indigenous women (official police counts of eighteen do not include several dozens of others noted by Indigenous communities) remain unsolved and sometimes not investigated, and in the northwestern Ontario city of Thunder Bay where police have been accused of systemic racism after lack of action in response to a growing number of serious injuries and deaths sustained by Indigenous people (Carrier Sekani Family Services, 2017; Nishnawbe Aski Nation, 2017). On a national scale, following several years of calls for action by Indigenous organizations and community members in relation to mounting numbers of unsolved cases in which Indigenous women were murdered or had disappeared under suspicious circumstances (well above official numbers of below two thousand), the federal government launched a National Inquiry into Missing and Murdered Indigenous Women and Girls in 2016 (Indigenous and Northern Affairs Canada, 2016).

These patterns point to a multilevel phenomenon. Indigenous people encounter high levels of victimization and discrimination, much of which is not acted upon or taken seriously by police, at the same time as they are susceptible to being profiled and victimized by police themselves. In many cases, these actions occur in relation to and also reinforce stereotypical conceptions – dressed sloppily or in revealing clothing; appearance of inebriation; dress style or accessories that appear to bear gang insignia; or walking/biking in predominantly non-Indigenous neighbourhoods; or driving between towns and Indigenous communities. Accounts by innocent individuals stopped by police who claim they resemble someone reported for committing a theft or assault are given meaning in relation to findings such as that of a survey in a major Western Canadian city that Indigenous women are ten times more likely than other women to be stopped for street checks by police (Huncar, 2017). Many such incidents are related to markers of social status, but other racialized factors are also significant. Another recent survey, in this case conducted with university students in the Prairie provinces, Indigenous respondents were 1.6 times more likely (once factors like age and gender were taken into account) than their non-Indigenous counterparts to report being stopped by police (Millar, 2016).

Although many of these reports and encounters rely on anecdotal evidence or focus on relatively specific regions or communities, they reveal a pattern that is relatively uniform and systemic in nature. Colonization and racialized forms of control represented in earlier generations through residential schooling and the child welfare system have been perpetuated especially through the criminal justice system (Macdonald, 2016; Satzewich & Wotherspoon, 2000: 110–11).

Racialized Policing and Over-Representation in Criminal Justice System Processes

Indigenous people in Canada have been impacted by a system of colonization and style of policing that has been racialized and harmful. Racialized discourse has been accompanied by the over-policing and increasing incarceration rates of Indigenous peoples. Spanning several decades, evidence of overrepresentation recurs in an array of statistics issued by numerous government agencies and research publications regarding disproportionately high levels of incarceration among Indigenous peoples, particularly in the Prairie region (Chartrand & Whitecloud, 2001; Hansen, 2015; Statistics Canada; TRC, 2015). Recent reconciliation processes have so far failed to reverse these trends.

Racialized policing is part of the broader fabric of control of Indigenous populations embedded within settler colonial foundations of nation-state-building processes. As Blaut (1992: 289) emphasizes, "racism most fundamentally is practice: the practice of discrimination, at all levels, from personal abuse to colonial oppression." Systems of policing and criminal justice are situated at the core of regulating minority populations, whether Indigenous or as newcomers, throughout White settler colonial nations (Blaut, 1993; Memmi, 1991; TRC, 2015). Such practices, Blaut (1993: 20) stresses, find justification through racist interpretations by Eurocentric historians and writers who considered Indigenous people to be, "naturally inferior to Europeans, naturally less brave, less freedom-loving, less rational and so on, and progress for them depended on European domination."

Modern racialized interpretations of Indigenous people are rooted in the discourse of domination and subjugation of Indigenous nations.

The racialization of Indigenous peoples in Canada and other colonized societies has contributed to extensive experiences of racism and other forms of social exclusion (Wotherspoon & Hansen, 2013: 32). These problems are especially evident in high rates of incarceration and other encounters within criminal justice systems. We observe elsewhere that "imperialism and racialization in the criminal justice system has been an important factor contributing to over-representation of Indigenous people in the justice system: its tools were the police, courts and racialization" (ibid.: 31).

Since the colonization of North America, Eurocentric interpretations have dominated official histories, educational materials and media in Canadian society. Early intellectuals constructed a unique Indigenous identity that was based on racialized constructs and myths, thereby framing the identity of Indigenous people in ways commonly seen and understood by much of the population. Peter Li (2003: 2–3) observes that, "the colonial history of the Aboriginal peoples and their present-day dependence on the state contribute to the social meaning of the term Indians to refer not only to a "racial" group of a remote past, but also a contemporary people that is economically burdensome, socially marginal and political militant."

This racialized version of Indigenous identity has fostered negative images – drunkards, addicts, criminal types, welfare frauds, and a burden to society draining public tax money – depicted in well-known stereotypes in Western society.

Such racialized images remain not only misleading but represent gross distortions that damage Indigenous identity and culture. Nonetheless, these representations often serve as framing devices played out regularly in social settings and institutional venues. In his analysis of the notion of visibility, Bronfenbrenner (1979), highlighting the sociological conception of the "definition of the situation," observes that one's perception of an encounter can have real consequences even if the objective environment is interpreted incorrectly. Particularly in cases where Indigenous people look physically different from the mainstream population or bear particular markers associated with Indigenous identity, their representation as "Indigenous" can shape their encounters with police officers, store clerks, school teachers or others. Although this influence may not always be negative, it is often likely to be so when there is such an extensive repertoire of disparaging cultural stereotypes to influence the interaction.

Police working within racialized communities do not have to justify familiar stereotypes; they are taken for granted. Racist beliefs seemingly constitute the actual criteria to determine the investigative situation. These assumptions are apparent in police investigative analysis, particularly in cases involving Indigenous people. Police working in inner cities, for instance, are assigned to patrol high-crime environments in which "carding" tends to be part of typical policing practices, putting Indigenous people and other racialized minorities at risk for involuntary stops and searches. Linden (2016: 132) observes that such practices can contribute to an escalating sequence of problems beginning with the likelihood that "the police may be influenced by race or ethnicity in the exercise of their discretion and authority. This includes decisions about whether or not to stop search, or arrest a suspect. Contact with the police is typically the first step in the criminal justice process."

While this may not be an astonishing revelation about policing, it points to forms of racialized policing that have invariably harmed many Indigenous people. Sometimes the consequences can be severe. Comack (2012: 13–14), in an analysis of racialized policing in Canada, cites, for instance, the case of Matthew Dumas, a young Indigenous male who was shot and killed by police in Winnipeg, Manitoba, because he fit the description; she emphasizes: "the death of Matthew Dumas had everything to do with race and racism ... Race and racism not only pervade the everyday lives of Aboriginal people, but also inform the wider public discourses and institutional processes ... including the processes of law enforcement."

In a prominent Nova Scotia case, the family of a murdered woman who had blond hair and fair features report that police became less responsive after they learned she was Indigenous (Tutton, 2017). These issues also point to why so many Indigenous people are disgruntled with differential treatment in the justice system. They experience racialization as a serious threat to that needs to be addressed systematically.

Racialized profiling assumes a particular view of Indigenous people: the perception of criminal types. Indigenous people – particularly those who look Indigenous, that is, those who cannot pass for a Western person – often encounter disempowering experiences. This phenomenon is reflected in Brighenti's (2007: 13) assertion that visibility "is a double-edged sword: it can be empowering as well as disempowering." Unfortunately, for many Indigenous people visibility often becomes disempowering, whether in inner-city environments or reserve communities environments where impoverished and racialized people are seen through the eyes of police who seem to be interpreting what they see in accordance with a belief in stereotypes (or criminal types). Comack (2012: 210) argues that the police often view Indigenous males – particularly those wearing a pony tail – as suspect drug dealers or gangsters, while Indigenous women are seen as prostitutes, stressing that, "Aboriginal men are regularly stopped by police, sometimes on a weekly basis, and asked to account for themselves." These stereotypes are lasting and continue to marginalize Indigenous people in their everyday lives. They reinforce perceptions among many Indigenous people that they are stereotyped by law enforcement and disproportionately subjected to unwarranted questioning (Chartrand & Whitecloud, 2001; Linden, 2016).

Some police departments espouse racialized policing in the hopes that it will limit crime. In other cases, especially in areas with high concentrations of minority populations, police officers may dismiss racial profiling as nonsense. Sanchez and Rosenbaum (2011: 169) cite the perspectives of an officer working in a Latino neighbourhood in a large city in the American Midwest: "There is no way you could be racial profiling in a minority neighborhood where there are only Hispanics and Blacks. Community don't really understand what racial profiling means. Mexicans say, 'you stopped me because I am Mexican,' when the neighborhood is Mexican."

As Cunneen (2006: 6) notes, "the main reason Aboriginal people are over-represented in prisons is because they commit many more offences than non-Aboriginal people" (2006: 6). Demographic and risk factors contribute to high levels of victimization among Indigenous people, but they do not fully account for rates of victimization that are more than double those among their non-Indigenous counterparts (Boyce, 2016). At the same time, common factors underlying criminal activity and perceptual differences, compounded by systemic bias in policing and justice systems, can heighten tensions in Indigenous–police relations. Indigenous people in many communities do not trust the police. Because many police forces lack diversity, relatively few minority neighbourhoods are staffed by police forces that reflect the populations that they serve. At the same time, racialized poverty and related factors that contribute to crime can intensify racialized policing, with the result that Indigenous people are over-policed or frequently stopped and asked to explain themselves in their everyday pursuits. These forms of racialized policing, in tandem with parallel processes related to detention, criminal trials and sentencing, represent systemic bias in the justice system resulting in over-incarceration of Indigenous people. According to Siegel, Brown, and Hoffman (2013: 46), "Aboriginal people are more likely than whites to be incarcerated for committing the same crimes, and are much less likely to be granted parole.

It is possible that some judges view many Aboriginal offenders as poor risks, considering them more likely to reoffend than white offenders."

In short, differential treatment, often beginning in communities or on the street, is perpetuated by and contributes to ongoing institutional discrimination reflected in systemic inequities throughout the justice system.

Regulating Indigenous Protest

Contemporary expressions of racialized policing are deeply rooted in earlier colonial structures and practices. The North-West Mounted Police (a forerunner of the national Royal Canadian Mounted Police force), like their Mounted Police counterparts in Australia, were created to maintain public order in emerging state territories, with much of their mandate focused on the containment of potential resistance by Indigenous populations (Nettelbeck et al., 2016: 57–59). Although many overt forms of state control of Indigenous people and cultures have been replaced by contemporary rights-based legal frameworks, regulation continues in various guises.

In the face of repeated violations of their rights and claims and actions that have undermined their well-being, Indigenous organizers and supporters have mobilized periodic protests to draw attention to their concerns. While most actions have been peaceful (typically involving organized marches, flash mobs, and occasionally blockages of roads, railways or contested economic development sites on their territories), they have frequently drawn anger from media and public accounts while exposing additional dimensions of race-based profiling and surveillance. Police and military forces have had a significant presence in many instances through undercover monitoring and surveillance and, at times, in visible shows of force. Although rarely as explosive as in cases like the Oka Crisis (in 1990 a provincial police officer was killed after heavily armed police stormed barricades mounted by Mohawk communities protesting a golf extension into traditional lands that included a burial site) or Ipperwash (where an unarmed First Nations man involved in a 1995 protest over incursion onto unceded territories was shot to death by police), it is not uncommon for official responses to be inordinately more coercive than warranted by actual circumstances (Hedican, 2012).

Unlike forms of racial profiling associated with street stops and other daily encounters, actions associated with protests tend to be driven by specific events or circumstances. Nonetheless, they do represent a broader pattern in which Indigenous individuals or groups are subject to high levels of surveillance and monitoring by virtue of their status as Indigenous (Dafnos, 2013; Wilkes, 2004). Individuals and communications associated with the Idle No More movement, which emerged as a grassroots initiative to draw attention to government policies that prioritized economic development in ways that jeopardized land, water and rights of Indigenous communities in late 2013 (Wotherspoon & Hansen, 2014), were subjected to continuous scrutiny by national security forces even though they posed no threat to public order (National Post, 2014). Since that time, documents reveal that the national police service (Royal Canadian Mounted Police) has continued to monitor Indigenous activists participating in various protest actions in different regions throughout the country (Craig, 2016). An analysis of protocols associated with these kinds of policing practices has suggested that guidelines sometime carry the implication that coercive security action is justified because "*any* incident involving an Indigenous person or relating to treaty or Aboriginal rights is considered 'high-risk'" (Dafnos, 2013: 64).

Such measures perpetuate longstanding colonial practices in which Indigenous rights are offset by strict scrutiny and regulation of Indigenous people by the state and its official agents (Satzewich & Wotherspoon, 2000; Smith, 2009). Legal recognition of Aboriginal rights has contributed to the removal of restrictions or bans on engagement in traditional cultural practices that prevailed into the mid-twentieth century. Nonetheless, as Simpson (2012) observes, even now Indigenous people who participate in ceremonies often encounter intimidation in interactions with both police and settlers. She stresses that, "these interactions have yet to be friendly. Most of the time they are aggressive and racist" (Simpson, 2012). Such interactions, built on ideas and practices of social exclusion that perpetuate colonial domination, are intended to undermine Indigenous culture and humiliate Indigenous people.

Is Indigenous Policing the Solution?

Although Indigenous communities have urged the Canadian government to support the inherent principle of Indigenous self-government on policing and other matters, progress in meeting these objectives has been slow. Indigenous communities across the country are policed through a patchwork of models. Whereas policing and justice systems are predominantly areas of provincial jurisdiction in Canada, the federal government assumed responsibility in the case of Indians and reserve lands, initially through a federal police force created in large part to enforce containment on reserves, residential schools and other state policies (Manitoba, 1991: 592–593). However, beginning in the late 1960s, various types of Indigenous policing programs have emerged throughout Canada typically through agreements involving different levels of government. These programs have been oriented to recruit and maintain more Indigenous people as police officers (Champagne, 2015; Chartrand & Whitecloud, 2001) and respond to distinct community conditions.

Although limited data exist to assess their effectiveness, there is some evidence that Indigenous policing has had some positive impact. Some changes in crime rates have been observed, but a more significant contribution has been reports of greater satisfaction with police–community relations and perceptions that safety and security have increased (Public Safety Canada, 2016: 14–15). In particular, policing models that demonstrate greater responsiveness to community needs and understanding of culturally appropriate relations are most effective (Kiedrowski, 2013: 11–12). Nonetheless, several problems remain. Most Indigenous communities continue to be policed by non-Indigenous officers, and many Indigenous police forces struggle with several issues, including funding constraints and the need for appropriate training and sufficient legal authority and legitimacy (Jones et al., 2014: 64ff.). According to Indigenous sociologist Duane Champagne (2015: 110), the development of culturally appropriate policing models for Canadian First Nations lags well behind tribal policing approaches in the United States. He observes: "Canadian law and policy greatly inhibits First Nations from forming their own police and courts, while the Canadian government does not provide culturally appropriate or effective court and legal services. A vacuum of lawlessness and social distress has been created, making many reserves unhealthy places to live" (2015: 110).

Despite some advances, several barriers have limited the capacity for Indigenous communities to be served by Indigenous policing and Indigenous models of justice.

CONCLUSION

Formal commitment to processes of reconciliation has facilitated greater understanding of the history and status of Indigenous people within the Canadian context. It has also fostered space for healing from severe damages many individuals, families and communities have experienced through residential schooling and other practices associated with colonization. However, many of them continue to have encounters with police and criminal justice systems that reproduce colonial relationships. Although being visible as Indigenous has become a source of pride in many contexts, it also contributes to produce vulnerability through exposure of signs and identities translated into harmful interactions shaped by powerful negative images and stereotypes.

Reconciliation, in this context, requires commitment to change on several levels. It requires an understanding of histories, cultures and relationships that will contribute to the erasure of images and identities shaped by colonial practices. However, it also means that Indigenous people have the capacity to achieve meaningful autonomy and self-government that includes models of justice, policing and other institutional sites grounded in Indigenous knowledge unencumbered by colonial traditions.

References

Angus Reid Institute. (2015, July 9). *Truth and reconciliation: Canadians see value in process, skeptical about government action.* Vancouver, BC: Angus Reid Institute.

Ash-Moccasin, S. (2014, December). I was racially profiled, roughed up, & detained by police for being Indigenous. *Briarpatch.* Retrieved from https://briarpatchmagazine.com/blog/view/i-was-racially-profiled.

Bahdi, R. (2003). No exit: Racial profiling and Canada's war against terrorism. *Osgoode Hall Law Journal, 41(2/3),* 293–317.

Bahdi, R., Parsons, O., & Sandborn, T. (2010). Racial profiling: B. C. Civil Liberties Association position paper. In R. Marcuse (Ed.), *Racial profiling* (pp. 31–53). Vancouver: B. C. Civil Liberties Association.

Blaut, J. M. (1992). The theory of cultural racism. *Antipode: A Radical Journal of Geography, 24(4),* 289–299.

(1993). *The colonizer's model of the world: Geographical diffusionism and Eurocentric history.* New York, NY: Guilford Press.

Boyce, J. (2016, June 28). Victimization of Aboriginal people in Canada, 2014. *Juristat.* Ottawa: Statistics Canada catalogue no. 85-002-X.

Brighenti, A. (2007). Visibility: A category for the social sciences. *Current Sociology, 55(3),* 323–342.

Bronfenbrenner, U. (1979). *The ecology of human development.* Boston, MA: Harvard University Press.

Brossard, L. & Pedneault, É. (2012, June 14). *Racial profiling and systemic discrimination of racialized youth: Report of the consultation on racial profiling and its consequences. One year later: Taking stock.* Québec City: Commission des droits de la personne et des droits de la jeunesse.

Canadian Race Relations Foundation. (2016). Raw Data, State of Relations 2016. Ottawa: Canadian Race Relations Foundation. Retrieved from https://crrf-fcrr.app.box.com/s/kgfnakrh5ttegbxjovwsmlky1xht9dbgp.

Carrier Sekani Family Services. (2017). Highway of tears: Preventing violence against women. Prince George, BC: Carrier Sekani Family Services. Retrieved from www.highwayoftears.ca/about-us/highway-of-tears.

Champagne, D. (2015). *Indigenous nations within modern nation states*. Vernon, BC: J. Charlton Publishing Ltd.

Chartrand, P. L. & Whitecloud, W. (2001). *The justice system and Aboriginal people: The Aboriginal Justice Implementation Commission Report of the Aboriginal Justice Inquiry of Manitoba*: Winnipeg: Aboriginal Justice Implementation Commission.

Comack, E. (2012). *Racialized policing*. Halifax: Fernwood.

Craig, S. (2016, November 13). RCMP tracked 89 indigenous activists considered 'threats' for participating in protests. *National Post*. Retrieved from http://nationalpost.com/news/canada/rcmp-tracked-89-indigenous-activists-considered-threats-for-participating-in-protests.

Cunneen, C. (2006). Racism, discrimination and the over-representation of Indigenous people in the criminal justice system: Some conceptual and explanatory issues. *Current Issues in Criminal Justice*, 17(3), 329–346.

Dafnos, T. (2013). Pacification and Indigenous struggles in Canada. *Socialist Studies*, 9(2), 57–77.

Environics Institute. (2016, June). *Canadian public opinion on Aboriginal peoples: Final report*. Toronto: The Environics Institute for Survey Research.

Ethno-Cultural Council of Calgary. (2011). *Racial profiling: The lived experience of ethno-cultural community members in Calgary*. Calgary: Ethno-Cultural Council of Calgary.

Friesen, J. (2016, October 20). The night Colten Boushie died: What family and police files say about his last day, and what came after. *The Globe and Mail*. Retrieved from www.theglobeandmail.com/news/national/colten-boushie/article32451940/.

Gabor, T. (2004). Inflammatory rhetoric on racial profiling can undermine police services. Canadian Journal of Criminology and Criminal Justice, 46(4), 457–466.

Gill, J. S. (2014). Permissibility of color and racial profiling. *WJ Legal Studies*, 5(3).

Grimard, C. (2017, September 27). FSIN chief says he was racially profiled by RCMP. CKOM radio website. Retrieved from www.ckom.com/2017/09/27/fsin-chief-says-was-racially-profiled-by-rcmp/.

Hansen, J. (2015). Indigenous–settler incarceration disparities in Canada: How tribal justice programming helps urban Indigenous youth. *Indigenous Policy Journal*, 25(3), 1–16. Retrieved from www.indigenouspolicy.org/index.php/ipj/article/view/290/281.

Harris, D. (1997). Driving while black and all other traffic offences: The Supreme Court and pretextual traffic stops. *Journal of Criminal Law and Criminology*, 87(2), 544–582.

Hedican, E. (2012). Policing Aboriginal protests and confrontations: Some policy recommendations. *The International Indigenous Policy Journal*, 3(2), 1–17.

Hier, S. P. & Walby, K. (2006). Competing analytical paradigms in the sociological study of racism in Canada. *Canadian Ethnic Studies*, 38(1), 83–104.

Huncar, A. (2017, June 27). Indigenous women nearly 10 times more likely to be street checked by Edmonton police, new data shows. CBC News website. Retrieved from www.cbc.ca/news/canada/edmonton/street-checks-edmonton-police-aboriginal-black-carding-1.4178843.

Indigenous and Northern Affairs Canada. (2016, Dec. 12). Terms of reference: National Inquiry into Missing and Murdered Indigenous Women and Girls. Ottawa: Government of Canada. Retrieved from www.mmiwg-ffada.ca/files/terms-of-reference.pdf.

Jones, N. A., Ruddell, R., Nestor, R., Quinn, K., & Phillips, B. 2014. *First Nations policing: A review of the literature*. Regina, SK: Collaborative Centre for Justice and Safety.

Kiedrowski, J. (2013). *Trends in Indigenous policing models: An international comparison*. Ottawa: Public Safety Canada.

Li, P. S. (2003, March 27–28). Social inclusion of visible minorities and newcomers: The articulation of "race" and "racial" difference in Canadian society. Paper presented at the Canadian Council on Social Development Conference on Social Inclusion.

Linden, R. (2016). *Criminology: A Canadian Perspective* (8th edition). Toronto: Nelson.

Macdonald, N. (2016, February 18.). Canada's prisons are the "new residential schools." *Maclean's*. Retrieved from www.macleans.ca/news/canada/canadas-prisons-are-the-new-residential-schools/.

Manitoba. Public Inquiry into the Administration of Justice and Aboriginal People. (1991). *Report of the Aboriginal Justice Inquiry of Manitoba*. Winnipeg: Queen's Printer.

McLean, C. (2015). *When police become prey*. North Vancouver, BC: Influence Publishing.

Meehan, A. & Ponder, M. (2002). Race and place: The ecology of racial profiling African American motorists. *Justice Quarterly*, 19(3), 399–429.

Melchers, R. (2003). Do Toronto police engage in racial profiling? *Canadian journal of Criminology and Criminal Justice*, 45(3), 347–366.

Memmi, A. (1991). *The colonizer and the colonized*. Boston, MA: Beacon Press.

Millar, E. (2016, February 18). Survey indicates Indigenous people targeted by police in Prairie provinces. *Discourse media*. Retrieved from http://discoursemedia.org/toward-reconciliation/survey-indicates-indigenous-people-targeted-police-prairie-provinces.

Narine, S. (2012). "Aboriginal organization set to collect anecdotal information on racial profiling," Saskatchewan Sage, 16 (8). Retrieved from www.ammsa.com/publications/saskatchewan-sage/aboriginal-organization-set-collect-anecdotal-information-racial-prof.

National Post. (2014, June 1). Canadian forces spent virtually all of 2013 watching Idle No More protestors. *National Post*. Retrieved from http://nationalpost.com/news/canada/canadian-forces-spent-virtually-all-of-2013-watching-idle-no-more-protesters.

Nettelbeck, A., Smandych, R., Knafla, L. A., & Foster, R. (2016). *Fragile settlements: Aboriginal peoples, law, and resistance in South-West Australia and Prairie Canada.* Vancouver, BC: UBC Press.

Nishnawbe Aski Nation. (2017, May 31). *First Nation leaders address Thunder Bay policing crisis around river deaths.* Toronto: Nishnawbe Aski Nation news release. Retrieved from www.nan.on.ca/upload/documents/nr-thunder-bay-policing-crisis-may-31-20.pdf.

Ontario Human Rights Commission. (2003). *The impact of racial profiling on the Aboriginal community.* Toronto: Ontario Human Rights Commission.

(2017, April). *Under suspicion: Research and consultation report on racial profiling in Ontario.* Toronto: Ontario Human Rights Commission. Retrieved from http://ohrc.on.ca/sites/default/files/Under%20suspicion_research%20and%20consultation%20report%20on%20racial%20profiling%20in%20Ontario_2017.pdf.

Owusu-Bempah, A. & Millar, P. (2010). Research note: Revisiting the collection of justice statistics by race in Canada. *Canadian Journal of Law and Society*, 25(1), 97–104.

Public Safety Canada. (2016, March 17). *2014–2015 Evaluation of the First Nations Policing Program. Final report.* Ottawa: Public Safety Canada.

Reber, S. & Renaud, R. (2005). *Starlight tour: The last, lonely night of Neil Stonechild.* Toronto: Random House.

Sanchez, C. G. V. & Rosenbaum, D. P. (2011). Racialized policing: Officers' voices on policing Latino and African American neighborhoods. *Journal of Ethnicity in Criminal Justice*, 9, 152–178.

Saskatchewan Public Complaints Commission. 2016. *Annual Report for 2016–16.* Regina: Public Complaints Commission, Ministry of Justice, Saskatchewan.

Satzewich, V. (Ed.). (1998). *Racism & social inequality in Canada.* Toronto: Thompson.

Satzewich, V. & Wotherspoon, T. (2000). *First Nations: Race, class, and gender relations.* Regina: Canadian Plains Research Centre.

Siegel, L. J., Brown, G. P., & Hoffman, R. (2013). *CRIM*, second Canadian edition. Toronto: Nelson Education.

Simpson, Leanne. (2012). Aambe! Maajaadaa! (What #IdleNoMore means to me). *Decolonization: Indigeneity, education & society.* Retrieved from http://decolonization.wordpress.com/2012/12/21/aambe-maajaadaa-what-idlenomore-means-to-me/.

Smith, K. (2009). *Liberalism, surveillance, and resistance: Indigenous communities in Western Canada, 1877–1927.* Edmonton: AU Press.

Statistics Canada. (2017, October 25). Aboriginal peoples in Canada: Key results from the 2016 census, *The Daily.* Ottawa: Statistics Canada catalogue no. 11–001-X.

Tator, C. & Henry, F. (2006). *Racial profiling in Canada: Challenging the myth of 'a few bad apples.'* Toronto: University of Toronto Press.

Trudeau, Justin. (2015, December 15). Statement by Prime Minister on release of the Final Report of the Truth and Reconciliation Commission. Ottawa: Government of Canada press release. Retrieved from https://pm.gc.ca/eng/

news/2015/12/15/statement-prime-minister-release-final-report-truth-and-rec onciliation-commission.

Truth and Reconciliation Commission of Canada. (2015). *Honouring the truth, reconciling for the future: Summary of the final report of the Truth and Reconciliation Commission of Canada.* Retrieved from www.trc.ca/web sites/trcinstitution/File/2015/Honouring_the_Truth_Reconciling_for_the_ Future_July_23_2015.pdf.

Tutton, Michael. (2017, October 30). Family says at MMIW hearings that a 'white-passing' appearance alters police reaction. CTV News. Retrieved from www.ctvnews.ca/canada/family-says-at-mmiw-hearings-that-a-white-passing-appearance-alters-police-reaction-1.3655730.

Wilkes, R. (2004). First Nation politics: Deprivation, resources, and participation in collective action. *Sociological Inquiry,* 74(4), 570–589.

Williams, C. (Ed.). (2006). *A companion to nineteenth-century Britain.* New York, NY: John Wiley and Sons.

Wortley, S. & Tanner, J. (2003). Data, denials, and confusion: The racial profiling debate in Toronto. *Canadian Journal of Criminology and Criminal Justice,* 45(3), 367–389.

(2005). Inflammatory rhetoric? Baseless accusations? Responding to Gabor's critique of racial profiling research in Canada. *Canadian Journal of Criminology,* 47(3), 581–609.

Wotherspoon, T. (2014). Seeking reform of Indigenous education in Canada: Democratic progress or democratic colonialism? *AlterNative,* 10(4), 323–339.

Wotherspoon, T. & Hansen, J. (2013). The "Idle No More" movement: paradoxes of First Nations inclusion in the Canadian context. *Social Inclusion,* 1(1), 21–36.

4

Black Lives Matter

The Watchdog for the Criminal Justice System

Lorenzo M. Boyd and Kimberly Conway Dumpson

*This chapter is dedicated to activist **Erica Garner** (May 29, 1990–December 30, 2017), daughter of the late Eric Garner*

Few things have polarized American culture more than the negative relationship between the police and communities of color. Many would argue that the term "justice" has been codified along racial lines, which in turn has caused disparate treatment within the criminal justice system. Additionally, several high-profile deaths of African-American citizens (many at the hands of White police officers) and the subsequent acquittals of, or lack of charges against, alleged perpetrators, have fueled a perceived lack of justice for people of color within the system. To many, when African-American citizens are killed by the police, the justice system affords the perpetrators more leniency than is afforded to those who are killed. This perceived lack of accountability gives the impression that the value of a Black life is *less than* that of a White life. Out of this level of frustration was born the social movement Black Lives Matter (BLM).

On the evening of February 26, 2012, 17-year-old high school student Trayvon Martin was walking alone back to the home of his father's fiancée's in the Twin Lakes neighborhood of Sanford, Florida after purchasing a bag of Skittles® and an Arizona® iced tea at a nearby convenience store. The Sanford neighborhood, which had suffered several robberies, enacted a neighborhood crime watch earlier that year. George Zimmerman, a member of the community watch, saw Martin and reported him to the Sanford Police Department (SPD) as looking suspicious. Because Martin had committed no crime, the SPD told Zimmerman to disengage and leave Martin alone. Nonetheless, Zimmerman, armed with a semiautomatic handgun, followed Martin, who was unarmed. Moments later, the two had a physical altercation and Zimmerman fatally shot Martin in the chest. Because of the confrontation, Zimmerman claimed self-defense. On July 13, 2013, a jury acquitted Zimmerman of second degree murder and manslaughter, sending shockwaves across the nation.

In the aftermath of the verdict, the BLM movement took social media by storm with the hashtag #BlackLivesMatter, highlighting "rampant and deliberate" "state-sanctioned violence" and "anti-Black racism." Guided by 13 principles, which include diversity, restorative justice, globalism and loving engagement, to name a few, the Black Lives Matter movement is a decentralized network comprised and led by a cadre of everyday freedom fighters, as diverse as the tapestry of America itself with membership that spans the intersections of race, gender, nationality, and identity. In contrast to other movements that were led by a strong, central, male figure, the Black Lives Matter movement, at its core, actively includes in its membership, and leadership, people who have previously been marginalized. Founded by three queer, African-American women – Alicia Garza, Opal Tometi, and Patrisse Khan-Cullors – the BLM movement offers a space where women, queer, and transgender citizens are actively engaged at the forefront of the movement (Smith, 2015).

Alicia Garza, Special Project Director for the National Domestic Workers Alliance, is a 32-year-old, African-American woman, writer and activist from Oakland, CA, who organized communities around themes of students' rights, health care, anti-racism, rights for domestic workers, and ending police brutality.

Opal Tometi, is a 29-year-old, New York-based, Nigerian-American writer, strategist, and community organizer from Phoenix, AZ. She is the Executive Director of the Black Alliance for Just Immigration. She regularly organizes community members in New York, Los Angeles, Oakland, Washington DC, and Phoenix. Ms Tometi is credited with creating the online platforms and initiating the social media strategy during the project's early days.

Patrisse Khan-Cullors, a 30-year-old artist and activist from Los Angeles, spends her time advocating for criminal justice reform. She is the director of Dignity and Power Now, an organization focused on helping incarcerated people and their families.

Garza, Tometi, and Cullors met while working with the national organization Black Organizing for Leadership & Dignity, which trains community leaders and organizers. In the aftermath of the Zimmerman verdict, these women started to question how they were going to respond to what they saw as the systemic devaluation of Black lives. Garza wrote a Facebook® post titled "A Love Note to Black People" in which she said: *Our Lives Matter, Black Lives Matter*. Cullors immediately added the hashtag: "#BlackLivesMatter." At that point, Tometi signed on to support the effort, and the social movement *Black Lives Matter* was born. Cullors stated that Black women have always led Black movements. Ella Baker, Diane Nash, and Fannie Lou Hamer are Black women leaders who were critical in developing movements, and their names aren't heard often. "We're leading the movement; we're the architects of the movement" (Dalton, 2015).

The Black Lives Matter movement builds upon the historical social, cultural, and legal experiences of Black people in the United States. Similar to David Walker's *Appeal to the Coloured Citizens of the World*, published in 1832 in Boston, MA, the BLM movement offers a call to action and challenges their "afflicted and slumbering brethren" to seek an end to "systemic racism and injustice as demonstrated through state-sanctioned violence" and anti-Black sentiment. In his *Appeal*, Walker, born free in North Carolina, sought to refute negative sentiments about Black character and used the *Appeal* as a clarion call to highlight the virtue and value of African-Americans. Like Walker's *Appeal*, the Black Lives Matter movement is working to highlight the value and validity of Black lives, and revitalizing the Black liberation movement.

In many ways, the BLM movement is akin to the "new" civil rights movement. Like other movements, the BLM message is one that it is rooted in equality and justice for all people, regardless of race, gender, sexual orientation, or economic status. The BLM movement also relies heavily on grassroots networks of ordinary citizens, who serve as foot soldiers to spread the movement's message in their local communities.

Though similar to prior social justice movements, this group-centered model of leadership is very different from the older charismatic leadership model of one central figure that characterized civil rights organizations of the past. For BLM, there is no central male leadership figure who purports to speak for the movement; rather, the movement, and its followers/ believers take up the call to action embodied in the movement and adjust their strategies in their local communities. In contrast to the Civil Rights Movement, the BLM movement is not rooted in "the church," and not reliant on massive support from large congregations of believers. Most significantly, however, BLM's primary method of engagement, motivation, and inspiration has been through social media, and its vast network of interconnected persons, connected through common ideologies across the globe who can act, nearly spontaneously, to acts of injustice wherever they may occur.

The Black Lives Matter movement focuses particularly on the disparate treatment of people of color in the criminal justice system and at the hands of the police. In 2014, just one year after its inception, the movement was jettisoned into the national spotlight as a result of its well-organized and well-attended street demonstrations following the deaths of two unarmed, African-American males at the hands of local police, for what many believe were minor infractions.

In Staten Island, New York on July 17, 2014, the police were called to a fight in the area, which was reportedly broken up by Eric Garner. When the police arrived, they saw what they believed was Garner selling individual cigarettes, in violation of NYC tax code. Prior to his arrest, Eric Garner was heard saying:

Get away [garbled] for what? Every time you see me, you want to mess with me. I'm tired of it. It stops today. Why would you. . .? Everyone standing here will tell you I didn't do nothing. I didn't sell nothing. Because every time you see me, you want to harass me. You want to stop me [garbled] selling cigarettes. I'm minding my business, officer, I'm minding my business. Please just leave me alone. I told you the last time, please leave me alone.

(Capelouto, 2014)

During the arrest, Officer Daniel Pantaleo put his arm around Garner's neck and took him down to the ground in what is described as an LAPD Style choke hold, which was in violation of NYPD policy. It is reported that Garner was heard saying; "I can't breathe" eleven times while lying face-down on the sidewalk. Eric Garner subsequently died at the hands of the police. On December 3, 2014, the Richmond County (NY) grand jury declined to indict Pantaleo for Garner's death. The BLM movement participated in later protests surrounding lack of indictments for the Eric Garner death. On July 13, 2015, an out-of-court settlement was reached in which the City of New York agreed to pay the Garner family $5.9M.

Less than a month after Garner's death, another incident fueling the Black Lives Matter movement occurred, this time in Ferguson, Missouri. On August 9, 2014, an unarmed, 18-year-old African-American, Michael Brown, was confronted by a 28-year-old White Ferguson police officer, Darren Wilson, while Brown was walking down the middle of a city street. A confrontation ensued between the two of them, and Brown allegedly reached inside Officer Wilson's vehicle and assaulted him.

Wilson then exited his vehicle and reportedly fired 12 shots at the unarmed teen, killing him. Reports say Brown's body was left on the sidewalk for roughly four hours in the unrelenting August sun before it was removed. Many residents of Ferguson, and nearby St Louis, protested in the streets. Cullors was one of the organizers who planned a national, Black Lives Matter Ride, to Ferguson during Labor Day weekend a few weeks later. Over 600 people gathered and people asserted that what happened in Ferguson was not an aberration, but in fact, a clear point of reference for what was happening in Black communities everywhere.

Since the Ferguson protests, participants in the movement have demonstrated against the deaths of numerous other African-Americans by police actions or while in police custody. The BLM movement claims inspiration from the Civil Rights movement, the Black Power movement, and other, more recent grassroots and social movements. The movement counts among its successes the ouster of Anti-Black elected officials, creation of legislation to protect citizens against state-sanctioned violence, and elevation of the national debate around these issues.

According to the group's website, "Black Lives Matter is an ideological and political intervention in a world where Black lives are systematically and intentionally targeted for demise. It is an affirmation of Black folks' humanity, our contributions to this society, and our resilience in the face of deadly oppression" (BlackLivesMatter.com. [n.d.]).

The organizers continue by stating that the space that #BlackLivesMatter occupies helped drive the conversation around unfettered state-sanctioned violence. They highlight the systematic, continuous, and egregious ways in which Black people are violated and the fact that the perpetrators are rarely brought to justice. #BlackLivesMatter was developed in support of all Black lives.

As the Black Lives Matter movement developed throughout 2013 and 2014, it was used by others as a platform and as an organizing tool. Other groups, organizations, and individuals used the Black Lives Matter Movement to expose anti-Black racism across the country, in all the ways it presented. Energized by the numbers of protesters in Ferguson, organizers from almost twenty different cities went back home and developed Black Lives Matter chapters in their local communities. This broadened the political exposure of the grassroots causes, and the movement continued to grow.

It was apparent that the organizers needed to continue establishing grassroots movements across the United States. It seemed obvious that people were hungry to galvanize their communities in order to end state-sanctioned violence against Black people. Shortly thereafter, the Black Lives Matter Global Network infrastructure was created. This global network is adaptive and decentralized, with a set of guiding principles. The goal is to support the development of new Black leaders, as well as create a network where Black people feel empowered to determine their own destinies in their communities.

Black Lives Matter has now become an international activist movement, with chapters in Asia, Australia, Canada, and Great Britain, among others. However, in many respects, the uproar around police shootings in the United States is uniquely an American issue. Few major Western nations suffer the epidemic of self-perpetuated gun violence that exists in the United States. Nor must they contend with the entrenched history of systemic racism that perpetuates life in the United States.

In the years since the advent of the BLM movement, news broadcasts are replete with stories of unarmed Black men who have been killed by police officers, many of them White officers. And similar to the aftermath of the tragic deaths of Michael Brown and Eric Garner, many of these incidents have resulted in no grand jury indictments, and no convictions for the officers involved:

Tamir Rice, 12 years old, killed by Cleveland police on November 22, 2014 while playing with a toy gun. A citizen called the police to report a Black male holding something that looked like a gun in a neighborhood park. The caller reported that the suspect was "probably a juvenile."

Walter Scott, a 50-year-old was shot in the back and killed by a North Charleston police officer on April 4, 2015 after a traffic stop for a broken brake light. Scott fled the officer because he had a warrant for child non-support. The officer claimed there was a struggle and hit Scott twice with a Tazer. Scott again fled and the officer shot him eight times in the back. The officer claimed self-defense until a bystander's video showed the truth. Nineteen months later, the officer pled guilty and was sentenced to 20 years in prison.

Freddie Gray, 25 years old, died as a result of injuries sustained while in custody in the back of a Baltimore Police Department transport van on April 12, 2015.

Alton Sterling, 37 years old, was shot and killed by White police officers while being held on the ground outside a convenience store in Baton Rouge, Louisiana, on July 5, 2016.

Philando Castile, 32 years old, was fatally shot while legally carrying a holstered, licensed firearm during a traffic stop in St Anthony, Minnesota, a suburb of St Paul, the day after the Sterling incident in Baton Rouge on July 6, 2016.

Terence Crutcher, a 40-year-old, was killed by a White police officer in Tulsa, Oklahoma on September 16, 2016. The police received a 911 call about an abandoned vehicle. Crutcher was unarmed during the encounter, and shot while standing with his hands raised near his broken-down vehicle in the middle of a street.

In all of these cases, to date only one officer has been convicted and sentenced, and only after a guilty plea. Most of the officers involved were not convicted for the death of these citizens, and many officers were never charged nor indicted. All of these deaths have galvanized the Black Lives Matter movement across the country.

As a result of these (and many other less publicized) killings, there has been a national uproar concerning the relationship between the police and the Black community, creating a state of civil unrest, and making police the focal point of protests. In response to a particular incident, citizens engaged in protests or demonstrations to express their frustrations toward the police. Unfortunately, these situations have the potential to become aggressive, and they can create an atmosphere for rioting and violence as was the case in the summer of 2016 following the deaths of Sterling and Castile.

After a peaceful Black Lives Matter march against the police killings of Alton Sterling, and Philando Castile in Dallas, Texas in July 2016, Micah Xavier Johnson allegedly shot at a group of 11 police officers, killing five of them and injuring nine other officers and two civilians. This shooting happened while many of these Dallas officers were protecting the peaceful protesters from the shooter. During this same time period, hundreds of people in cities across the country were arrested for protesting the deaths of Sterling and Castile.

Critics of the Black Lives Matter movement believe that the movement's tactics are confrontational, divisive, and lacking a coherent strategy and outcomes. Still other critics believe that the Black Lives Matter movement is responsible for inciting violence, particularly violence aimed at law enforcement. In response to the movement's tacit premise that Black Lives Matter, the outcry from critics was a retort of "Blue Lives Matter" and "All Lives Matter." This has had a polarizing effect and detracted from the issue at hand, being the deaths of unarmed people of color.

In 2017, the case of *Officer John Doe Smith* v. *Deray McKesson, et al.* was filed anonymously by Baton Rouge police officers against the Black Lives Matter movement, claiming the group's civil unrest gave way to actions that physically caused officers harm (Canfield, 2017). According to a *Washington Post* article, the lawsuit claimed that the Black Lives Matter movement and the rhetoric of its leaders inspired a decorated former US Marine sergeant to ambush Baton Rouge police officers on July 17, 2016. The result of that shooting left three officers dead and three others injured, including the plaintiff, who was only identified as John Doe Smith (Hawkins, 2017).

In September 2017, in Baton Rouge, Louisiana, US District Court Judge Brian Jackson threw out the lawsuit and ruled that "Black Lives Matter" is a social movement and therefore cannot be sued. He went on to say that "in a similar way that a person cannot plausibly sue other social movements such as the Civil Rights movement, the LGBT rights movement, or the Tea Party movement," Black Lives Matter cannot be sued. The judge reiterated that #BlackLivesMatter is not an entity capable of being sued (Canfield, 2017).

One month earlier, in August 2017, the Federal Bureau of Investigations (FBI) issued a report stating that it is the Bureau's assessment that "it is very likely Black Identity Extremist (BIE) perceptions of police brutality against African Americans spurred an increase in premeditated, retaliatory lethal violence against law enforcement and will very likely serve as justification for such violence," according to an FBI Intelligence Assessment (FBI, 2017). In its report, the FBI asserts that "premeditated acts of violence" may be inspired by, and/or motivated by "black separatist rhetoric" and also by "a mix of anti-authoritarian, Moorish sovereign citizen ideology, and BIE ideology" (FBI, 2017).

While some may assert that there is a proverbial "war on cops," potentially caused by the Black Lives Matter Movement, the numbers do not bear witness to those claims. According to the National Law Enforcement Memorial Fund (NLEOMF), there are over 900,000 sworn officers in the United States. As of Christmas week in 2017, 128 officers had died in the line of duty, with 44 of the officers shot and killed (44 percent). That is down 10 percent from 2016, when 143 officers died, with 66 gunned down (Hayes, 2017; see also *USA Today*, 2017).

More than half of officer deaths were caused by circumstances other than being feloniously shot by assailants. Those incidents included suicide, aircraft crashes, drowning, electrocution, falls, fire-related incidents, job-related illness, and poisoning (NLEOMF, 2017). Moreover, the number of police officers killed in the line of duty dropped sharply in 2017, making it the second-lowest toll in more than 50 years. While shootings of officers played a major role in these numbers, it was traffic accidents that caused the largest number of officer deaths (Forbes, 2016).

According to the National Law Enforcement Memorial Fund, Line of Duty Deaths in 2016 were down 6 percent over 2015. In fact, According to *Forbes* magazine, the number of police fatalities has decreased significantly since the early 1970s (McCarthy, 2016). So the idea of a war on cops since the founding of the Black Lives Matter movement has not yielded increases in police fatalities. Indeed, although policing remains a dangerous job, 2016 was a safer year than the previous several years.

According to the Mapping Police Violence Project, and a report from "Campaign Zero," police officers in the United States killed at least 104 unarmed Black people in 2015, nearly two people each week. The report further states that 1 in 3 Black people killed by police in 2015 were identified as "unarmed," though the actual number is likely higher due to underreporting. Thirty six percent of unarmed people killed by police were Black in 2015 despite Black people being only 13 percent of the U.S. population. Moreover unarmed Black people were killed at five times the rate of unarmed Whites in 2015 (mappingpoliceviolence.org [n.d.]). These statistics are a major reason that the Black Lives Matter movement continues to shine a light on injustices perpetrated against people of color.

There tends to be very few indictments or convictions of officers when unarmed people of color are killed by the police or while in police custody. And when an indictment is handed down, seldom are the officers convicted, even when the victim is unarmed and the events have been recorded. Often officers claim that they used deadly force against an unarmed suspect because they feared for their lives

We are hearing the "fear for their lives" claim more and more as a justification of the killing of unarmed people of color, but that is not a new phenomenon. Policing pioneer Jerome Skolnick penned the term "symbolic assailant" to describe what the police often label many of the people of color who are stopped, searched, and often killed by the police. In the mid-1960s, Skolnick constructed the term *symbolic assailant* to identify certain people whose behavior, appearance, or characteristics was thought to be threatening to the police. Skolnick went on to say that the police develop a technique for identifying *undesirables* or *potential law violators*. These techniques are based mainly on physical appearance and have less to do with actual criminal behavior. These characteristics, such as a person's clothing, their hairstyle, mannerisms, etc. amount to a vague indication of danger suggested by *appearance* (Skolnick & Fyfe, 1993). The Black Lives Matter movement rails against this sort of systemic and biased policing.

Many officers rationalize their escalation of force by stating that the suspects tried to flee from the encounter. Officers have stated if the suspect would have complied, or did not flee, then the suspect would still be alive. The American Civil Liberties Union (ACLU) documented over 204,000 Boston Police Department reports of police–civilian encounters (or field interrogations) from 2007 to 2010; it was found that Blacks were subjected to 63 percent of the stops and searches, even though they made up only 24 percent of Boston's population.

This cannot be explained by levels of crime, nor calls for service. When controlling for such variables as level of crime, alleged gang affiliation, and other non-race factors, the number of field interrogations was driven by a neighborhood's concentration of Black residents. In short, that means that as the percentage of Black population increased, so did the number of police encounters. Young Black men were more likely than young White men to be repeatedly targeted for police–civilian encounters such as stops, frisks, searches, observations, and interrogations.

These stops of citizens were not based on reported crimes or suspected guilt; instead, in three-quarters of these reports for the period 2007–2010, the officer's stated reason for initiating the encounter was simply to "investigate the person." This reason cannot provide a constitutionally permissible reason for stopping or frisking someone. This rationale only describes what the officer *decided* to do (ACLU, 2015). In September 2016, the Massachusetts Supreme Judicial Court ruled on the indignities associated with Black males repeatedly being stopped, searched, and harassed by the police for no articulable reason. In the 2016 case *Commonwealth* v. *Jimmy Warren*, the Court ruled that state law gives individuals the right to not speak to police and even walk away if they are not charged with anything. The Court further stated when an individual does flee, the action does not necessarily mean the person is guilty. And when it comes to Black men, the Boston Police Department and ACLU documents a pattern of racially profiling Black males in the city of Boston. The Massachusetts Supreme Judicial Court ruled:

We do not eliminate flight as a factor in the reasonable suspicion analysis whenever a black male is the subject of an investigatory stop. However, in such circumstances, flight is not necessarily probative of a suspect's state of mind or consciousness of guilt. Rather, the finding that black males in Boston are *disproportionately and repeatedly targeted* for FIO [Field Interrogation and Observation] encounters

IMAGE 3. Reverend Dr Martin Luther King in jail (Getty Images)

suggests *a reason for flight totally unrelated to consciousness of guilt.* Such an individual, when approached by the police, might just as easily be motivated by the desire to avoid the recurring indignity of being racially profiled as by the desire to hide criminal activity. Given this reality for black males in the city of Boston, a judge should, in appropriate cases, consider the report's findings in weighing flight as a factor in the reasonable suspicion calculus.

Commonwealth v. *Jimmy Warren.* MA SJC (9/20/16, emphasis added; Enwemeka, 2016)

Improved relationships between police and the communities of color they serve could improve these disturbing trends. Building on the strengths and successes of President Obama's Task Force on 21st Century Policing, it would be wise and prudent to adhere to the recommendation of the report. A 2017 report from the Community Oriented Police Services (COPS) office in the Department of Justice provides insight from policing, members of civil rights groups, media and advertising executives, researchers, and university students who worked together to discuss challenges and suggested improvements to current practices in the police (Copple, 2017).

In order to successfully bridge the gap between the police and communities of color, step one is building trust and legitimacy, which is the mainstay in the Task Force's report. The Task Force found that "people are more likely to obey the law when they believe that those who are enforcing it have the legitimate authority to tell them what to do... The public confers legitimacy only on those they believe are acting in procedurally just ways" (COPS Office, Task Force Report, 2015).

If there were more legitimacy and accountability, and less bias in policing, perhaps there would be fewer violent encounters between the police and communities of color. If we could achieve this, then fewer Black people, unarmed or otherwise, would die at the hands of the police. If we could make this thing happen, then there would not be a global outcry asserting the fact that Black Lives Matter.

References

American Civil Liberties Union. (2015). Black, brown, and targeted: A report on Boston Police Department street encounters from 2007–2010. Retrieved from https://aclum.org/wp-content/uploads/2015/06/reports-black-brown-and-targeted.pdf.

BlackLivesMatter. (n.d.). Retrieved from https://blacklivesmatter.com/about/herstory.

Canfield, S. (2017, October 30). Judge tosses injured cop's claims against Black Lives Matter. Retrieved from www.courthousenews.com/wp-content/uploads/2017/10/MeKessonBLM.pdf.

Capelouto, S. (2014, December 8). Eric Garner: The haunting last words of a dying man. Retrieved from www.cnn.com/2014/12/04/us/garner-last-words/index.html.

Commonwealth v. *Jimmy Warren*. (2016). 475. Mass. 530.

Copple, J. E. (2017). *Law enforcement recruitment in the 21st century: Forum proceedings*. Washington, DC: Office of Community Oriented Policing Services.

Dalton, D. (2015, May 4). The three women behind the Black Lives Matter movement. Retrieved from http://madamenoire.com/528287/the-three-women-behind-the-black-lives-matter-movement/.

Enwemeka, Z. (2016, September 20). Mass. high court says Black men may have legitimate reason to flee police. WBUR News. Retrieved from www.wbur.org/news/2016/09/20/mass-high-court-black-men-may-have-legitimate-reason-to-flee-police.

Federal Bureau of Investigations (2017, August 3). Black identity extremist likely motivated to target law enforcement officers. Retrieved from https://info.publicintelligence.net/FBI-BlackIdentityExtremists.pdf.

Forbes. (2016). 124 police officers killed in the U.S. last year. Retrieved from www.statistica.com.

Hawkins, D. (2017, September, 29). Black Lives Matter cannot be sued by Louisiana police officer, federal judge rules. Retrieved from www.washigntonpost.com/news/morning-mix/wp/2017/07/10/permanently-disabled-baton-rouge-officer-sues-black-lives-matter-for-2016-ambush-shooting/.

Hayes, C. (2017, December 28). Number of officers killed hits 2nd-lowest in more than 50 years. *USA Today*. Retrieved from www.usatoday.com/story/news/2017/12/28/number-officers-killed-2017-hits-nearly-50-year-low/984477001/.

Mapping Police Violence.org. (n.d.). Retrieved from https://mappingpolcievio lence.org/unarmed/.

McCarthy, N. (2016, July 8). U.S. police deaths in the line of duty over the years [Infographic]. Retrieved from www.Forbes.com/sites/niallmccarthy/2016/07/08/124-u-s-police-officers-died-in-the-line-of-duty-last-year-infographic/$436432d51bf5.

National Law Enforcement and Memorial Fund. (2017). Law enforcement officer fatality report. Retrieved from www.nleomf.org/assets/pdfs/reports/fatality-reports/2017/2017-End-of-Year-Officer-Fatalities-Report_FINAL.pdf.

Skolnick, J. & Fyfe, J. (1993). *Above the law: Police and the use of excessive force*. New York, NY: Simon and Schuster.

Smith, M. D. (2015, June 2). #BlackLivesMatter. A conversation about building an inclusive movement, the importance of identity, and how to shift the narrative of justice away from jailing killer cops. *The Nation*. Retrieved from www.thenation.com/article/qa-opal-tometi-co-founder-blacklivesmatter/.

Task Force Report. (2015). Community Oriented Police Services, U.S. Department of Justice. Retrieved from https://cops.usdoj.gov.

USA Today. (2017). Retrieved from www.usatoday.com/story/news/2017/12/28/number-officers-killed-2017-hits-nearly-50-year-low/984477001/.

Walker, D. (1832). *Appeal to the coloured citizens of the world*. University Park, PA: Pennsylvania State University Press.

5

An Absence of Appearance Identifiers

The Misguided Moral Crusades in Anti-Human Trafficking

Billy James Ulibarrí

In early 2017, an Alaskan Airlines flight attendant noticed that one of her passengers was a disheveled-looking teenage girl with greasy blonde hair who was traveling with an older, well-dressed man. The flight attendant was noted as saying, "She looked like she had been through pure hell," estimating the girl's age at 14 or 15 years old (Dillon, 2017). She notified her pilot who immediately contacted on-ground authorities. When the plane landed in San Francisco, it was met by police. Later the same year, two female Delta airline passengers, both of Asian descent, were detained for questioning because someone suspected that they were both human trafficking victims. One of the passengers, Stephanie Ung, said that she and her friend likely looked to other passengers like "two little girls on the plane" (Ortiz, 2017).

These stories suggest two social facts: One is that the general public is on the lookout for human trafficking victims, and the second is that they know what to look for. However, how do any of us know what human trafficking victims look like? How would we be able to recognize a human trafficking victim? What would we look for? I suggest that although we may have never actually encountered a human trafficking victim, we may have a general idea of what to look for. The physical appearance of human trafficking victims, real or perceived, is the focus of this chapter.

I will describe the changes over time in definitions of human trafficking victims, the false depiction in gender ratios of human trafficking victims, the wrongheadedness of assuming ubiquity in victims and perpetrators, and, in a general statement, the almost total absence of discriminating features of victims and traffickers. As to changes in trafficked victims, among the United States' first encounter in modern times of discussing

IMAGE 4. Missing Children advertisements on milk cartons (Getty Images)

trafficked women, we find that women from formerly Communist societies were markedly prominent among those trafficked to the United States; indeed, this version of trafficking was termed the "Natasha Trade" as these women came from Russia and parts of Eastern Europe (Moldova, Slovenia, and the Czech Republic). In addition to these women seeking a better life, we find that women from Mexico and Thailand were commonly brought to the United States under false pretenses and kept in horrifying conditions as domestic servants, sex workers, and laborers in the beauty industry, with some three-fourths of these women engaged in nonsexual labor. These women were young, which added to their vulnerability and desirability. However, while the bulk of trafficked victims before 2012 were foreign-born, the concern, if not the reality, after 2012 was that "anybody" could be a trafficking victim. That is, the construction of this social problem of human trafficking was broadened to include any racial, ethnic, and nationalistic category of any age, but with an especial focus on children. After 2012, we find a panic associated with the abduction of children from playgrounds, shopping malls, or anywhere children might commonly be found. And we find that "have you seen me" advertisements for missing children are common (see Image 4).

By contrast, men who came to the United States illegally constitute about three-fourths of all trafficked victims and yet receive little public attention. Part of the reason, as will become clear, is that men are assumed to arrive in the United States voluntarily. They arrive willingly from Mexico, Central America, India, and Bangladesh, seeking work. They are visible by several means, one being their ethnic features (Hispanic, Indigenous, and South Asian) and another being the context in which they are found. Men assumed to be "illegals," for instance, can be found gathered together in the early morning to be transported away for their day laborer jobs. But, because they presumably came to the United States willingly, they are considered "criminal immigrants" subject to deportation rather than "victim immigrants" who are worthy of our sympathy and protection.

One of the most significant interpretations for this text on physical appearance and crime is the lack of discrimination found in present-day anti-human trafficking measures. In other words, while we usually think of the appearance and crime interaction as one of misjudgments about physical appearance (for example, Blacks are automatically suspects, attractive White women are innocent, and so on), in the human trafficking phenomenon in today's terms, *all* of us are subject to abduction and abuse and *all* of us are potential traffickers. If trafficking is perceived to be ubiquitous, then we can all be rightly suspected (as when parents warn their children of "stranger danger") and all of us are in danger, particularly women and children. Human trafficking, as it is currently conceptualized, can happen to anyone, regardless of appearance.

APPEARANCE STRATIFICATION AND VICTIMIZATION

I describe how physical appearance cues perpetuate a stratified hierarchy of human trafficking victims, where those individuals who correspond with an easily recognizable and stereotypical victim-image are considered deserving of sympathy and rescue, and those who do not are barely considered at all by the anti-human trafficking campaign and are subsequently left out of anti-human trafficking discourse. In this analysis, I focus on the question, "What do human trafficking victims look like?"

I draw from 12 years of newspaper coverage to demonstrate how depictions of what human trafficking victims look like is a crucial dimension of the anti-human trafficking (AHT) campaign in the United States. As a symbol, the human trafficking victim is a linchpin that brings many claimsmaking and framing processes into contact with one another. Victim-images, which are stereotypical and often sensationalized portrayals of human trafficking victims, are invoked to create public awareness of human trafficking and to develop a sense of urgency in implementing possible solutions. However, the victim-image that characterizes the US AHT campaign does not correspond with how social scientists have come to understand human trafficking, but it does correspond with widely held ideological beliefs about victimization. As this chapter will show, the victim-image is characterized by physical appearance cues that signify helpless, vulnerable women or children who are unambiguously blameless in their own harm and are deserving of rescue. I argue that victims, actual or hypothetical, that do not correspond with this image, namely men exploited for nonsexual labor, are thereby excluded as nonvictims unworthy of sympathy or assistance. I agree with constructionist assertions that social problems in-the-making are "problems in search of victims" in the sense that the problems themselves are not fully constituted until their victims are made apparent (Holstein & Miller, 1997: 41). Constructing a class of injured persons is integral to shaping the public perception of human trafficking, and physical appearance provides the observable data for recognizing a hidden social problem.

SOCIAL CONSTRUCTION OF HUMAN TRAFFICKING VICTIMS

When social movement actors (also called claimsmakers) make public statements about social problems, they create and contribute to a discourse that embodies a perception of what the social problem is, and more importantly, understandings of who has been injured via a socially constructed process of "victimization" (Holstein & Miller, 1997: 29). In the context of the United States, someone is categorized as a victim only when others perceive that person to be deserving of sympathy (Best, 1997). People who are most often deemed worthy of sympathy and support are those people who are unambiguously not responsible for the harm they experience (Loseke, 1993: 78–79).

VICTIMIZATION IDEOLOGY

Coined by Joel Best (1997), a victimization ideology is a collection of propositions about the nature of victimization. The propositions suggest how claims of victimization are to be made and how audiences should respond. The ideology is based on the assumption that victimization is not an individual characteristic or personal trait, but rather it is an interactional achievement; it is a status that is conferred (Holstein & Miller, 1997). Best's model is comprised of seven propositions (see Best, 1997: 11–13), and while all seven are relevant to understanding the social construction of human trafficking, I only focus on three in this chapter as they best illustrate the operation of appearance bias in the AHT campaign.

The first is the proposition that victimization is common and frequent. To support this assumption, claimsmakers will emphasize the large number of people affected and routinely argue that victimization is widespread, sometimes almost ubiquitous. Claimsmakers frequently make statements about the "hundreds of thousands" of women and children who are sold into the sex industry each year around the world and within the United States. These numbers are quite dubious, but their real value is rhetorical. When it comes to mobilizing resources and competing in the social problems marketplace, the specific numbers may not matter; what matters is that the numbers are big and suggest a need for serious and sustained policy attention (Andreas & Greenhill, 2010). The second tenet complements the first: victimization often goes unrecognized. Relating these propositions to human trafficking, they would suggest that human trafficking victims are everywhere, albeit invisible; they are hidden in plain sight. They are both everywhere and nowhere.

If trafficking victimization is both ubiquitous and hidden, it follows that if strategic actors (law enforcement officers and other well-positioned individuals) are educated to recognize the signs of trafficking, they may be able to identify victims and aid in their rescue. This is the third proposition: the public must be trained to recognize their own victimization and the victimization of others. The campaign's push to create public awareness of human trafficking, and specifically how to identify victims is where appearance bias is most influential. The campaign tells us what human trafficking looks like and where to look. The concepts of victims and victimization are social constructions in that they are based on the attributes and meanings that come to be associated with particular kinds of people. The victim is a symbol evoked by claimsmakers to suggest what a problem "looks-like," whom it affects, and what solutions are most appropriate. "As an act of interpretive reality construction, victimization unobtrusively advises the audience in how they should understand persons, circumstances, and behaviors under consideration" (Holstein & Miller, 1997: 29). In the next section, I outline three important developments of the AHT campaign in the United States to show how physical appearance came into the forefront of anti-human trafficking discourse.

The US anti-human trafficking campaign and the Trafficking Victims and Protection Act of 2000

In the United States, the AHT campaign is the collection of actors who participate in claimsmaking activities with the shared goals of prosecuting human traffickers and providing support to trafficked individuals. Campaign actors include government actors, such as government officials, policymakers, law enforcement agencies, and other entities that work within the political arena to pursue the campaign's goals. The campaign also includes nongovernmental organizations that advocate on behalf of trafficked individuals, provide services, and lobby for their causes to regulatory bodies. Prior research (McDonald, 2004; Soderlund, 2005; Stolz, 2005) has characterized the AHT campaign's activity up to 2001 as a sequence of initiatives by various groups with somewhat differing agendas, but with a common concern about protecting women from sexual exploitation. Feminist, religious, refugee, labor, human rights, and other interest groups have educated decisionmakers at the United Nations and the United States executive and legislative branches on the scope of the trafficking problem and have lobbied for specific solutions. While human trafficking technically refers to any exploitive and unfair labor conditions, in which an individual is forced to labor under mechanisms of indentured servitude, debt bondage, or slavery, the campaign's message appears to have coalesced around sex trafficking of women and children as its focus (Ulibarrí, 2015). The campaign's first major legislative achievement was the Trafficking Victims and Protection Act of 2000 (TVPA).

The director of the Coalition Against the Traffic of Women, stated in a position statement,

The sexual exploitation of women and children by local and global sex industries violates the human rights of all women and children whose bodies are reduced to sexual commodities in this brutal and dehumanizing marketplace. While experienced as pleasure by the prostitution consumers and as lucrative sources of income by sex industry entrepreneurs, prostitution, sex trafficking, and related practices are, in fact, forms of sexual violence that leave women and children physically and psychologically devastated.

(Leidholdt, 2000: 1)

The quotes cited above are representative of the framing activity that characterized the early days of the AHT campaign. The campaign used broad strokes to create an image of what human trafficking victims look like: they are women and children caught up in impossible-to-escape situations of sexual exploitation. However, these depictions of human trafficking and victims did not go unchallenged.

CHANGES IN FOCUS ON TYPES OF VICTIMIZATION

Between 2000 and 2012, newspaper coverage of human trafficking demonstrates a sustained and almost exclusive focus on sex trafficking and sex trafficking victims. There were three primary sources of criticism.

First, international researchers and diplomats called out discrepancies between the claims about human trafficking made by campaign leaders and the observations made by quantitative analysis and diplomatic investigation. Beginning in 2005, reliable quantitative estimates regarding the scope and prevalence of human trafficking around the globe challenged some of the basic assumptions of the AHT campaign. The estimates by International Labor Organization (ILO) have been among the most reliable and transparent. In 2012, the ILO estimated that, of the nearly 21 million people that are forced laborers, only 4.5 million are estimated to be "victims of forced sexual exploitation." Thus, over three-fourths of the people around the globe estimated to be in forced labor are not involved in sex trafficking, but are in industries such as agriculture, construction, domestic work, or manufacturing (ILO, 2012). Referring to the United States specifically, similar conclusions were reached by the United Nations Special Rapporteur on Human Trafficking who conducted a special mission at the US–Mexico border in 2005. She concluded that she observed an overemphasis on sex trafficking interventions, especially in the US Southwest, where she said labor trafficking was a more significant problem than sex trafficking (Pizarro, 2002).

Second, claimsmakers from within the campaign itself brought attention to what they perceived as misguided, and potentially harmful, claims that were based on unsupported assumptions. They took issue with the selection of individuals who spoke at press conferences to share their personal trafficking experiences (i.e., rescued trafficking victims), arguing that were not representative of trafficking victims more broadly and further perpetuate the mythology that all sex workers are trafficking victims and that human trafficking is predominantly a problem of sexual exploitation. They decried the lack of visibility for labor trafficking victims and questioned the conflation of all sex work with sexual exploitation (Ulibarrí, 2015).

Thirdly, national media outlets (namely *The Washington Post*, *The New York Times*, *The Atlanta-Constitution Journal*, and others) conducted their own investigations into the integrity and efficacy with which federal anti-trafficking dollars were spent. Investigative journalists launched a heavy critique of the AHT campaign by calling into question its "sensationalized and often unfounded" depictions of human trafficking. As one journalist writes, "As part of the fight [against human trafficking], President Bush has blanketed the nation with 42 Justice Department task forces and spent more than $150 million – all to find and help the estimated hundreds of thousands of victims of forced prostitution or labor in the United States. But the government couldn't find them. Not in this country" (Markon, 2007).

Collectively, these sources of criticism are a major force in the social construction of human trafficking victims. Together, these challengers ask, "Where are they?" In response, the campaign invokes the third proposition of the victimization ideology: we have to learn how to recognize victimization.

The campaign responds: "You have to know what to look for"

In the mid-2000s, what victims look like comes to the forefront of AHT discourse. With few victims identified and even fewer cases prosecuted, campaign actors pushed forward with their claims that human trafficking victimization is both ubiquitous and hidden. The campaign, support by federal and state-level funds, undertook large-scale education campaigns that focused on teaching targeted professionals such as law enforcement officers how to recognize the signs of trafficking. However, this effort went beyond law enforcement. Since trafficking victims may be hidden in the private homes of their traffickers, home-service professionals such as cable installers are well-positioned to uncover a trafficking case. In Los Angeles, city workers (electric meter readers, etc.) were being trained to "know what to look for." "There are people right now that are living in people's homes that are enslaved. They are petrified and in fear. This training will help (city workers) know what to look for" (Uranga, 2005).

Before describing the findings of the analysis, I briefly describe the importance of media as a data source.

DATA SOURCES AND ANALYSIS

Claimsmakers use mass media as vehicles for publicizing social problems and for stirring up public support for any associated interventions. Historically, mass media have been very instrumental in social reform campaigns, especially those that are based on moral claims, such as prohibition, white slavery, and pornography. In these cases, newspaper media have been a common stage for publicizing specific events or actions in order to garner enough publicity to incite public discussion in the hopes of achieving a public mandate that "something must be done!" (Jenness & Grattet, 1996).

To this end, the data for this study comes from several years of newspaper coverage of human trafficking. Following Altheide and

Schneider's (2012) approach to analyzing media discourse, I collected electronic versions of newspaper articles from LEXIS-NEXIS (LN), an electronic archive of print media. LN allows researchers to use key search terms to search periodical sources from around the globe. I limited cases to articles from English-language newspapers that were published in the United States from 2000 to 2012. The starting year of 2000 reflects the point at which human trafficking became commonly covered in the mass media. Prior to 2000, even though AHT activity was occurring, it did not frequently appear in the mass media (Farrell & Fahy, 2007). The resulting dataset includes 1655 newspaper articles, which I believe capture the bulk of public discourse on human trafficking in the United States between 2000 and 2012, and therefore saturation of the topic (Glaser & Strauss, 1967).

I conducted a qualitative content analysis (QCA). Unlike traditional content analysis, which uses predetermined coding categories, coding sheets, and numerical counts, QCA is an inductive methodology in which the researcher's interpretation emerges through sequential open, axial, and theoretical coding phases (Creswell, 2004). The focus of this analysis was statements given by campaign actors about the physical appearance of human trafficking victims. As previous sections indicate, the campaign was put in the hot seat when few victims were identified after millions of dollars were spent to locate them. In response, the campaign highlighted physical cues that would signify human trafficking victimization. These physical cues are discussed in the next section.

PHYSICAL CUES TO LOOK FOR IN HUMAN TRAFFICKING VICTIMIZATION

Efforts to train individuals to spot human trafficking were broad-reaching initiatives that focused on what teaching members of the public what human trafficking victims look like. At the federal level, government agencies sought to collaborate with travel and transportation industries, such as Amtrak and commercial airlines like Delta, so that individuals working in these industries can identify trafficking victims on trains and airplanes. Former Homeland Security Secretary Janet Napolitano described the major initiative: "Transportation workers, including Amtrak police, train conductors and ticket counter staff and others come into contact with thousands of people on a daily basis, making them well positioned to identify situations that don't seem quite right" (Seper, 2012).

Our empirical question becomes, what exactly constitutes a situation that does not "seem quite right"? The physical cues that signify human trafficking victimization are threefold. First, they are female. Second, they behave or look to be obviously abused or imprisoned. Finally, they have these behaviors or appearances in physical locations commonly associated with sex trafficking. I argue that victimization status is ascribed based not on one of these cues, but rather based on an interplay of physical appearance with the expectations and social settings associated with this appearance.

In framing the physical appearance of human trafficking victims, the campaign highlights physical cues that signify depictions of gender violence, extreme vulnerability, and dependence on others for rescue. As the number of challenges to the official human trafficking narrative increased, campaign actors argued that the best way to find victims was to train professionals and members of the general public on how to recognize the signs. Most obviously, the first common indicator of a victim was they that they were a woman and/or a child.

"They are women and children"

The ubiquitous phrase, "women and children," represents the gender and age characteristics most often associated with trafficked individuals. No surprise here as women and children are often represented as being the most vulnerable of victims in several human rights arenas (Carpenter, 2005), and they are easy populations to envision as being unable to control or influence the situations in which they exist (Holstein & Miller, 2007) and therefore deserving of protection (Dunn, 2001; Schneider & Ingram, 1993). Campaign claims repeatedly invoke the phrase "women and children" to equate women's and children's vulnerability and lack of agency (Chapkis, 2005; Weitzer, 2007). In sum, age and gender are observable cues that signify vulnerability.

However, assuming that women and children are by definition vulnerable is not the complete story. Rather, because of their gender and age, they are especially vulnerable to being tricked, lured, or forced into human trafficking arrangements. The news media data is rich with stories, specific and hypothetical, as to how victims are forcibly or deceptively recruited into trafficking situations. The most commonly depicted way of being recruited into trafficking is through deception or fraud. Statements that highlight deception and fraud describe how women are lured into exploitative arrangements with promises of a better life resulting from a new job or a move to a new geographical location where economic opportunities are perceived to be better. For instance, a major proponent of the AHT campaign, Congressman Smith said, "[M]any young women are lured to the United States with the promise that they will obtain legitimate jobs, but when they arrive, '[t]heir passport is pulled and then they realize the nightmare that they're in for'" (Seper, 2001: p. A9).

While women may be vulnerable to trafficking by believing the promises of lucrative employment, teenage girls and other young women are depicted as susceptible to the honeyed words of a trafficker posing to be a potential boyfriend. A key part of the vulnerability narrative is that women and girls may be trafficked by someone they "thought they loved or trusted",

[M]any teenage girls never really intended to leave home for good. They were enticed by the traffickers with offers of nice clothes or good treatment, and then taken far away from home and quickly subjected to their new 'lifestyle.' They sweet talk them until they get them in the car, and then it's over.

(Trigg, 2012)

The implications of a discourse that emphasizes women and children as likely victims is that it excludes other categories, namely adult men, from being considered victims. The women-and-children focus is obvious, but its importance can be overstated. When victims are primarily and exclusively women and children, a mechanism is created for instantly testing the face validity of victimization claims. Discursively, the category of "women and children" means victimization. Men are often not considered legitimate victims because in the same way that women and children means victimization (because they are vulnerable), the category of men implies agency, physical autonomy, and resourcefulness that does not resonate with the helpless victim-image championed by the AHT campaign.

Existing empirical research has suggested that women and children are not the most common targets of human trafficking because sex trafficking (which does primarily target these categories of people) comprises only a minority of human trafficking (Belser & Cock, 2005; ILO, 2002, 2012). Trafficking of migrant laborers, mostly men, is much more common globally than sex trafficking. Male migrant workers caught in labor trafficking are probably the least understood group of trafficked persons (Ruwanpura & Rai, 2004), even though in many regions of the world, including Europe and Africa, adult males appear to be the primary subjects (ILO, 2001), and this may be true of the United States as well (Pizarro, 2002). Yet such complexity, even though consistent with empirical evidence, does not readily enter the public discourse.

"They look abused and imprisoned"

The women-and-children signifier becomes an even more salient indicator of victimization when it is combined with additional physical cues that suggest physical abuse, a lack of physical autonomy, and even the inability to speak freely. Indicators of physical abuse usually refers to injurious marks on the face, such as bruises or cuts. Signs of malnutrition and hunger may indicate starvation and neglect. A Utah police officer counsels the public on what to watch for in the following terms: "Observers should watch for telltale signs such as broken bones, bruises or poor hygiene. Victims also show symptoms of post-traumatic stress disorder, avoiding eye contact in social situations and crying easily" (Deseret Morning News, 2012).

In a police-led training session, an officer highlights poor hygiene as a possible indicator: "Women may make furtive attempts at contact with neighbors. Children may appear dirty and malnourished. All are signs. 'All of these little details ... if you know what they mean, they can add up'" (Guthrie, 2006).

Other indicators, again attached to women and children, refer to particular behaviors consistent with abuse such as a hesitation to speak, a disinclination to make eye contact, a skittish demeanor, or a fear of uniformed authorities. In New York, victim identification training was facilitated by Petra Hensley, a survivor of trafficking. She identified the following red flags, which include body language, "[A]n older man traveling with a young girl who does not appear to be his daughter and the two carry passports from different countries. 'Ask the girl where she is going ... If she is reluctant to answer, something is not right. It's about body language'" (Mohn, 2012).

Signs of coercion and a lack of control are indicated by the omnipresence of men, who never leave the room or allow the woman or girl to be alone. Similarly, one police officer suggested, "Look for the signs, he said, including young girls spending time with older boys or men. Girls who have low self-esteem, avoid eye contact, show signs of abuse and struggle with substance abuse also could be victims, he said" (Miller, 2012).

It appears that the first dimension, women and children, is complemented by the second dimension, the appearance of abuse, coercion, and helplessness. According to the AHT campaign, the women and children that we ought to be looking for appear helpless and trapped. Finally, we must ask, where are these abused and trapped women and children?

"They are in the places where trafficking occurs"

If we consider victimization an interactional achievement, it is important to consider the settings in which appearance signifiers of victimization occur. According to Goffman (1974), the setting of interpersonal inter-actions also contributes meaning and interpretation to the behaviors and appearance of any social actor. The image of a woman or child who appears abused or captured is further validated when it coincides with a gendered physical locale commonly associated with sex trafficking.

The newspaper data suggest that trafficking victims can be found in private homes, in hotels or brothels, massage parlors, nail salons, and on trains and airplanes. These locales imply the occurrence of forced labor, primarily sexual, for women and children. Locales such as fields and factories were comparatively missing from the news coverage. For instance, one law enforcement officer in Florida explained to a journalist how to identify a potential human trafficking situation in a nail salon:

[S]ay a customer notices that every single day, the same person is working at the nail salon. The customer might try to spark a friendly conversation with the worker, who seems evasive. The boss will then come over and put a stop to the chat, acting like a gatekeeper. That's probably a sign the worker might be a victim of human trafficking.

In New Jersey, in another example, law enforcement officers were training members of the public on how to identify trafficking victims in service establishments,

In service and hospitality establishments such as massage parlors, if a citizen notices an employee does not have their own identification, is spoken for by someone else, and has visible marks such as bruises from physical harm or appears as if they have been deprived of basic necessities such as sleep, food, water or medical care, these are all red flags ...

(Marciniak, 2012)

In a very similar fashion, hotel workers are also told what to look for:

Front desk employees, for example, are encouraged to look for visual clues like signs of abuse or fear among potential victims; young people made up to look older; and clients who pay with cash, are reluctant to provide identification or have no luggage.

(Mohn, 2012)

As the two stories at the very beginning of this chapter suggest, the public is looking for trafficking victims on airplanes. This makes sense because human trafficking evokes images of victims being transported like products, so it follows that trafficked victims could be found along major transportation routes. As then US Secretary of Transportation Ray LaHood explained, "... [A]nytime someone travels by plane, train, bus or car, they have a responsibility to keep an eye out for these activities. It can be as simple as a passenger alerting staff that they see a child on a train that doesn't appear to know the people she is with or an Amtrak employee calling in with a tip" (Alcindor, 2012).

In sum, the newspaper data suggest that human trafficking victims look like women or children with obvious signs of physical abuse or imprisonment who are located in gendered work places such as hotels and nail salons or in transit.

THE DIALECTIC OF IDENTIFYING HT VICTIMS

According to the AHT in the United States, when trying to identify a hidden trafficking victim, one should look in hotels or nail salons for a young woman who has obviously been abused and imprisoned. She might be timid and reluctant to speak, but that is testament to her victimization. The image of the defenseless human trafficking victim has been effective in drawing public attention to the issue, but it homogenizes victimization into a vague, broad-strokes stereotypical profile. As a result, we will continue to spend resources looking for victims in the wrong places and turn up empty-handed. Eventually, the public is likely to feel manipulated or conclude that their tax dollars were wasted and take back their support of the campaign, perhaps wondering if human trafficking is actually happening at all.

The AHT campaign is engaged in a dialectic. By capitalizing on the ideologically sound victim-image of the defenseless and abused female, it successfully keeps public attention on the problem of human trafficking. At the same time, however, the campaign may be worsening the situation for most trafficking victims, who do not look like abused women engaged in the sex industry, by directing attention away from their plight. Others, such as men, are excluded from the discourse. The AHT campaign engages in appearance stratification as it confers social power to those victims who correspond with the imprisoned, abused, and hidden women stereotype. "A failure to understand the contrasts and continuities, whether on the part of scholars, researchers, policymakers, law enforcers, or the public at large, works to the advantage of traffickers while under-mining victims' welfare" (Tiano, 2012: 8). I fear that as the discrepancy between the campaign's common portrayals of trafficking and the observed reality of trafficking grows, it will only be a matter of time before "trafficking fatigue" (Feingold, 2010: 74) sets in, and "people ask why we have spent so much to achieve so little."

In summary, demeanor, context, and physical signs of abuse are all important markers of possible trafficking; those who were the focus of trafficking have changed over time by nationality and age; although men are far more likely to illegally immigrate to the United States, the concern is over women and children; and we are now in a situation where there is no discriminatory powers exercised to uncover the social problem of human trafficking since we view this problem as likely to occur anywhere, at any time, against anyone. As to this last point, I find that appearance bias as it operates in human trafficking is rather the opposite of what the other contributors to this book are finding, since the focus is usually on obvious and agreed-upon physical features that set criminal offenders and criminalized victims apart from nonoffenders and nonvictims. This absence of appearance discrimination in which everyone is a suspect and everyone a potential victim speaks to an ineffective social control system. In this way, it mirrors a control system that relies on mistakenly judging people on their appearance.

References

Alcindor, Y. (2012, October 5). Amtrak on board to fight trafficking; Rail service joins effort by airlines. *USA Today*, p. 3A.

Altheide, D. L. & Schneider, C. J. (2012). *Qualitative media analysis*. Thousand Oaks, CA: Sage.

Andreas, P. & Greenhill, K. (Eds.). (2010). *Sex, drugs, and body counts: The politics of numbers in global crime and conflict*. Ithaca, NY: Cornell University Press.

Belser, P., Cock, M., & Mehran, F. (2005). *ILO Minimum estimate of forced labor in the world*. Geneva: International Labor Organization.

Benford, R. & Snow, D. (2000). Framing processes and social movements: An overview and assessment. *Annual Review of Sociology*, 26, 611–639.

Berry, B. (2007). *Beauty bias: Discrimination and social power*. Westport, CT: Praeger Publishers.

    (2008). *The power of looks: Social stratification of physical appearance*. Hampshire, UK: Ashgate.

Best, J. (1997). Victimization and the victim industry. *Society*, 34(4), 9–17.

Carpenter, C. (2005). Women, children, and other vulnerable groups: Gender, strategic frames and the protection of civilians as a transnational issue. *International Studies Quarterly*, 49(2): 295–334.

Chapkis, W. (2005). Soft glove, punishing fist: The Trafficking Victims Protection Act. In E. Bernstein & L. Shaffner (Eds.), *Regulating sex* (pp. 51–65). New York, NY: Routledge.

Clarkson, B. (2012, September 18). Palm Beach county is a "perfect storm" of human trafficking. *Sun Sentinel.* Retrieved from http://articles.sun-sentinel.com/2012-09-15/news/fl-boca-trafficking-lombardi-20120916 1human-farm-work-carmen-pino.

Creswell, J. W. (2007). *Qualitative inquiry and research design: Choosing among five approaches.* Thousand Oaks, CA: Sage.

Deseret Morning News. (2012, October 17). End human trafficking. *Deseret Morning News,* Retrieved from www.deseretnews.com/article/765612414/ending-human-trafficking-is-a-group-effort.html.

Dillon, N. (2017, February 6). Flight attendant uses secret message to rescue teen girl from human trafficking on Calif. flight. *New York Daily News.* Retrieved from www.nydailynews.com/news/national/flight-attendant-rescues-teen-girl-human-trafficking-article-1.2965478.

Dunn, J. L. (2001). Innocence lost: Accomplishing victimization in intimate stalking cases. *Symbolic Interaction,* 24(3), 285–313.

Farrell, A. & Fahy, S. (2007). The problem of human trafficking in the US: Public frames and policy responses. *Journal of Criminal Justice,* 37(6), 617–626.

Feingold, D. A. (2010). Trafficking in numbers: The social construction of human trafficking data. In P. Andreas & K. Greenhill (Eds.), *Sex, drugs and body counts: The politics of numbers in global crime and conflict* (pp. 46–74), Ithaca, NY: Cornell University Press.

Glaser, B. & Straus, A. (1967). *The discovery of grounded theory: Strategies for qualitative research.* New Brunswick, NJ: AdineTransaction.

Goffman, E. (1974). *Frame analysis: An essay on the organization of experience.* Boston, MA: Harvard University Press.

Guthrie. M. (2005, October 23). "Trafficking" in sex slaves. *New York Daily News.* Retrieved from: www.nydailynews.com/archives/nydn-features/trafficking-sex-slaves-article-1.571300.

Holstein, J. A. & Miller, G. (1997). Rethinking victimization: An interactional approach to victimology. In G. Miller and J. A. Holstein (Eds.), *Social problems in everyday life: Studies of social problem work* (pp. 25–47). Greenwich, CT: Jai Press.

International Labor Organization. (2001). Stopping Forced Labor. Geneva, Switzerland: International Labor Office.

(2012). ILO Global Estimate of Forced Labour: Results and Methodology. Geneva, Switzerland: International Labor Office.

Jenness, V. & Grattet, R. (1996). The criminalization of hate: A comparison of structural and polity influences on the passage of "bias-crime" legislation in the United States. *Sociological Perspectives,* 39(1), 129–154.

Leidholdt, D. (2000). Analysis of International Trafficking of Women and Children Victim Protection Act. Retrieved from: www.uri.edu/artsci/wms/hughes/catw/ans600.htm.

Loseke, D. (1993). Constructing conditions, people, morality, and emotion: Expanding the agents of constructionism. In J. Holstein & G. Miller (Eds.), *Challenges and choices: Constructionist perspectives on social problems* (pp. 120–129). New York, NY: Aldine de Gruyter.

Marciniak, B. (2012, December 13). *Pascack Valley Community Life*, p. A.26.

Mariano, W. (2012, December 31). An AJC special investigation; Crime effort lacks clarity. *The Atlanta Journal-Constitution*, p. 1A.

Markon, J. (2007, November 23). How widespread is human trafficking?; U.S. estimates thousands of victims, but efforts to find them fall short. *The Washington Post*, p. A01.

McDonald, W. (2004). Traffic counts, symbols and agendas: A critique of the campaign against trafficking of human beings. *International Review of Victimology*, 11, 143–176.

Miller, V. (2012, September 21). Human trafficking discussion warns, "It does happen here." Retrieved from www.the gazette.com/2012/09/20/human-trafficking-discussion-warns-it-does-happen-here.

Mohn, T. (2012, November 9). The travel industry takes on human trafficking. *The New York Times*, p. F12.

Ortiz, E. (2017, November 28). Woman on Delta flight says she was mistaken for a human trafficking victim. NBC News. Retrieved from www.nbcnews.com/storyline/airplane-mode/woman-delta-flight-says-she-was-mistaken-human-trafficking-victim-n824456.

Pizarro, G. (2002). Human rights of migrants addendum: Mission to the border between Mexico and the United States of America (E/CN.4/2003/85/Add.3). Office of the United Nations High Commissioner for Human Rights. Retrieved from http://ap.ohchr.org/documents.alldocs.aspx?doc_id=3384.

Roebuck, K. & Wereschagin, M. (2006, June 26). Task force to fight human trafficking. *Pittsburgh Tribune Review*. Retrieved from http://triblive.com/x/archive/1390181-74/archive-story.

Ruwanpura, K. N. & Rai, P. (2004). Forced labour: Definition, indicators and measurement. International Labor Organization. Retrieved from www.ilo.org/global/topics/forced-labor/publications/WCMS_081991/lang–en/index.html.

Schneider, A. & Ingram, H. (1993). Social construction of target populations: Implications for politics and policy. *American Political Science Review*, 87(02), 334–347.

Seper, J. (2001, July 19). Ashcroft targets human trafficking. *The Washington Times*, p. A9.

(2012, October 5). Feds team up with Amtrak to fight human trafficking. *The Washington Times*, p. A2.

Soderlund, G. (2005). Running from the rescuers: New US crusades against sex trafficking and the rhetoric of abolition. *NWSA Journal*, 17(3), 64–87.

Stolz, Barbara A. (2005). Educating policymakers and setting the criminal justice policymaking agenda: Interest groups and the "Victims of Trafficking and Violence Act of 2000." *Criminal Justice*, 5(4): 407–430.

Tiano, S. (2012). Human Trafficking: A perfect storm of contributing factors. In S. Tiano and M. Murphy Aguilar (Eds.), *Borderline slavery: Mexico, United States, and the human trade* (pp. 15–50). Surrey, UK: Ashgate.

Trigg, L. (2012, March 8). SOAP program offers young girls a way out of trafficking. *The Tribune-Star*. Retrieved from www.tribstar.com/news/local_news/soap-program-offers-young-girls-a-way-out-of-trafficking/article_d5a0876a-93ef-500c-a420-7dbb2ef4794d.html.

Ulibarrí, B. (2015). Human trafficking victims are everywhere and nowhere: A qualitative content analysis of the United States anti-human trafficking campaign 2000–2012. (Doctoral dissertation). University of New Mexico, Albuquerque, New Mexico.

Uranga, R. (2005, December 14). Training starts to spot slaves. *The Daily News of Los Angeles*, p. N4.

Weitzer, R. (2007). The social construction of sex trafficking: Ideology and institutionalization of a moral crusade. *Politics & Society*, 35(3), 447–475.

PART III

THE PROCESS OF SOCIAL CONTROL AS INFLUENCED BY APPEARANCE

From Mugshots to the Death Penalty

This section will attend to the process of crime control (corrections, policing, courts) as influenced by the physical appearance of the controlled (crime suspects, prisoners, crime victims) and of the controllers (for example, the police).

As Johnson and King (2017) remark in their work on facial appearance, mugshots, and decisions to punish, we (everyone but not excluding criminal justice personnel) make immediate judgments about people based on their physical appearance. Specific to their work on judgments about booking photos, we assess the faces depicted as associated (or not) with dangerousness, and thus we appropriate punishment necessary to keep these suspects (because that is all they are at the booking stage) from posing a threat to the community. Of the eight hypotheses that Johnson and King pose, the two that were unsupported were: "Offenders who were perceived to be more threatening in appearance will be more likely to be sentenced to prison" and "Threatening appearance will mediate the association among offender race, physical appearance characteristics, and imprisonment decisions" (p. 18).

Per Johnson and King's methodology a threatening countenance can refer to darkness of skin tone (read Blackness), tattoos, and scars. The authors had originally assumed that physical appearance in terms of overall attractiveness and a "baby-faced" appearance would serve as the independent variable, mediated by the intervening variable of a threatening appearance, which would then influence the dependent variable punishment assigned (imprisonment). To their surprise and mine, a threatening appearance is not a mediating factor in sentencing. Instead, facial appearance *directly affects* punishment decisions. This finding is groundbreaking since, obviously, it shows that appearance (attractiveness) by itself is enough of a judgment call that guilt and punishment decisions are based upon it.

To elaborate, Johnson and King found support for their six other hypotheses:

> Hypothesis 1 states that: "Racial and ethnic minorities, particularly Blacks, will be more likely than Whites to be perceived to be more threatening in appearance."
> Hypothesis 2 states: "Racial and ethnic minorities, particularly Blacks, will be more likely than White offenders to be sentenced to prison."
> Hypothesis 3 states: "Offenders who are more attractive or baby-faced will be perceived to be less threatening in appearance."
> Hypothesis 4 states: "Offenders who are more attractive or baby-faced will be less likely to be sentenced to prison."
> Hypothesis 5 states: "Offenders with visible tattoos or scars will be perceived to be more threatening in appearance."
> Hypothesis 6 states: "Offenders with facial tattoos or scars will be more likely to be sentenced to prison." (p. 18)

One could argue that tattoos, scars, and Blackness all serve to issue a perception of threat in the minds of many citizens and criminal justice personnel (police, juries, and judges). None of these findings affirming Hypotheses 1–6 are surprising but they reaffirm what we already know in criminology about judgments regarding race, facial appearance, and threat perception. Yet, apparently, attractive faces and youthful baby faces instill a perception of innocence, rightly or wrongly, resulting in fewer findings of guilt and less punishment.

The public, incidentally, also can have reactions to booking photos that may or may not impact what happens to the suspects in the photos. Here, I would point to the internet sensation, Jeremy Meeks, aka "Mug Shot Heartthrob" and "Hottie Thug." Mr Meeks is an attractive man who inspired women (and a few men) to remark online about their romantic interest in him (Manuel-Logan, 2017). Like Mr Meeks, Mekhi Alante Lucky, another attractive man depicted in a mug shot, was offered modeling jobs (Inside Edition, 2017). Mr Lucky was luckier than Mr Meeks: the latter served a 27-month sentence.

One would think that, given the importance of physical appearance in booking photos, and the sharing of those photos among criminal justice personnel such as attorneys, that exact representation of the suspect would be helpful. Instead, color printers are not necessarily available or used for sharing photos (Lageson, 2017a, personal communication; see also Lageson, Bacak, & Powell, 2017b). Color prints would show not only depth of skin tone but also, significantly, signs of trauma. Signs of trauma (knocked-out teeth, missing eyes, bruises, burns, scars, etc.) can be indications of police brutality or abuse and neglect at the hands of others. As an attorney interviewed by Lageson's team remarked, with "dark complexions, bruises don't show very well. When a bunch of cops beat up my black client, it's impossible to show the jury my client look[ing] beat up unless I show a very, very detailed color photo" (Lageson, 2017a).

Mugshots, helpful or not helpful to the suspect/offender (in other words, depicting an attractive and innocent-looking face or not), can follow an individual for life. They are costly to have erased and their persistent presence can haunt the individual represented in the booking photo as well as the family of that individual (Lageson, 2017c, 2016a, 2016b).

Chapters 6 and 7 focus on the appearance of female prisoners and of female victims, two subsets that commonly overlap. A question that was raised in the first section of this book about "ugly criminals" applies here: does living a criminal life cause unattractiveness or does unattractiveness lead to criminal involvement? And does physical appearance lead us to blame victims for their victimization?

Chapter 6, Brenda Chaney's chapter on prisoners' appearance is unique on several dimensions. For one, there is a complete dearth of literature on the topic. When I searched for data, literature, and finally data collectors to find out about prisoners' appearance, I came up empty-handed. Yet, as a volunteer sponsor at the Women's Corrections Center in Washington and as someone who spends too much time looking at mugshots, it seemed obvious that suspects and convicted offenders commonly do not resemble non-suspects and non-convicts. Disproportionately, people who are caught up in the criminal justice system are poor, nonwhite, and have been subject to physical abuse; all of these factors influence their appearance before, during, and after criminal involvement. Moreover, many are or have been heavy users of alcohol and drugs, both leading to premature aging, especially noticeable on the face. The use of methamphetamines takes a highly visible toll on facial appearance through the destruction of teeth and gums ("meth mouth," see Image 5) and the shredding of facial flesh by the users' abnormal

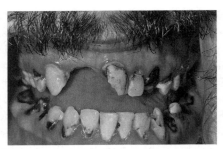

IMAGE 5. A photograph of meth mouth, courtesy of Dr Chris Heringlake, DDS, St Cloud Correctional Facility, St Cloud, Minnesota

scratching and skin picking. (Formication, the sensation that insects are crawling on or under the skin, causes meth users to pick at their skin.) Professor Chaney pinpoints her focus on the appearance and demeanor of women suspects during trial, which then determines whether they end up in the Midwestern women's prison where Chaney leads the Inside-Out program.

Many women prisoners were once abused (sexually and otherwise) themselves, from childhood onward, and that fact alone alters their appearance. Roxane Gay, feminist author, is a good example of what women do to protect themselves by altering their appearance after having been assaulted. In her latest book (*Hunger*, 2017), she described having been gang-raped by a group of boys at the age of 12. Of course this experience had a profound effect on her, complete with self-blame and self-punishment. She dealt with it by putting on massive amounts of weight; by her 20s, she weighed 577 pounds (on a 6'3" frame). She wanted to protect herself by becoming unattractive, which would certainly work in a fat-phobic society.

Chapter 7, by Jennifer Wareham, Brenda Sims Blackwell, Denise Paquette Boots, and me, attempts to understand the relationship between the appearance of victims of interpersonal violence and their blame-worthiness. It has long been supposed that women who groom themselves and dress themselves in a particular way (wearing cosmetics, wearing tight-fitting clothes, and so on) are "asking for it" (see Image 6). And it is somewhat well-known that unattractive women are not viewed as worthy of protection; their social capital is small compared to attractive women, and thus they are seen as not deserving of equal treatment as victims. Among the questions raised in this study are whether attractive-ness of the victim directly affects the determination of guilt for the

IMAGE 6. Slutwalk: My little black dress does not mean yes! (Getty Images)

defendant, the harshness of the recommended sentence, and the blame-worthiness of the victim in cases of sexual and domestic (nonsexual) assault. Appearance, of course, is an extra-legal factor and should not be integral to determining victim blameworthiness or perpetrator guilt, but it does impact these perceptions and decisions.

Chapter 8 by Brent Teasdale, Taylor Gann, and Dean Dabney ana-lyzed data from their observational study of a police force in the South-eastern United States. University students went on ride-alongs with police officers and coded their reactions to many forms of violations (traffic and criminal), specifically looking for appearance cues that may lead the officers to release the suspect without arrest, warn the suspect, issue a ticket, or make an arrest. This chapter, one analysis of several from this study, pertains to the response of police officers to the appearance of suspected female and male traffic violators, and finds, against expect-ations, that attractive female traffic violators get away with their offenses *less* often than attractive male violators. Teasdale et al. also find that a conventional appearance versus one that is unusual in terms of grooming and clothing styles ("grills" on the teeth, Black-centric hairstyles, etc.) works in favor of the suspect, reaffirming the literature I cited in the

Introduction to this book that ordinary rather than stand-out appearance is generally preferred. In other words, attractive male citizens were less likely to be ticketed than less attractive male citizens and less likely to be ticketed than female citizens, including attractive ones.

Finally, Chapter 9 captures the importance of the appearance of crime controllers (law enforcement) as escalating or diminishing public outbursts. Steve Bishopp, a sergeant with the Dallas, Texas Police Department, describe the wide array of police "presence" in terms of clothing, weaponry, grooming, race, and so on in respect of its effect on how the public view law enforcement. Specifically, Bishopp describes varying images of intimidation shown by police accoutrements, such as a militarized appearance versus a calmer, subtler, and more public-service image. In this chapter, appearance traits of the police (their size, skin color, facial hair, etc.) as well as their protective/assaultive law enforcement tools are offered as dimensions in determining reactions by the public and criminal suspects. Besides the intimidating versus service images, Bishopp additionally examines police race by suspect race in terms of effective and fair law enforcement. As we saw in Chapter 4, the racial intermixes are of grave importance. The visible physical features may include police clothing (casual versus militaristic), weaponry (ordinary guns, stun guns, shields, body armor, tanks, robots, drones, etc.), and means of conveyance as insulators from the public (cars, horses, bicycles, feet).

Basically, the image of the police and their police tools speaks to power. Knowing that, the effect of police attire and equipment may escalate or de-escalate emotional and behavioral reactions in public encounters. After the Ferguson incident, the Black community protested the killing of an unarmed Black citizen, resulting in a police presence that was truly intimidating to the point of overkill. This police presence, with tanks and other evidence of militarism, infuriated the Black citizens even more. Of course, the reason for a frightening police presence is to intimate the public into submission, but it can have the opposite effect of causing more violence.

We might assume that police tools, such as tanks, shields, and guns, make the police feel invulnerable to attack. However, the reverse may be true when police are unidentified as police through wearing non-official attire. Stolberg (2017) reports that un-uniformed police officers are more likely to mistreat suspects and otherwise engage in unethical behavior (stealing, etc.). In Baltimore, Maryland, where there have been numerous cases of police misconduct, the police commissioner disbanded plainclothes teams. Police officers wearing jeans and T-shirts are anonymous to the public, which means they are unidentifiable as police officers and makes it easier for them to fool the public and, therefore, discover criminal activity through, for example, stings. So far, this sounds like a good thing: Being unknown as officers creates the element of surprise. "The uniform is a signal to the public and to the officer who wears one that the police represent law and order" (Stolberg, p. 13). But some police officers prefer to be "out of the bag" (not wear a uniform) because it is a sign of status. Some plainclothes officers feel that they can dress as they want and that means they can do what they want. Not surprisingly, there is a racial component to all this. In 2016, a US Justice Department investigation documented "frequent complaints about plainclothes officers 'as particularly aggressive and unrestrained in their practice of stopping individuals, without cause and performing public humiliating searches'" (p. 13). It encourages a culture of discretionary policing. There is a very large difference in the behavior of uniformed police, with a badge and a name clearly visible, and officers who are not immediately identifiable.

The author Kurt Andersen is correctly concerned about "Americans' accelerating penchant for blending the fantastical into the real world," especially as to how that phenomenon pertains to law enforcement's militarization (2017, p. 25). He gives a brief history of how law enforcement in the United States since the 1960s has become more militarized in behavior and, importantly for this text, appearance. This has culminated in the above-mentioned 2014 appearance of the police presence in Ferguson, Missouri after the killing of an unarmed Black citizen by a white police officer. To deal with citizen protest, the police showed up armed with AR-15s and, Ballistic Engineered Armored Response Counter-Attack Trucks. In the 1990s, the US federal government "began supplying the police with surplus military helicopters, armored troop carriers, semi-automatic rifles" etc. (p. 25). Overlapping with my comments to Part IV in this volume, Andersen remarks that "costumed and armed racists with torches and Nazi flags" as we saw in the August 2017 White supremacist march in Charlottesville, Virginia, also speaks to the imagery of military-appearing fantasies. He concludes by stating that such imaging promotes the fallacy that policing is the same as fighting wars.

Public Reporting based on Appearance

Bear in mind that the public and schools can and do serve as the initiators of calls to the police. Here also appearance bias plays a significant role.

Shaban, Bott, Villarreal, and Carroll (2017) find that California schools report Black students with disabilities to the police far more than White children with disabilities. Disabilities can be visible or not, as Scherer and Reyns discuss in Chapter 13, but the combination of nonwhite appearance and even invisible disabilities (depression, learning disabilities, and the like) are known to magnify notice by social control agencies as well as by those who would criminally victimize these minorities. Shaban and colleagues found that, nationally, Black students are three times more likely to be arrested than White students, and disabled students are likewise three times more likely to be arrested than nondisabled students. Legislation and guidelines are absent yet necessary to correct this form of bias as it occurs in the schools, against children, by educators and by law enforcement.

QUESTIONS

If a militaristic police presence serves to intimidate and thus quell public rebellion, should it be used?

If prisoners' health and appearance improve while incarcerated, can we say that imprisonment is beneficial? It occurred to me when I served as a volunteer sponsor at the Washington Corrections Center for Women, that, according to the prisoners, their drug and alcohol problems declined even while in jail and continued to decline while incarcerated. Their teeth were repaired. They gained weight, which many did not like, but at least they were healthier. And they were absent from the abusive conditions under which most of them lived. I am not arguing that being incarcerated outweighs the freedom of the outside or the separation from their children and other loved ones; I am echoing the benefits, as remarked upon by prisoners, that time away from poor environments can prove advantageous.

If victims of interpersonal violence are blamed for their abuse because of their appearance, what can be done?

References

Andersen, K. (2017, September 8). Hands up: It's showtime. *New York Times*, p. A25.

Gay, R. (2017). *Hunger: A memoir of (my) body*. New York, NY: HarperCollins.

Inside Edition. (2017, September 4). North Carolina man's "hot mugshot" gets him a modeling job. Retrieved from http://nbc41.com/author/inside-edition.

Johnson, B. D. & King, R. (2017). Facial profiling: Race, physical appearance, and punishment. *Criminology*, 55, 520–547.

Lageson, S. E. (2017a, November 28). Personal communication.

Lageson, S. E., Bacak, V., & Powell, K. (2017b). Assessments of public defenders attrition. Paper presented at the American Society of Criminology annual meetings, Philadelphia.

Lageson, S. E. (2017c). Crime data, the Internet, and free speech: An evolving legal consciousness. *Law and Society Review*, 15, 8–41.

 (2016a). Digital punishment's tangled web. *Contexts*, Winter, 22–26.

 (2016b). Found out and opting out: The consequences of online criminal records for families. *Annals (The Annals of the American Academy)*, 665, 127–141.

Manuel-Logan, R. (2017, January 28). Mug shot heartthrob Jeremy Meeks sentenced to federal prison. Retrieved from https://newsone.com/3089289.

Shaban, B., Bott, M., Villarreal, M., & Carroll, J. (2017, February 27). California schools call police on black students with disabilities far more often than other children. Retrieved from www.nbcbayarea.com/investigations.

Stolberg, S. G. (2017, April 15). Does a uniform keep officers in line? Baltimore thinks so. *New York Times*, pp. A1 and A13.

6

Becoming and Being a Woman Prisoner

Does Appearance Matter?

Brenda Chaney

In January 2016, Tara Lambert, a former model, was found guilty of hiring a hit man to kill her husband's ex-partner. Each day of her trial, the local newspapers gave detailed descriptions of the clothing and shoes the woman wore to court. The jury reportedly felt that she was manipulating them and said they didn't buy her (innocent) version of the story. One commentator noted that "her appearance was stunningly well put together, her hair and makeup simply flawless. Wearing animal prints and tight-fitting dresses with thigh-high slits, carrying a Coach purse on the same arm that sported an Apple smartwatch, she radiated confidence. The courtroom appeared to be her stage" (Zachariah, 2016).

After the verdict was overturned by an appeals court, Ms Lambert said that in her retrial, she would dress differently, not in designer clothing. Her new lawyer commented, "Juries pick up on things and when you are in a court of law you are not at a discotheque. You ought to dress accordingly" (Preston, 2017).

Women who face jury trials are judged on more than the evidence. If they are too attractive, they face bias. If they are unattractive, they face bias. This chapter is a discussion of the pitfalls of being a woman facing a jury and possibly being sent to prison for years or even for life. In Ohio, just 2.5 percent of felony criminal cases go before a jury trial (Futty, 2014). Therefore, only a few women face jury trials but when they do, they likely have serious charges that could result in incarceration for many years, life in prison, or in a few cases, death. The question is, then, are these women judged on the quality of the evidence or on subjective evaluations about their appearance?

THE PRESENTATION OF SELF IN EVERYDAY LIFE

The presentation of self in everyday life refers to the way individuals guide and control the impression that others form of them. Erving Goffman was interested in the influencing that takes place between people who are physically in each other's presence (1959, 1967). He introduced the dramaturgical perspective to explain how we interact and control the impression we give to others. Control of the impression that we present to the outside world will allow us to achieve individual or social goals (Jacobsen & Kristiansen, 2015). The other participants in the encounter, the social audience, will "attempt to form a picture of his or her identity and for that purpose they use a number of different types of sign vehicles, each saying something about the person in question" (Jacobsen & Kristiansen, p. 68). In the courtroom, the jury will be looking at the defendant and using information given by the physical presentation and demeanor of the individual to draw conclusions about the guilt or innocence of that person.

One type of information used by the observer is verbal or nonverbal symbols used to convey a meaning. Actors attempt to influence how others perceive the situation through the use of a front. The front consists of attitudes, presence, and expressions used to convey a certain image. The crucial task in any encounter is to control the definition of the situation. Goffman believed that definitions of the situation contain a moral component: as interpreted by Jacobsen and Kristiansen, Goffman meant that "individuals have a morally founded right to expect to be treated according to the social markers they implicitly or explicitly present" (p. 70).

The question now is, how can women have any control over their presentation of self if their physical appearance is interpreted as a sign of guilt, or when their demeanor is interpreted as a sign of guilt? Goffman told us that backstage we prepare for our performance frontstage. But if women lack the social power to control the backstage, they cannot control their frontstage appearance (Berry, 2007). Women facing criminal trials are stigmatized by subjective factors that they cannot control and that will influence the outcomes of their trials and determine their futures.

Goffman investigated the management of a spoiled identity and how the stigmatized interact with the normal (Jacobsen & Kristiansen, 2015). Individuals who display culturally nonaccepted attributes are discredited. These attributes can be physical, character, or tribal, with tribal referring to belonging to a race or religion or nationality that is discredited

(Jacobsen & Kristiansen, p. 98). The appearance biases I will discuss are the result of physical traits (dentition and other attractiveness dimensions, demeanor, facial expressions, etc.), character (facing serious criminal charges) and tribal (belonging to racial/ethnic groups that are stereotyped as deviant/criminal).

TEETH

In the late 1980s, I worked in one of the prison pre-release centers for women in Ohio. During a discussion with a woman one day, I asked her if she could change anything about herself before she left prison what would she change. Her reply, "My teeth and my language." Like many women who grew up in families with poorly educated caretakers who did not encourage success in school, she had poor grammar and didn't understand basics like subject–verb agreement. Over time, we could have fixed the grammar. But, how to fix teeth that have been ruined by lack of dental care while a child and the effect of drug use as an adult?

As Otto (2017) described in her book, *Teeth*, adults who have lacked dental care during their childhoods find it difficult to improve their lives. More than 114 million Americans lack access to dental care. These Americans are the poor, the minority, and those most likely to find their way into the criminal justice system (Otto, p. 35). Many longtime drug users also have black, rotten teeth, and when these women are in court, they face a jury that believes their poor teeth are a sign of their guilt.

In the way that they disfigure the face, bad teeth depersonalize the sufferer. They confer the stigma of economic and even moral failure. People are held personally accountable for the state of their teeth in ways that they are not held accountable for many other health conditions (Otto, pp. vii, viii).

APPEARANCE BIAS

In 2012, Smithsonian.com published an article on women's appearance and bias. The article concluded that women who are blonde and beautiful are less likely to get any sympathy from a jury. In fact, "physical attractiveness increased the perception of the defendant's responsibility in committing the crime" (Eveleth, 2012). In a mock swindle trial, an attractive defendant was sentenced more harshly because the mock jurors believed the defendant was using her attractiveness to bias them while an unattractive burglar was given a harsher sentence than an attractive burglar, strongly suggesting that the level of attractiveness is mediated by the type of crime for which the defendant is accused (Hollier, 2017).

However, this type of finding is an anomaly. In 1997, *Psychology Today* published an article concluding that attractive defendants are perceived as more credible, are acquitted more often, and receive lighter sentences than those who are unattractive (Paul, 1997). The Law Project found that the more unattractive the criminal, the harsher the sentence. While jurors do not make sentencing decisions, this research shows that appearance makes a difference. Further, women were more likely to find a defendant guilty if the victim was attractive (Hollier, 2017). In summary, women are judged more harshly if they are unattractive and if they are attractive (Hollier, 2017).

REMORSE

Remorse is one of the most important factors in a juror's decision on whether to sentence a defendant to death. Lack of remorse plays a critical role in criminal justice decisionmaking, from arrest to charges by the prosecutor, to jury decisionmaking, to sentencing (Bandes, 2015). But, what does remorse look like? Here is a description of Karla Faye Tucker's demeanor at her capital trial: "(Her lawyer) had told her to look dignified and calm and so she was trying to look unmoved by the proceedings and when she did they said she was cold" (Bandes, 2015, p. 16).

Determining remorse can be a process filled with error. Jurors from subcultures other than that of the defendant may make judgments based on their, often faulty, interpretation of differences in demeanor. In *Code of the Street*, Anderson described how informal rules of behavior governed the everyday lives of young people in violent neighborhoods. These young people believed that they must maintain the respect of others through a violent and tough identity accompanied by a willingness to get revenge if they are disrespected (Anderson, 1999).

Jones (2008) described the experience of inner-city girls as not being different from that of inner-city boys. They share with the boys an "understanding about how to survive in a setting where your safety is never guaranteed" (Jones, p. 69). Also, like the boys, they are committed to managing their presentation of self in a way that masks vulnerability (p. 71). The presentation of self as required by young, urban, black women contrasts with the desired traits of femininity for young white women. Passive and submissive are not desirable characteristics for young women who have to present a front of toughness and strength in order to survive in their neighborhoods. When jurors see the tough, aggressive, passive stare of young black women in court, their appearance is interpreted as a lack of remorse rather than a means of survival in tough urban neighborhoods.

One year, a young black woman sat in my office and told me about her experiences in court, accused of murder and facing life imprisonment. She said she grew up in a tough, high-crime neighborhood and she had been told since she was very young to not show emotion and to not cooperate with the police. During her trial, the prosecutor used her silence with the police as a sign of guilt rather than a common attitude for young people in inner-city areas who are likely to have frequent contact with the police.

In another example of appearance bias, a woman in the pre-release center where I previously worked was severely obese and was targeted by a staff member as a personal project. The staff member forced the young woman to walk laps around the basketball court in hot, humid weather "for her own good." The woman frequently walked around the court sobbing due to the humiliation and physical pain she was experiencing. Berry has written about fat shaming, and this is an example of a person with power humiliating a woman because of her size (Berry, 2007).

TRIBAL MEMBERSHIP AS SIGNS OF GUILT

One semester I taught a class on social stratification, and one of the assigned books was Bonnie Berry's *Beauty Bias*. The small class was made up of students I knew well from previous classes. One woman was very large, and during her first pregnancy weighed 300 pounds. We were discussing fat shaming, and the conversation turned to race. My student said that she faced plenty of judgmental stares and believed that a fat Black woman would be treated even more poorly than a fat White woman. The research supports her opinion of the treatment of Black women and for women involved in the criminal justice system who are African-American and thought to be unattractive (with obesity being one dimension of socially determined unattractiveness); the outcome is harsher treatment in court (DeSantis & Kayson, 1997).

Goffman defined tribal as belonging to a particular race, religion, or nationality. For this chapter, I am specifically referring to women of color and the disadvantage that presents when facing a jury. It is essential to understand that skin tone has nothing, technically, to do with attractiveness; that is, Black, Asian, and Indigenous features are not more or less attractive than White features. However, society has assigned a favored status of attractiveness to whiteness. Attractiveness has traditionally been linked to looking White, and women who are not White have tried, through the use cosmetics, hair straightening, even plastic surgery, to look less ethnic (Berry, 2007). Berry writes that, "lighter skin tone is associated with greater likelihood of being married, and to being married to spouses with greater income" (Berry, p. 35). Cultural stereotypes of desirable looks have an effect cross-culturally, as is discussed in the Introduction to this volume.

There are many examples of women of color facing public resentment and condemnation because of their appearance. For example, in 2011, a blogger for *Psychology Today* posted an article on why Black women are less attractive: though the relationship between race and attractiveness is a shared cultural understanding, more pointedly, being Black is equal to being unattractive (Lennard, 2011). When Leslie Jones, a Black woman, played a character in the *Ghostbuster* movie, she was harassed and condemned, with national media reporting on the complaints about her appearance (Ukoha, 2016). There are consequences to women for this condemnation: depression, increased rates of suicide, increased self-medication through drugs, and involvement with criminal justice. Research shows that in recent years, "African American women have experienced the greatest increase in criminal supervision of all demographic groups, with their rate of supervision rising by 78% from 1989–94" (Mauer & Huling, 1995). I have already described the bias that women face because of their appearance when involved in the criminal justice system. The stigma attached to being a racial/ethnic minority results in dual discrimination.

CONCLUSION

When women face a jury they are not only being tried for the quality of the evidence and the defense attorney's arguments but also on their appearance. If they are too attractive, they are attempting to manipulate the jury. If they are considered too unattractive, they look guilty, deserving of punishment, blameworthy. If they had the misfortune of growing up in a poor family that had no access to dental care, they are found to be morally suspect. If they grew up in urban, poor neighborhoods filled with violence that taught them to not show signs of weakness, they are seen as remorseless. When prosecutors instruct the jury to look at the defendant's faces for a lack of remorse, the street-hardened women are being condemned for a learned survival tactic.

Over the past thirty years I have worked in and led groups in women's prisons. During this time I have heard many stories from the women about their experiences when they went to trial. These women were facing long prison sentences and hoped for fair treatment from their jury. One Black woman recounted that the prosecutor told the jury to look at her scarred face and asked if that was the face of an innocent woman. The woman said to me, "I know I am ugly but what does that have to do with my case?" A teenager facing life wore jeans and a T-shirt to court, and the prosecutor told the jury she was trying to manipulate them by looking cute. Other women told me stories of not being allowed makeup or clothing from their closets at home while they sat in the county jail, unable to make bail. The women were not making claims of innocence. They were asking why they were judged on their appearance and not on the facts.

During months of reading and thinking about disadvantages that women face in jury trials, I have also thought of remedies. Surely, there must be a way to ensure that women are found guilty based on evidence and not appearance. I am not optimistic. The biases that accompany racial, class, and gender stereotyping are not easy to overcome. Some authors have suggested explicit trial instructions from the judge that asks the jury to ignore subjective factors (Ingriselli, 2015). But, we know that asking a person to not be prejudiced is not a cure for prejudice. If it were, this book would not be needed.

References

Anderson, E. (1999). *Code of the street: Decency, violence, and the moral life of the inner city*. New York, NY: W. W. Norton.

Bandes, S. A. (2016). Remorse and criminal justice. *Emotion Review*, 8, 14–18.

Berry, B. (2007). *Beauty bias: Discrimination and social power*. Westport, CT: Praeger.

DeSantis, A. & Kayson, W. (1997). Defendants' characteristics of attractiveness, race, and sex and sentencing decisions. *Psychological Reports*, 81, 679–683.

Eveleth, R. (2012, October 10). Trial by judgmental jury – Attractive women seem more guilty. Retrieved from www.smithsonianmag.com/smart-news/trial-by-judgmental-juryattractive-women-seem-more-guilty-69048349/.

Futty, J. (2014, January 13). Trials a rarity in Ohio. Retrieved from www.dispatch.com/content/stories/local/2014/01/13/trials-a-rarity-in-ohio-u-s-.html.

Goffman, E. (1959). *The presentation of self in everyday life*. New York, NY: Doubleday.

(1967). *Interaction ritual*. New York, NY: Doubleday.

Hollier, R. (2017). Physical attractiveness bias in the legal system. Retrieved from www.thelawproject.com.au/blog/attractiveness-bias-in-the-legal-system.

Ingriselli, E. (2015). Mitigating jurors' racial biases: The effects of content and timing of jury instructions. *The Yale Law Journal, 5,* 1– 32.

Jacobsen, M. H. & Kristiansen, S. (2015). *The social thought of Erving Goffman.* Los Angeles, CA: Sage.

Jones, N. (2008). Working the code: On girls, gender, and inner-city violence. *The Australian and New Zealand Journal of Criminology, 4,* 63–83.

Lennard, N. (2011). "Why are black women less attractive?" asks *Psychology Today.* Retrieved from www.salon.com/2011/05/17/psychology_today_racist_black_women_attractive/.

Mauer, M. & Huling, T. (1995). Young Black Americans and the criminal justice system: Five years later. Retrieved from www.sentencingproject.org/publications/young-black-americans-and-the-criminal-justice-system-five-years-later/.

Otto, M. (2017). *Teeth: The story of beauty, inequality, and the struggle for oral health in America.* New York, NY: The New Press.

Paul, A. M. (1997, November 1). Judging by appearance. Retrieved from www.psychologytoday.com/articles/199711/judging-appearance.

Preston, K. (2017, September 25). Model claims "sexy" courtroom outfits turned a jury against her. Retrieved from https://honey.nine.com.au/2017/09/25/11/18/tara-lambert-court-outfits.

Robertson, K. (2016, January 25). Tara Lambert wears designer shoes during her trial. Retrieved from www.dispatch.com/photogallery/OH/20170608/NEWS/608009993/PH/1?start=2.

(2016, January 27). Tara Lambert listens to the guilty verdict. Retrieved from www.dispatch.com/photogallery/OH/20170608/NEWS/608009993/PH/1?start=2.

Ukoha, E. (2016). Why the societal harassment of Leslie Jones exposes the ugly black woman syndrome. Retrieved from https://medium.com/@nilegirl/why-the-societal-harassment-of-leslie-jones-exposes-the-ugly-black-woman-syndrome-6fcc888f9dfb.

Zacharaiah, H. (2016, April 18). The inside story of Circleville femme fatale Tara Lambert. Retrieved from www.dispatch.com/article/20160418/LIFESTYLE/304189620.

7

The Impact of Victim Attractiveness on Victim Blameworthiness and Defendant Guilt Determination in Cases of Domestic and Sexual Assault

Jennifer Wareham, Bonnie Berry, Brenda Sims Blackwell, and Denise Paquette Boots

INTRODUCTION

The criminal justice system in the United States is intended to be fair and equitable. Justice is said to be "blind" to any and all personal characteristics that would result in disparity and impeach this fair treatment. Accordingly, the US Constitution has numerous amendments, with the Sixth Amendment guaranteeing citizens the right to trial by an impartial jury of their peers, to enforce this intent. Despite this, jurors do make discriminating judgments based on nonevidential, or extralegal, factors that are not legally relevant to the criminal case before them. Extralegal factors such as race and ethnicity (e.g., Sargent & Bradfield, 2004), gender (e.g., Hodell, Wasarhaley, Lynch, & Golding, 2014), and age (e.g., Bergeron & McKelvie, 2004) have been shown to subvert fairness in case processing in both real-life and mock trials. Jurors may also discriminate based on the physical appearance of the defendant and/or complainant/victim. It is important to acknowledge the terms "victim" and "complainant" have different yet overlapping meanings; the terms tend to be used interchangeably in research testing attractiveness bias in juror judgments, and will be used interchangeably throughout this chapter.

In sum, by law what one looks like should not impact the likelihood of being believed as a victim or judged culpable as a defendant. Yet it does. Appearance influences how the public views individuals in terms of their blameworthiness, the degree of public empathy received, and the public feeling of what should happen to the culprit who instigated the offense. Specifically, "beauty," as a form of social capital, favorably influences social interactions and perceptions. Indeed, Dion, Berscheid, and Walster (1972) reported in their seminal study that attractive people are viewed as more sociable, kind, and interesting, and capable of achieving greater occupational prestige, happier marriages, and happier lives than less attractive people. They concluded, "What is beautiful is good" (p. 289). A large body of research corroborates this claim.

Most research on attractiveness bias in jurors' decisionmaking focuses on the defendant's appearance, but ignores the appearance of the victim. Overall, the research exploring whether defendants' attractiveness influences jurors' perceptions of guilt and blame is mixed. Some studies find attractive defendants are less likely to be judged guilty than are unattractive defendants (e.g., Castellow, Weunsch, & Moore, 1990; Darby & Jeffers, 1988; Jacobson, 1981; Shechory-Bitton & Zvi, 2016). Meanwhile, other studies report no significant effect for attractiveness on juristic judgments of defendants' guilt and blameworthiness (e.g., Ahola, Christianson, & Hellström, 2009; Burke, Ames, Etherington, & Pietsch, 1990; Erian, Lin, Patel, Neal, & Geiselman, 1998; Gerdes, Dammann, & Heilig, 1988; Stewart, 1980). These mixed results highlight the need for further research, suggesting that additional variables yet to be examined may exert influences on the attractiveness–blame relationship. For example, the impact of attractiveness on guilt ratings may depend on juror gender, especially in cases of sexual harassment and assault (Moore, Wuensch, Hedges, & Castellow, 1994).

A much smaller body of research has examined attractiveness bias for victims in juristic judgments. Similar to attractiveness bias toward defendants, studies of jurors' attractiveness bias toward victims are mixed. In cases of sexual assault and rape, mock jurors in some studies attribute more blame to attractive victims (Calhoun, Selby, Cann, & Keller, 1978; Jacobson & Popovich, 1983), while others find either more blame directed toward unattractive victims (Seligman, Brickman, & Koulack, 1977; Thornton & Ryckman, 1983) or no bias in either direction (Gerdes et al., 1988; Thornton, 1977). While some studies report that jurors in rape cases are more likely to judge defendants as guilty when the victim is more attractive (Jacobson, 1981), a larger number of studies find victim's appearance has no effect on perceptions of the defendant's guilt (e.g., Erian et al., 1998; Gerdes et al., 1988; Thornton, 1977; Thornton & Ryckman, 1983; Villemur & Hyde, 1983). Contradictory findings also exist for studies depicting sexual harassment scenarios (Castellow et al., 1990; Moore et al., 1994) and other crimes such as theft, robbery, and criminal negligence (e.g., Callan, Powell, & Ellard, 2007; Kerr, 1978;

MacCoun, 1990; Seligman et al., 1977). Further, Burke et al. (1990) found attractiveness of the victim had no effect on blameworthiness of the victim or the defendant's guilt in cases of domestic assault. In sum, there is considerable inconsistency in research on attractiveness bias for juristic judgments and little of this research examines the impact of the attractiveness of the victim/complainant.

It is important to note the aforementioned research separately examined attractiveness bias on blameworthiness of the victim and guilt of the defendant. Research to date has not considered the mediating role played by jurors' blame toward the victim in the relationship between victim attractiveness and the perceived guilt of the defendant. While a couple of studies identified significant negative correlations between blameworthiness of the victim and defendant's guilt (Gerdes et al., 1988; Shechory-Bitton & Zvi, 2016), these studies did not consider how attractiveness affected this relationship. We posit that when jurors determine a defendant is not completely responsible for an assault, then they may be placing part of the responsibility on the victim or elsewhere (e.g., society, chance). As well, we recognize that the impact of attractiveness may vary depending on the gender of the agent under consideration.

The present study explores the mediating role of jurors' blame toward the complainant on the relationship between complainant's attractiveness and judgments of the defendant's guilt. We specifically hypothesize that the attractiveness of the complainant will affect jurors' judgments of blame toward the complainant, which will in turn affect jurors' judgments about guilt of the defendant. Second, we hypothesize this mediating process will vary by gender of the research respondent.

SAMPLING AND PROCEDURES

Data for this study were collected from surveys of students attending a large urban state university in the Midwestern US. The focus of the survey was to examine attractiveness bias in mock jurors' perceptions of domestic and sexual assault against women. Factorial survey design, a quasi-experimental approach often used in psychology and other social sciences for examining judgments of social situations (see Rossi & Nock, 1982), was utilized to randomly assign images of complainants, extralegal factors of complainant's race, and mitigating and aggravating factors of criminal history, specifically suspected intoxication, injury severity, and presence of witnesses (except in sexual assault scenarios), within a written description of details for the assault vignettes. Hence, each vignette represented a random construction of all specified extralegal and legal factors.

The attractiveness of the complainants' images was pre-tested on a separate sample of similar students at the university. Computer software (FaceGen© Modeller) was used to generate 99 color images of women appearing to be either Black or White in race, with each image presenting a portrait-style image (full, forward face of head and neck), including similar hairstyles, and displaying a non-smiling or neutral expression. In the pre-test, students were electronically surveyed and asked to rate the attractiveness (scale of 1 to 10) of 35 randomly selected images from the pool of 99 images. The images that received the highest, average, and lowest ratings were selected to represent the attractive, average, and unattractive images, respectively, used in the assault vignettes.

In the fall semester of 2015, students (N = 450) were electronically surveyed about their judgments for the assault vignettes and other beliefs. Two vignettes presented a situation of domestic assault and two described a situation of sexual assault. The design of the vignettes was loosely based on the work of Burke and associates (Burke et al., 1990) for factorial vignettes and physical appearance in that they presented ambiguous assault scenarios in which either the defendant or complainant could be blamed. The assault scenarios were described from police officers' viewpoints upon arrival at the scene and included both the female complainant's and male defendant's perspectives, with no description from witnesses to corroborate either version. Hence, blame and fault are ambiguous and interpreted as "my word against yours." After reading each vignette, students were asked to indicate the degree of blame for the complainant and defendant and what the punishment level should be for the defendant.

MEASUREMENT

Dependent Variables

The two dependent (endogenous) variables are self-reported opinions/judgments of the *blame of complainant* (domestic violence or DV: $M = 3.31$, $SD = 2.25$; sexual assault: $M = 1.32$, $SD = 2.18$) and *guilt of defendant* (DV: $M = 6.06$, $SD = 2.36$; sexual assault: $M = 7.70$, $SD = 2.11$) in the domestic and sexual assault scenarios. Responses ranged from 0 = not blameworthy/guilty to 9 = blameworthy/guilty.

Independent Variables

The key independent (exogenous) variable of interest is the experimental treatment condition of attractiveness. As described above, respondents were randomly assigned one of three conditions for the complainant's facial appearance: attractive, average, or unattractive. This multicategorical variable was dummy coded (0/1) into two variables for the analyses: *attractive* (DV: $M = .33$, $SD = .47$; sexual assault: $M = .38$, $SD = .49$) and *unattractive* (DV: $M = .30$, $SD = .46$; sexual assault: $M = .32$, $SD = .47$). The reference category was average appearance.

Other Covariates

Several covariates for the respondent's demographic characteristics and the crime scenario extralegal and legal factors were included in the analyses. These covariates include: gender of the respondents, race of the respondents, and characteristics of the assault scenario (race of the complainant, intoxication of the complainant, intoxication of the defendant, prior calls to the residence and criminal history of the defendant, presence of witnesses, and level of injury sustained by the complainant).

STATISTICAL ANALYSIS

Path analyses were conducted to examine the mediating role of blame of the complainant on the relationship between attractiveness (attractive vs. average and unattractive vs. average) and judgments of guilt for the defendant. Group-based models were estimated to examine gender differences in the mediation model.

RESULTS

Descriptive statistics for the key variables of interest are reported in Table 7.1. A single-factor ANOVA on the guilt of defendant measure indicates no significant mean differences in attractiveness for domestic assault, $F(2, 502) = .39$, $p = .68$, but marginally significant mean differences for sexual assault, $F(2, 444) = 2.98$, $p = .05$. Pairwise comparisons between means reveal that those assigned an attractive image of the complainant ($M = 7.92$) placed significantly more guilt on the defendant for the sexual assault scenario than those assigned an average image ($M = 7.33$). Thus, it seems perceptions of guilt of the defendant were affected

TABLE 7.1. *Descriptive Statistics for Attractiveness Bias Study*

| | | Domestic assault | | | | |
| | | Blame complainant | | Guilt of defendant | | |
	n	*M*	*SD*	*M*	*SD*	*M**
Attractive	167	3.44	2.31	6.07	2.37	6.10
Average	186	3.35	2.32	5.86	2.40	5.86
Unattractive	152	3.29	2.12	5.90	2.29	5.87
All Groups Combined	505	3.36	2.25	5.94	2.36	5.94
		Sexual assault				
		Blame complainant		Guilt of defendant		
	n	*M*	*SD*	*M*	*SD*	*M**
Attractive	171	1.13	1.95	7.92	1.71	7.81
Average	126	1.46	2.30	7.33	2.44	7.39
Unattractive	150	1.49	2.41	7.73	2.21	7.81
All groups combined	447	1.34	2.21	7.69	2.11	7.67

$M*$ = adjusted mean, adjusted to the sample mean of blame of complainant.

by the attractiveness of the complainant in a limited way. Whether blame of the complainant is one of the mechanisms driving the attractiveness bias on perceptions of guilt is examined next.

Mediation Model of Attractiveness Bias for Guilt

It was hypothesized that complainant's attractiveness would directly affect perceived guilt of the defendant for domestic and sexual assault scenarios, and indirectly affect guilt through blame placed on the complainant. The path analyses for a mediation model of attractiveness on guilt through blame controlled for the effects of respondents' gender and race, along with vignette characteristics for complainant race, intoxication of both complainant and defendant, defendant's prior criminal history, severity of injury the complainant sustained, and presence of witnesses (for the domestic assault vignettes only); for simplicity in reporting the path models, the effects of the covariates are not reported in this chapter.

As shown in Figure 7.1, mediation models were estimated for the effect of being assigned an attractive or unattractive image of the complainant

(A) Domestic assault (*n* = 422)

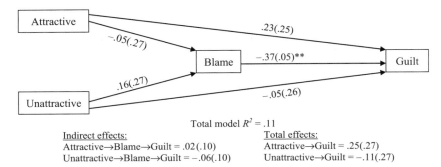

Indirect effects:
Attractive→Blame→Guilt = .02(.10)
Unattractive→Blame→Guilt = −.06(.10)

Total effects:
Attractive→Guilt = .25(.27)
Unattractive→Guilt = −.11(.27)

(B) Sexual assault (*n* = 410)

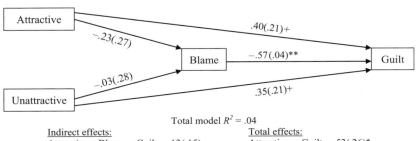

Indirect effects:
Attractive→Blame→ Guilt = .13(.15)
Unattractive→Blame→ Guilt = .02(.17)

Total effects:
Attractive→ Guilt = .53(.26)*
Unattractive→Guilt = .37(.27)

FIGURE 7.1. Mediation model results for attractiveness of complainant condition (attractive or unattractive vs. average) on perceived guilt of defendant, mediated by blame of complainant. Unstandardized coefficients are reported (standard errors in parentheses). Covariates were controlled for, but are not presented in the model. +$p < .$10; *$p < .$05; **$p < .$01.

(reference category = average) on mock jurors' judgments of the defendant's guilt for domestic and sexual assault scenarios, mediated by jurors' judgments of the complainant's blame for the incident. Blame of the complainant was inversely related to guilt of the defendant for both forms of assault. In other words, when mock jurors attributed more blame to the complainant, they concurrently assigned less guilt to the defendant.

In addition, within the domestic assault vignettes (Model A in Figure 7.1), the attractiveness condition had no significant direct effect on guilt of the defendant, nor did it indirectly affect guilt through blame of the complainant. However, within the sexual assault vignettes (Model B in Figure 7.1), marginal direct effects indicated that attractiveness does affect guilt determination of the defendant. Specifically, compared to those assigned an average-looking complainant, those assigned an attractive or unattractive complainant's image were marginally more likely to find the defendant guilty for the sexual assault. (It should be noted the effects of the attractive and unattractive conditions were significant below the $p = .05$ level when the covariates were excluded.) These findings suggest attractiveness of the complainant has a weak direct impact on perceived guilt of the defendant, controlling for respondent's race and gender and key extralegal and legal factors related to the case. As such, the results support previous research finding no attractiveness bias on juristic judgments when considering the victim's/complainant's appearance.

Gendered Effect of Mediation Model of Attractiveness Bias for Guilt

Given findings in prior research that the gender of the juror influences the attractiveness bias effect on juristic judgments, we examined the mediation model across gender of respondents. Results for the gender-based path analyses for domestic assault yielded no significant effects for the attractiveness condition by gender; therefore, those findings are not reported.

However, as seen in Figure 7.2, gender differences in the mediation model for sexual assault were found. Among male respondents, no attractiveness bias on blame toward the victim or guilt of the defendant was found. For women in the study, though, attractiveness mattered. Compared to female respondents assigned average-looking complainants, women assigned images of attractive complainants were significantly more likely to find the defendant guilty of sexual assault. This finding underscores the importance of considering gendered effects when examining the extralegal impact of complainant's attractiveness. Furthermore, these findings support the likeability perspective (Alicke, 2000; Mitchell & Byrne, 1973) that purports jurors identify better – and in this case wish to protect – with those they find more socially appealing or good. As such, the findings also contradict the "Beliefs in a Just World" perspective (Lerner, 1965, 1980), which asserts that jurors place more blame on attractive victims based on the need to invent some unknown reason or justification for the tragedy befalling the victim. That is, sexual assault would not occur for "good" women because good things happen to good people; therefore, women who are sexually assaulted must have done something to deserve it (Jones & Aronson, 1973). In support of the Beliefs

(A) Males (*n* =105)

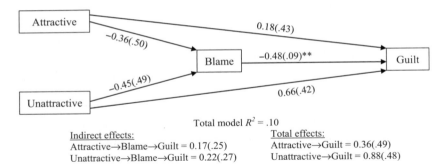

Total model R^2 = .10

Indirect effects:	Total effects:
Attractive→Blame→Guilt = 0.17(.25)	Attractive→Guilt = 0.36(.49)
Unattractive→Blame→Guilt = 0.22(.27)	Unattractive→Guilt = 0.88(.48)

(B) Females (*n* = 305)

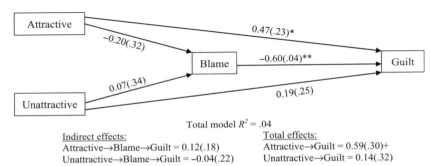

Total model R^2 = .04

Indirect effects:	Total effects:
Attractive→Blame→Guilt = 0.12(.18)	Attractive→Guilt = 0.59(.30)+
Unattractive→Blame→Guilt = -0.04(.22)	Unattractive→Guilt = 0.14(.32)

FIGURE 7.2. Gender-based mediation model for sexual assault results for attractiveness of complainant condition (attractive or unattractive vs. average) on perceived guilt of defendant, mediated by blame of complainant. Unstandardized coefficients are reported (standard errors in parentheses). Covariates were controlled for, but are not presented in the model. +*p* < .10; **p* < .05; ***p* < .01.

in a Just World perspective, Villemur and Hyde (1983) reported mock jurors were less likely to find defendants guilty of sexual assault of attractive complainants, yet our findings contradict the Beliefs in a Just World perspective (see Figure 7.2).

CONCLUSIONS, LIMITATIONS, AND IMPLICATIONS

In contrast to the underlying principles of justice, equity, and fairness that philosophically shape the criminal justice system, the system is not always impartial; complainants and defendants often are judged based on extra-legal factors such as their race, gender, socioeconomics, or age.

Individuals involved in the criminal justice system are also judged by their physical attractiveness. While research suggests attractiveness is an inconsistent and weak factor affecting jurors' decisionmaking, it still matters.

We tested the hypothesis that complainants' attractiveness directly affects guilt of the defendant for domestic and sexual assault scenarios. Guilt of the defendant was not influenced by the complainants' attractiveness in cases of domestic assault but was affected, marginally, by complainants' attractiveness in cases of sexual assault. In other words, attractiveness of the complainant has a limited direct impact on perceived guilt of the defendants. When we explored this direct effect across gender of the mock juror (student), attractiveness only mattered for female jurors for the sexual assault scenarios. Interestingly, women were more likely to perceive the male defendant for the sexual assault scenarios as guilty when the image of the female complainant was more attractive compared to average, but there was no substantive difference in guilty verdicts when comparing average and unattractive complainants.

We also hypothesized that complainants' attractiveness indirectly determines defendants' guilt via blame placed on a complainant. While blame for the complainant was consistently inversely related to guilt of the defendant, blameworthiness of the complainant did not act as a mediating variable in the model, for either domestic assault or sexual assault or for men versus women.

A number of limitations are present in this study. For example, the computer-generated images used to depict complainants' attractiveness may yield problems. Although skin tone was fairly easily ascertained in the color images presented to participants in the study, attractiveness assessments were rather artificial given the technology of computer-generated images. Future studies would benefit from the use of more realistic images, for instance, actual photos of human faces illustrating varying levels of attractiveness or photos of human faces that had been cosmetically altered to represent varying levels of attractiveness.

In considering how this study's findings have implications for criminal justice policy, it is recommended that juries and judges be made aware of the manner in which complainants' levels of attractiveness affect judgments about the complainants' blameworthiness, as well as judgments about defendants' guilt. In other words, blame assigned to complainants and guilt assigned to defendants should be independent of the victims' level of attractiveness. This is true not only for cases of sexual and domestic assault as discussed here, but a recognition of the meaninglessness of attractiveness should be applied regardless of offense type.

The absence of strong effects linking attractiveness of the victim to blameworthiness and to guilt determination of the defendant is confirmatory of previous research. While we found only marginal effects of complainant attractiveness on blameworthiness and guilt, which were specifically limited to sexual assault, even this modest impact is a contribution toward better understanding how appearance impacts judgments regarding sexual assaults by the public within the court system.

References

Ahola, A. S., Christianson, S. Å., & Hellström, Å. (2009). Justice needs a blindfold: Effects of gender and attractiveness on prison sentences and attributions of personal characteristics in a judicial process. *Psychiatry, Psychology, and Law*, 16, S90–S100.

Alicke, M. D. (2000). Culpable control and the psychology of blame. *Psychological Bulletin*, 126, 556–574.

Bergeron, C. E. & McKelvie, S. J. (2004). Effects of defendant age on severity of punishment for difference crimes. *Journal of Social Psychology*, 144, 75–90.

Burke, D. M., Ames, M. A., Etherington, R., & Pietsch, J. (1990). Effects of victim's and defendant's physical attractiveness on the perception of responsibility in an ambiguous domestic violence case. *Journal of Family Violence*, 5, 199–207.

Calhoun, L. G., Selby, J. W., Cann, A., & Keller, G. T. (1978). The effects of victim physical attractiveness and sex of respondent on social reactions to victims of rape. *British Journal of Social and Clinical Psychology*, 17, 191–192.

Callan, M. J., Powell, N. G., & Ellard, J. H. (2007). The consequences of victim physical attractiveness on reactions to injustice: The role of observers' belief in a just world. *Social Justice Research*, 20, 433–456.

Castellow, W. A., Wuensch, K. L., & Moore, C. H. (1990). Effects of physical attractiveness of the plaintiff and defendant in sexual harassment judgments. *Journal of Social Behavior and Personality*, 5, 547–562.

Darby, B. W. & Jeffers, D. (1988). The effects of defendant and juror attractiveness on simulated courtroom trial decisions. *Social Behavior and Personality*, 16, 39–50.

Dion, K., Berscheid, E., & Walster, E. (1972). What is beautiful is good. *Journal of Personality and Social Psychology*, 24, 285–290.

Erian, M., Lin, C., Patel, N., Neal, A., & Geiselman, R. E. (1998). Juror verdicts as a function of victim and defendant attractiveness in sexual assault cases. *American Journal of Forensic Psychology*, 16, 25–40.

Gerdes, E. P., Dammann, E. J., & Heilig, K. E. (1988). Perceptions of rape victims and assailants: Effects of physical attractiveness, acquaintance, and subject gender. *Sex Roles*, 19, 141–153.

Hodell, E. C., Wasarhaley, N. E., Lynch, K. R., & Golding, J. M. (2014). Mock juror gender biases and perceptions of self-defense claims in intimate partner homicide. *Journal of Family Violence*, 29, 495–506.

Jacobson, M. B. (1981). Effects of victim's and defendant's physical attractiveness on subjects' judgments in a rape case. *Sex Roles*, 7, 247–255.

Jacobson, M. B. & Popovich, P. M. (1983). Victim attractiveness and perceptions of responsibility in an ambiguous rape case. *Psychology of Women Quarterly*, 8, 100–104.

Jones, C. & Aronson, E. (1973). Attribution of fault to a rape victim as a function of respectability of the victim. *Journal of Personality and Social Psychology*, 26, 415–419.

Kerr, N. L. (1978). Beautiful and blameless: Effects of victim attractiveness and responsibility on mock jurors' verdicts. *Personality and Social Psychology Bulletin*, 4, 479–482.

Lerner, M. J. (1965). Evaluation of performance as a function of performer's reward and attractiveness. *Journal of Personality and Social Psychology*, 1, 355–360.

(1980). *The belief in a just world: A fundamental delusion.* New York, NY: Plenum Press.

MacCoun, R. J. (1990). The emergence of extralegal bias during jury deliberation. *Criminal Justice and Behavior*, 17, 303–314.

Mitchell, H. E. & Byrne, D. (1973). The defendant's dilemma: Effects of jurors' attitudes and authoritarianism on judicial decisions. *Journal of Personality and Social Psychology*, 25, 123–129.

Moore, C. H., Wuensch, K. L., Hedges, R. M., & Castellow, W. A. (1994). The effects of physical attractiveness and social desirability on judgments regarding a sexual harassment case. *Journal of Social Behavior and Personality*, 9, 715–730.

Rossi, P. H. & Nock, S. L. (Eds.). (1982). *Measuring social judgments: The factorial survey approach.* Beverly Hills, CA: Sage Publications.

Sargent, M. J. & Bradfield, A. L. (2004). Race and information processing in criminal trials: Does the defendant's race affect how the facts are evaluated? *Personality and Social Psychology Bulletin*, 30, 995–1008.

Seligman, C., Brickman, J., & Koulack, D. (1977). Rape and physical attractiveness: Assigning responsibility to victims. *Journal of Personality*, 45, 554–563.

Shechory-Britton, M. & Zvi, L. (2016). Does offenders' facial attractiveness affect police officers' judgment? *Psychiatry, Psychology and Law*, 23, 588–601.

Stewart, J. E., II. (1980). Defendant's attractiveness as a factor in the outcome of criminal trials: An observational study. *Journal of Applied Social Psychology*, 10, 348–361.

Thornton, B. (1977). Effect of rape victim's attractiveness in a jury simulation. *Personality and Social Psychology Bulletin*, 3, 666–669.

Thornton, B. & Ryckman, R. M. (1983). The influence of a rape victim's physical attractiveness on observers' attributions of responsibility. *Human Relations*, 36, 549–562.

Villemur, N. K. & Hyde, J. S. (1983). Effects of sex of defense attorney, sex or juror, and age and attractiveness of the victim on mock juror decision making in a rape case. *Sex Roles*, 9, 879–889.

8

Do Attractive Women "Get Away" with Traffic Violations? An Observational Study of Police Responses to Traffic Stops

Brent Teasdale, Taylor Gann, and Dean Dabney

INTRODUCTION

Surprisingly little empirical work has examined the effects of attractiveness on police decisionmaking. Advancing thinking in this regard requires one to enlist a broad tapestry of extant literature. To begin with, a large literature exists documenting the extensive social benefits of being more physically attractive (Hosoda, Stone-Romero, & Coats, 2003; Jackson, Hunter, & Hodge, 1995; Lorenzo, Biesanz, & Human, 2010; Mulford, Orbell, Shatto, & Stockard, 1998; Patzer, 2012). These studies show physical attractiveness to be predictive of outcomes such as increased earnings, marital stability (Jaeger, 2011), perceived competence (Jackson et al., 1995), and overall positive health outcomes (Mathes & Kahn, 1975).

Within a criminal justice context, a small body of research has focused on how physical appearance is predictive of courtroom outcomes (e.g., Johnson and King, 2017). A number of studies have shown victim and defendant physical attractiveness to be predictive of the outcomes of rape trials (Feild, 1978; Feild, 1979; Gerdes, Dammann, & Heilig, 1988). It has long been established that police processes function as a funnel selecting those who appear before the courts (President's Commission on Law Enforcement and Administration of Justice, 1967). It stands to reason that there may be a narrowing of the range of appearance traits that occurs before courtroom actors ever see defendants. Furthermore, there is pop culture wisdom suggesting that more attractive women "get away" with traffic violations, by not receiving tickets. In this chapter, we systematically examine this pop culture wisdom using quantitative data coded from an observational study we conducted with a metropolitan police department in the southeastern United States.

LITERATURE REVIEW

Prior literature suggests that physically attractive individuals typically have better health outcomes, are perceived to be socially competent and likeable, and are viewed more positively compared to their "unattractive" counterparts (Patry, 2008). These perceptions are formulated through facial features that incite snap judgments of an individual's character (Johnson & King, 2017). Benefits associated with this physical attractiveness bias include increased monetary earnings, status attainment, and overall well-being. Moreover, these benefits are present not only in daily life, but are reproduced in sentencing and other judicial outcomes within the legal system (Darby & Jeffers, 1988; Mazzella & Feingold, 1994; Patry, 2008; Stewart, 1985). Prior research has documented the significance of physical appearance bias in a number of judicial arenas such as perceived guilt, less severe punishments, and outcomes for rape trials. For example, Efran (1974) examined the extent to which attractiveness bias influences potential outcomes, based on the characteristics that jurors believed were important to evaluate in potential defendants. Initial survey results suggested that a defendant's character and prior history should be the driving factors influencing court decisions; however a simulated jury task demonstrated the importance of attractiveness over and above these important factors. That is, defendants who were perceived as more attractive were viewed with less certainty of guilt, and received less severe recommendations for punishment (Efran, 1974).

In addition to perceived guilt, other research has emphasized the importance of appearance bias in sentencing severity (Leventhal & Krate, 1977; Sigall & Ostrove, 1975; Stewart, 1980). In a recent study on facial profiling and punishment, Johnson and King (2017) found that physically attractive individuals experienced 33 percent lower odds of being sentenced to imprisonment as compared to their less attractive counterparts. Physical attractiveness remained significant when controlling for other factors that may affect sentencing outcomes such as presumptive sentence, criminal history, current offense type, having a private attorney, and defendant race.

Similar to sentencing outcomes and perceptions of guilt, appearance bias has been documented to play a significant role in judicial outcomes for different types of crime (Castellow, Wuensch, & Moore, 1990;

Maeder, Yamamoto, & Saliba, 2015; Sigall & Ostrove, 1975; Zebrowitz & McDonald, 1991). With regard to sensitive trials that involve crimes such as rape, research has shown the significant effects of physical appearance on both sentencing outcomes and attribution of blame to rape and sexual assault victims (Castellow et al., 1990; Maeder, Yamamoto, & Saliba, 2015; Thornton & Ryckman, 1983). For example, Thornton and Ryckman (1983) examined the relationship between victim attractiveness and blame attribution for rape. Analysis found that attractive victims were not only assigned less responsibility for their assault, but unattractive victims were considered to possess a more provocative appearance that contributed to their assault. This appearance bias toward rape and sexual assault victims has also been shown to be important in juror decisionmaking for sexual assault trials (Maeder et al., 2015). One study explored the combined effects of sex and victim physical attractiveness on sexual assault outcomes. The results demonstrated a positive correlation between male jurors' certainty of guilt and the unattractiveness of the defendant. That is, male jurors perceived defendants to be guilty more often if they were viewed as unattractive (Maeder et al., 2015).

This significant relationship can also be seen for other types of crime (Castellow et al., 1990; Sigall & Ostrove, 1975; Zebrowitz & McDonald, 1991). For example, Sigall and Ostrove (1975) found differences in appearance bias across different types of crime. The authors assigned types of crime to two groups: attractiveness-related and unrelated to attractiveness (i.e., swindling and burglary, respectively). The analysis denoted that attractive offenders were given lenient sentences for crimes unrelated to attractiveness (Sigall & Ostrove, 1975). Conversely, attractive defendants received harsher punishments for attractiveness-related crimes.

Appearance bias has also been documented in a civil court context. Namely, Zebrowitz and McDonald (1991) examined different tort claims and how attractiveness played a role in case outcomes of a small claims court. They found that attractive plaintiffs were more likely to win their cases when they were accusing an unattractive defendant (Zebrowitz & McDonald, 1991). Similar findings were found for civil cases involving sexual harassment claims (Castellow et al., 1990).

Before individuals make it to the legal system, police officers serve as a funnel for inclusion in the criminal justice system (President's Commission on Law Enforcement and Administration of Justice, 1967; Smith, Visher, & Davidson, 1984). There are several determinants that influence an officer's decision to arrest, and ultimately appearance within the courts.

These factors include: race, sex, suspect demeanor, and seriousness of the offense. Studies have highlighted the significance of racial bias in policing (Bronson et al., 2003; Smith & Visher, 1981; Smith et al., 1984; Weitzer & Tuch, 2005). In addition to race, research has also documented the effects of gender on police discretion (Smith & Visher, 1981; Visher, 1983). That is, females are less likely to be arrested when they adhere to stereotypical behaviors centered on gender norms (Visher, 1983). All of these determinants may be serving as a narrowing effect for inclusion within the criminal justice system. Stated differently, physical characteristics of suspects may serve as cues for developing perceptions of attractiveness, which, in turn, may impact police discretion.

Although there is not much research on appearance bias in police discretion, one recent study examined the influence of physical appearance through hip-hop culture and discretionary outcomes in policing (Dabney, Teasdale, Ishoy, Gann, & Berry, 2017). This study found that suspects who embodied stereotypical hip-hop attire (i.e., baggy pants, gold teeth, having dreadlocks, etc.) experienced higher odds of receiving a ticket or being arrested as opposed to the officer taking no action. Drawing upon the same dataset, the present study examines how attractiveness could have the same impacts on the discretionary actions of police officers. That is, there is a pop culture myth asserting attractive women "get away" from tickets owing to appearance bias. Employing observational data collected within a metropolitan police jurisdiction, this study will examine the relationship between perceived physical attractiveness and police discretionary outcomes.

METHODS

Sample

The data for this chapter were drawn from a larger data collection effort focused on discretionary outcomes within a large metropolitan police department located in the Southeast. The department employs over 200 employees who provide comprehensive law enforcement service for a population of slightly less than 100,000 residents, spread across an area of just less than 100 square miles. The jurisdiction experiences robust levels of crime as evidenced by the fact that, in 2016, there were over 7,000 reported Part I offenses recorded by the department. More than 1,000 of these reports involved violent offenses.

Over the course of a 35-month period (2014–2017), a team of trained research assistants participated in ride-alongs with police officers employed by the department under study. This effort was facilitated by a structured data template designed to systematically record the events that occurred during all formal police–citizen contacts. This included all officer- and citizen-initiated interactions with a person in a vehicle or on foot. Data collection was restricted to interactions where a crime was alleged to have occurred and a suspect was present who might be subjected to a formal police action. The data template was designed to capture a detailed record of a host of legal and extralegal factors shown to be predictive of police decisionmaking. These included various aspects of the suspect's physical appearance (i.e., race, sex, age, attire, grooming) and behavior (suspect demeanor, level of compliance, etc.), the demographics of the officer (i.e., race, sex, and age), relevant legal factors (the seriousness of the offense, suspect's prior criminal history, mandatory search or arrest policies, etc.) and the formal outcome of the incident (no action, verbal warning, citation, arrest). All data was captured using survey software that was installed on smartphones or tablets and allowed for daily uploading to a central database file. Ride-alongs were scheduled during all days and shifts, and were conducted with officers assigned to patrol, traffic, and crime suppression units. A total of 934 formal interactions between officers and citizens were recorded by the team of 23 observers over the course of the 35-month data collection effort. For the purposes of this chapter, we use data from 183 observations collected when a suspected traffic offense was committed.

Prior to data collection, each research assistant underwent multiple training sessions. These sessions included training on how to access and use the online software, how to code suspect behavior and subsequent interactions with officers, proper ride-along etiquette, and a safety debriefing with the police department. These efforts were supplemented by several training sessions aimed to ensure inter-rater reliability. This was accomplished by conducting multiple tests in coding suspect appearance where several photographs and social observations of a variety of individuals were coded and a consensus was reached by the research staff.

The jurisdiction is unique, in that it is majority African-American. Since our ride-along data was producing a preponderance of cases that were either Black or Latino, we went to great lengths to examine the jurisdiction's demographic make-up. First, research assistants were dispatched to the parking lot of two Walmart stores located in the jurisdiction to develop an unbiased demographic profile of the population.

We reasoned that these retail locations attract a high volume of persons on foot, in personal vehicles, and mass transit riders who represent a broad cross-section of the local citizenry. Research assistants systematically documented the age, race, and sex of 3,073 individuals entering the stores. This data collection effort lasted a month and was spread across all days of the week and at various time intervals. The results of these observations suggested that 82.4 percent of the area population was African-American, 7.5 percent were Hispanic, and the other 8 percent comprised of Whites and Asian/Pacific Islanders. Slightly more than half (52.2 percent) of the persons entering Walmart were females and the average age was assessed to be in the 30–34-year-old range. Second, we pulled 2010 census data for the study jurisdiction, and found that these numbers closely approximated the demographic patterns produced through our Walmart data collection efforts. In other work (Dabney and Ishoy, 2016), we have documented that there is surprisingly little racial or gender bias going on in the jurisdiction.

Measures

The outcome measure was recorded in terms of whether the officer issued a traffic citation or not. The key independent variable, physical attractiveness, was coded on a 10-point Likert-type scale with anchors of Very Attractive (10) and Very Unattractive (1). Independent observers coded their assessment of the citizen, and then they asked officers to rate the citizen from their own perspective. These two responses correlated highly ($r = .77$ for men and $r = .72$ for women). The results presented later in this chapter are based upon the officer's subjective perception of the citizen, since the officer is ultimately the one deciding whether to issue a ticket or not, and the results from the independent observer mirror those presented in this chapter. In addition to the dependent and independent variables of interest, we also include in the analysis below information on the sex and race of the citizen, and the sex, race, and age of the officer. Given the small sample size of traffic stops ($n = 183$), we chose not to include other available predictors in the models detailed below.

RESULTS

As shown in Table 8.1, in most circumstances (69 percent), officers gave a traffic citation to the citizen. However, there was some evidence of discretion, as 31 percent of encounters resulted in only a verbal warning

TABLE 8.1. *Descriptive Data for the Ride-Alongs (N = 183)*

	Mean or %	Standard Deviation	Min	Max
Ticketed	69.4%		0	1
Attractiveness	4.48	2.18	1	10
Female	42.6%		0	1
Black/Brown Citizen	89.0%		0	1
Male Officer	76.5%		0	1
Black Officer	70.0%		0	1
Officer Age	32.1	6.02	23	52

or no action taken. Most of the citizens encountered for traffic violations were male (57.4 percent). This represents a slight overrepresentation of males relative to the baseline demographic data detailed above. As we noted earlier, since the demographics of the jurisdiction skew heavily toward minorities, it is not surprising that most of the citizens encountered for traffic violations were nonwhite (89 percent). The observed officers were most male (76.5 percent), Black (70 percent), and averaged 32 years of age. The average citizen was about 4.5 on a 1–10 scale, suggesting the average person is pretty close to the midpoint on our attractiveness scale, based on officer's perceptions. Most citizens clustered within two points of the center, indicating the typical person was between a 2.5 and a 6.5 in attractiveness.

Officers did not discriminate based on the sex of the driver in terms of traffic citations: 68.6 percent of males received a citation, while 70.5 percent of females did. This difference was not statistically significant. Moreover, officers did not perceive the women they encountered as significantly more attractive than the men. Women were on average rated a 4.5, while men were on average rated a 4.25. Again, this difference was not statistically significant.

There does, however, appear to be an attractiveness bias in the disposition of traffic cases in our sample. That is, more attractive men seem to be less likely to get a traffic citation than less attractive men. There does not appear to be a similar process at work for women. As shown in Table 8.2, the average man receiving a citation was 1.5 points lower in attractiveness than the average man who did not receive a traffic citation. This difference was statistically significant ($p < .01$). No difference in the average attractiveness of cited and not cited women was shown in the data.

In order to probe this pattern further, we examined whether it was male or female officers that produced this pattern for male and female

TABLE 8.2. *Average Officer Perceptions of Citizen Attractiveness Split by Sex and Ticketed*

	N	Ticketed	Not Ticketed	T
Male	105	3.89	5.27	2.98**
Female	78	4.73	4.61	.81 NS

NS = not significant, t statistic tests whether the difference between the ticketed mean and the not ticketed mean is statistically different in the population, for males and females separately.

citizens. The patterns held for both male and female officers. Next, we examined whether it was Black or non-Black officers that produced these patterns. Again the patterns held for both Black and non-Black officers alike. Thus we conclude that it is truly the attractiveness (or not) of the male citizen that is producing these findings; whereas the attractiveness of female traffic violators seems irrelevant to their receipt of a citation.

CONCLUSIONS

We highlight that pop culture wisdom does not always translate into reality. In fact, in this case, we find the opposite of what pop culture wisdom would suggest. The attractiveness of women seems largely irrelevant to the police officer's decision to issue a citation. In contrast, it is the attractiveness of the men that significantly reduced the likelihood of getting a traffic citation. This was based on the officer's evaluation of whether the suspect was attractive or not, but the coding of the citizen's attractiveness by our trained independent observers mirrored this pattern. The pattern held regardless of officer characteristics, as well.

The benefits of attractiveness generally have been well established in the literature. More attractive people earn greater salaries, have better wellbeing scores, greater marital stability, are perceived as more trustworthy, and are less likely to receive punishment. There is no doubt that being more attractive is a key characteristic that creates social stratification (Berry, 2008). In this chapter, we examine whether these benefits appear in police decisions to impose traffic citations, and whether those benefits are gendered. Indeed, we find there are benefits, but contrary to pop culture wisdom, we find that the benefits of attractiveness are primarily for men, not women in our study.

We interpret this finding in terms of what sociologists have termed intersectionality (Crenshaw, 1991; McCall, 2005). That is, we cannot simply consider the sex of the citizen in isolation. Recall that we earlier described the jurisdiction as primarily Black and Latino. Most of the officer encounters with traffic violators involved Black male officers and Black or Latino citizens. Thus, we are talking about minority men and women in this chapter, not just men and women. Consequently, it is important to consider what it means to be an attractive Black man, in this context. We speculate that it may mean "conventional" and therefore not ticket-worthy. In our other empirical work, for example, we have documented that unconventional appearance traits, those associated with hip-hop culture significantly increase the risk of arrest, holding constant a large number of both legally relevant and extralegal factors (Dabney et al., 2017). It may be that the converse is also true. That is, while unconventional appearance may result in more formal criminal justice sanction, conventional appearances may lessen the likelihood of those sanctions. What it means to be an attractive Black woman in this jurisdiction may be different. It may not connote conventionality, as others have discussed. Black women's sexuality and perhaps their physical attractiveness is often hypersexualized (DuRant et al., 1997; Turner, 2011). For example, in an analysis of the main characters in music videos, Turner (2011) found that African-American women were more likely to be in provocative clothing (36.3 percent) than White women (22.7 percent). The pattern was even more exaggerated for background characters (those who were not the lead-actor in the video). Here, Turner finds that 68.7 percent of African-American and 30.9 percent of White background characters were dressed in provocative clothing. If this influenced officer's perceptions of what is attractive for Black women, this nontraditional conceptualization may have influenced Black male officers to view more attractive Black women as no more and no less deserving of a ticket than less attractive Black women. If, on the other hand, attractive Black men were viewed as conventional, perhaps this explains their lower rate of ticketing compared with less attractive/conventional Black men.

Another possible explanation is the overstatement of the pop culture myth that attractive women "get away" with more. Perhaps, because this myth is widely acknowledged, officers police women differently in order not to adhere to the stereotype. Another possibility is our choice of outcome. As Visher (1983) has indicated, women who engage in gender nonconforming behaviors are punished, while women who are gender conforming may be more likely to avoid punishment. Since traffic violations are not particularly gendered activities, this may have had an influence on our results, as well. Finally, the choice of jurisdiction is key here.

We collected data in a primarily African-American jurisdiction, with primarily African-American law enforcement officers. It would be interesting for future work to see if the patterns found in this study generalize to White populations and White officers. In addition, it would be interesting to see if these patterns hold in more suburban and rural jurisdictions, since most of the current study is in an urban area. Finally, we leave you with the thought that pop culture wisdom may or may not have truth to it, but empirical research is an essential tool in challenging these untested beliefs.

References

Berry, B. (2008). *The power of looks: Social stratification of physical appearance.* Hampshire, UK: Ashgate.

Bronson, C., Lawson, K., Clingman, J., Gerhardstein, A., Gibson, J., Greenwood, S., & Mingo, R. P. (2003). Racial Bias and Policing. Retrieved December 20, 2017, from: www.acluohio.org/assets/issues/PolicePractices/CincinnatiAgreement/Racial_Bias_and_Policing.pdf.

Castellow, W. A., Wuensch, K. L., & Moore, C. H. (1990). Effects of physical attractiveness of the plaintiff and defendant in sexual harassment judgements. *Journal of Social Behavior and Personality,* 5(6), 547.

Crenshaw, K. (1991). Mapping the margins: Intersectionality, identity politics, and violence against women of color. *Stanford Law Review,* 43(6), 1241–1299.

Dabney, D. A. & Ishoy, G. A. (2016). *An audit of the racial profiling data collected by the Fulton County Police Department from 2008–2014.* Atlanta, GA: Georgia State University.

Dabney, D. A., Teasdale, B., Ishoy, G. A., Gann, T., & Berry, B. (2017). Policing in a largely minority jurisdiction: The influence of appearance characteristics associated with contemporary hip-hop culture on police decision-making. *Justice Quarterly,* 34(7), 1310–1338.

Darby, B. W. & Jeffers, D. (1988). The effects of defendant and juror attractiveness on simulated courtroom trial decisions. *Social Behavior and Personality: An International Journal,* 16(1), 39–50.

DuRant, R. H., Rome, E. S., Rich, M., Allred, E., Emans, S. J., & Woods, E. R. (1997). Tobacco and alcohol use behaviors portrayed in music videos: A content analysis. *American Journal of Public Health,* 87(7), 1131–1135.

Efran, M. G. (1974). The effect of physical appearance on the judgment of guilt, interpersonal attraction, and severity of recommended punishment in a simulated jury task. *Journal of Research in Personality,* 8(1), 45–54.

Feild, H. S. (1978). Juror background characteristics and attitudes toward rape: Correlates of jurors' decisions in rape trials. *Law and Human Behavior,* 2(2), 73.

(1979). Rape trials and jurors' decisions: A psycholegal analysis of the effects of victim, defendant, and case characteristics. *Law and Human Behavior,* 3(4), 261.

Gerdes, E. P., Dammann, E. J., & Heilig, K. E. (1988). Perceptions of rape victims and assailants: Effects of physical attractiveness, acquaintance, and subject gender. *Sex Roles*, 19(3), 141–153.

Hosoda, M., Stone-Romero, E. F., & Coats, G. (2003). The effects of physical attractiveness on job-related outcomes: A meta-analysis of experimental studies. *Personnel Psychology*, 56(2), 431–462.

Jackson, L. A., Hunter, J. E., & Hodge, C. N. (1995). Physical attractiveness and intellectual competence: A meta-analytic review. *Social Psychology Quarterly*, 108–122.

Jaeger, M. M. (2011). "A thing of beauty is a joy forever"? Returns to physical attractiveness over the life course. *Social Forces*, 89(3), 983–1003.

Johnson, B. D. & King, R. D. (2017). Facial profiling: Race, physical appearance, and punishment. *Criminology*, 55(3), 520–547.

Leventhal, G. & Krate, R. (1977). Physical attractiveness and severity of sentencing. *Psychological Reports*, 40(1), 315–318.

Lorenzo, G. L., Biesanz, J. C., & Human, L. J. (2010). What is beautiful is good and more accurately understood: Physical attractiveness and accuracy in first impressions of personality. *Psychological Science*, 21(12), 1777–1782.

Maeder, E. M., Yamamoto, S., & Saliba, P. (2015). The influence of defendant race and victim physical attractiveness on juror decision-making in a sexual assault trial. *Psychology, Crime & Law*, 21(1), 62–79.

Mathes, E. W. & Kahn, A. (1975). Physical attractiveness, happiness, neuroticism, and self-esteem. *The Journal of Psychology*, 90(1), 27–30.

Mazzella, R. & Feingold, A. (1994). The effects of physical attractiveness, race, socioeconomic status, and gender of defendants and victims on judgments of mock jurors: A meta-analysis. *Journal of Applied Social Psychology*, 24(15), 1315–1338.

McCall, L. (2005). The complexity of intersectionality. *Signs: Journal of Women in Culture and Society*, 30(3), 1771–1800.

Mulford, M., Orbell, J., Shatto, C., & Stockard, J. (1998). Physical attractiveness, opportunity, and success in everyday exchange. *American Journal of Sociology*, 103(6), 1565–1592.

Patry, M. W. (2008). Attractive but guilty: Deliberation and the physical attractiveness bias. *Psychological Reports*, 102(3), 727–733.

Patzer, G. L. (2012). *The physical attractiveness phenomena*. New York, NY: Plenum Press.

President's Commission on Law Enforcement and Administration of Justice. (1967). *Task Force Report: Science and Technology*. Washington, DC: Government Printing Office.

Sigall, H. & Ostrove, N. (1975). Beautiful but dangerous: Effects of offender attractiveness and nature of the crime on juridic judgment. *Journal of Personality and Social Psychology*, 31(3), 410.

Smith, D. A. & Visher, C. A. (1981). Street-level justice: Situational determinants of police arrest decisions. *Social Problems*, 29(2), 167–177.

Smith, D. A., Visher, C. A., & Davidson, L. A. (1984). Equity and discretionary justice: The influence of race on police arrest decisions. *The Journal of Criminal Law and Criminology (1973)*, 75(1), 234–249.

Stewart, J. E. (1980). Defendant's attractiveness as a factor in the outcome of criminal trials: An observational study. *Journal of Applied Social Psychology*, 10(4), 348–361.

—— (1985). Appearance and punishment: The attraction–leniency effect in the courtroom. *The Journal of Social Psychology*, 125(3), 373–378.

Thornton, B. & Ryckman, R. M. (1983). The influence of a rape victim's physical attractiveness on observers' attributions of responsibility. *Human Relations*, 36(6), 549–561.

Turner, J. S. (2011). Sex and the spectacle of music videos: An examination of the portrayal of race and sexuality in music videos. *Sex Roles*, 64(3–4), 173–191.

Visher, C. A. (1983). Gender, police arrest decisions, and notions of chivalry. *Criminology*, 21(1), 5–28.

Weitzer, R. & Tuch, S. A. (2005). Racially biased policing: Determinants of citizen perceptions. *Social Forces*, 83(3), 1009–1030.

Zebrowitz, L. A. & McDonald, S. M. (1991). The impact of litigants' baby-facedness and attractiveness on adjudications in small claims courts. *Law and Human Behavior*, 15(6), 603–623.

9

The Police "Presence"

Public Service versus Intimidation

Stephen A. Bishopp

The effect of police appearance (e.g., militaristic attire) on citizens' perceptions and behaviors has received only sporadic attention over the last few decades (Simpson, 2017). From prior research, several themes are present and include perceptions of officers by citizens, perceptions of citizens by officers, and situational variables as major correlates that influence one group's perception of the other. Within this body of research, there are two points of departure among academics concerning appearance and its relationship to various police behaviors – police uniforms and citizen/officer race.

Despite disagreements among academics on the direction of the influence, police attire and equipment influence escalation or de-escalation of emotional and behavioral reactions during encounters with the public (Johnson, 2005). Because uniforms and equipment are what citizens see first, their perceptions of police rely on aesthetical factors as much or more than the actions police take during an interaction (Johnson, 2005; Simpson, 2017; Singer & Singer, 1985; Volpp & Lennon, 1988). Though narrowly focused on police attire, this area of police research is vitally important in lieu of recent citizen clashes with police where police respond with military-grade equipment. Over the last few years, the militarization of the police has become a particularly divisive point of contention (Bove & Gavrilova, 2017; Institute for Intergovernmental Research, 2015; Turner & Fox, 2017).

Policing encompasses many functions including patrol, traffic, SWAT (special weapons and tactics; aka police paramilitary units), helicopter pilot, bicycle officer, among others. Each job requires specific uniform schemes to perform the tasks at hand. Examples include patrol officers in

IMAGE 7. Recruitment vehicle, Dallas Police Department, courtesy Sgt Steve Bishopp

IMAGE 8. Dallas Police Department Plain Clothes Unit, Sgt Steve Bishopp center in shorts

traditional police uniforms, bike officers wearing reflective gear and shorts in warm weather, and specialized units clothed in battle-dress uniforms (BDUs). In this way, the incident itself often dictates the appearance – uniforms, weapons, mode of transportation – of police (Simpson & Hipp, 2017). Few variations in police uniforms, however, create more controversy than ones presenting a militaristic appearance (Kraska & Kappeler, 1997; Turner & Fox, 2017). Thus, the first section in this chapter discusses the research on relationship between appearance and police/citizen interaction outcomes (arrests, coercion, [de]escalation, etc.) beginning with a brief history of police militarization (see Images 7 and 8).

A second point of departure for academics is the impact of race on how people perceive police/citizen encounters. After four decades of analyzing the connection between citizen race and the criminal justice system (Warren, Tomaskovic-Devey, Smith, Zingraff, & Mason, 2006), research is beginning to reevaluate the influence of race on police decisionmaking. Race is a prominent fixture in policing research as a predictor of arrest, use-of-force, and deadly force (Dabney, Teasdale, Ishoy, Gann, & Berry, 2017; Jetelina, Jennings, Bishopp, Piquero, & Reingle-Gonzalez, 2017; Klinger, Rosenfeld, Isom, & Deckard, 2016; Miller et al., 2017). Yet, race inhabits a prominent position in academia and is one of the most important predictor variables in policing research (Wu, Sun, & Triplett, 2009). The second section, therefore, examines the prominence of race as a major predictor of perception-based police/citizens interactions.

THE EFFECT OF A MILITARISTIC APPEARANCE ON POLICE–CITIZEN ENCOUNTERS

At the beginning of modern policing in London, England in 1829, an important first step was to distinguish police officers from military personnel. Differentiating the two services meant redesigning the uniform to separate the red and white of the English military and replacing it with a distinctive blue. Despite uniform changes, organizational structures and ranks mirrored the military. Although issuing new directives to change the primary policing mission to crime prevention (Auten, 1981), the London Metropolitan Police retained militaristic organizational structures (e.g., hierarchical rank) and uniformed appearance. The color of uniform and mission changed but the police remained inherently linked to the military, with a uniformed public appearance representing the government's authority. Even today, the police uniform serves as the most visible sign of the police/military relationship (Kraska & Kappeler, 1997).

Reflective of Sir Robert Peel, the originator of England's police force, Peelian policing concepts of a military-like organizational structure with distinctive uniforms set the ground work for budding police organizations in the United States. With urbanization growing, police agencies formed, and scores of uniformed police officers patrolled large urban areas. Beginning in New York City in 1845, large metropolitan areas instituted organized uniformed police forces. Other cities' development of police forces soon followed, including Boston, Philadelphia and Detroit (Johnson, 2005). Not until the 1960s, however, did militaristic uniforms and equipment become problematic for US citizens. During civil unrest, police regularly used riot shields, tear gas, and lined up in military formation when approaching large crowds of protesters. However unfortunate, past police actions drive current research aimed at understanding interactions between police officers and citizens (see Alpert & Dunham, 2010). There is, however, much work to be done.

There is large gap in research owing to the dearth of studies evaluating citizens' perceptions of police legitimacy based on the aesthetics of police uniforms and/or equipment. That is unfortunate since over the last 20 years the police have acquired a large quantity of military equipment via US Government initiatives (Turner & Fox, 2017). In a move toward fighting the war on drugs and improving conditions in urban areas, President Clinton authorized police agencies to purchase military surplus with the federal "1033 Program" (Kraska, 2007; Turner & Fox, 2017). The President's authorization of military equipment was to aid local, county, and state law enforcement against the growing threat of drug trafficking. Regardless of the size of the population served, police agencies were now able to buy equipment that included MP5 submachine guns, M16s, sniper rifles, MRAP (mine-resistant, ambush protected) troop transport vehicles, Kevlar helmets, and so on (see Kraska, 2007; Kraska & Cubellis, 1997). Tactically, this equipment is useful in protecting officers when confronted with the potential for an armed conflict with suspected criminals. Nevertheless, lasting perceptions from the Branch Davidian raid in Waco (Texas) in 1993 are that the operation was indistinguishable from a military operation with heavily armed and fatigue-wearing law enforcement officers using armored vehicles to serve search/arrest warrants.

Twenty-one years later, the 2014 police shooting in Ferguson, Missouri, reignited public and political outcry for police to reexamine their procedures and strategies for handling mass demonstrations. Indeed, the debate over the appropriateness of police dressed as soldiers and using military apparatus to contain a lawful protest rose as far as the White House (White, Gaub, & Todak, 2017). As a result, the President's Task Force on 21st Century Policing (herein Task Force) (2015, p. 25) suggested changes to police policy to address militaristic-looking police officers and to improve public trust: "Law enforcement agencies should create policies and procedures for policing mass demonstrations that employ a continuum of managed tactical resources that are designed to minimize the appearance of a military operation and avoid using provocative tactics and equipment that undermine civilian trust."

Reflected here is that when police confront protesters with military formation, dress in military BDUs (battle-dress uniforms), and wield military weaponry, they communicate power and violence rather than safety and security (see also Kraska & Cubellis, 1997; Paul & Birzer, 2004). The Task Force's recommendations, however, do not discourage police from attaining or utilizing military-grade equipment. In fact, police are encouraged to purchase certain pieces of equipment such as anti-ballistic vests (those meant to stop high-caliber rifle rounds) and medical kits for triaging critically injured police and civilians. The goal of the Task Force is lowering chances that police show up to a mass demonstration dressed for war.

Aside from technical reports, however, the impression that militarized uniforms and equipment leave on civilian populations is unexamined. More broadly, the militarization of policing is under-studied, and we have little insight into the effects of police appearance, military or otherwise, on perceptions of the police (see Simpson, 2017). There are, of course, descriptive ruminations regarding the aesthetics of a militarized police (e.g., Balko, 2013; Kraska, 2007) that provide little more than a colorful one-sided view. That said, prior research provides the backdrop for understanding how police attire might affect citizens' perceptions of police.

The work of Kraska and colleagues (see Kappeler & Kraska, 2015; Kraska, 2007; Kraska & Cubellis, 1997; Kraska & Kappeler, 1997; Kraska & Paulsen, 1997) gives considerable insight into the manifestation of militaristic principles, academic perceptions, and equipment in policing. The etiology of police militarization of police is found in the development of the first SWAT teams in the LAPD in the 1960s. Beginning as elite units responding to high-risk incidents in large agencies (Kraska, 1997), SWAT teams have since become ubiquitous in policing, even existing in smaller agencies (Kraska & Cubellis, 1997; Waddington, 1999). Moreover, special operations teams are increasingly more proactive, so much so that Kraska and Paulsen (1997) noted substantial increases in the proactive use of SWAT over the course of more than a decade, 1982–1995.

Police decisions to utilize military equipment should involve officer safety and effectiveness as well as the health and welfare of the community (Kraska, 2007). Two events in Dallas highlight the gravity of the decision, and the subjective lens through which these decisions are viewed. In June 2015, a gunman driving an armored truck attacked Dallas Police headquarters with automatic weapons and explosive devices (Merchant, 2015). He was later shot and killed by SWAT snipers armed with large-caliber rifles capable of penetrating the suspect's vehicle. One year later, Dallas Police used a robot to kill a barricaded suspect who had just murdered four Dallas Police officer and one Dallas Area Rapid

Transit officer, and wounded seven others (Thielmann, 2016). The decision to use the robot as an instrument of deadly force was a first in history (Thielmann, 2016), and it was used to end the deadliest day in the history of US law enforcement except for the September 11 2001 terror attacks.

Notably, both incidents were ended by the intervention of SWAT using equipment and technology that is generally in the purview of the military. Yet, despite the dynamic situation unfolding during the shooting of five officers, the use of a robot prompted criticisms about the appropriateness of using drone technology to deliver deadly force (see Joh, 2016). Though they were anomalies, the two events illustrate the types of emergencies that SWAT is designed to address. In other words, SWAT responds to violent and dangerous crimes that require more training and tactics than patrol officers are equipped to handle.

In light of the growing military arsenals in police possession, utilizing SWAT to fight crime (the role of basic law enforcement) is a polemical issue. On one side of the spectrum, police militarization evokes hostility from citizens and encourages police to use force to solve problems. Further, Kraska and Cubellis (1997) found that violent crime explains very little of the work SWAT responds to. Balko (2013) observed that SWAT teams are over-utilized and too often lead to needless deadly encounters.

On the other hand, researchers argue that military equipment enhanced officer and community safety and lowers crime (Turner & Fox, 2017) as well as encouraging professionalism and accountability (Bieler, 2016). Still others suggest that we move beyond relying on SWAT teams in certain situations and call for greater military involvement in local policing when dealing with certain matters such as terrorism (Klinger & Grossman, 2001; Schmidt & Klinger, 2005). Bieler (2016) posits that the disparity among findings is largely related to definitional disagreements associated with the term "militarization." Militarization is differentially operationalized across studies leading Bieler (2016, p. 596) to suggest, "[I]t may well be that both sides are right, with certain elements associated with militarization having positive impacts and other elements having negative ones."

The lack of consensus notwithstanding, success of A&E's[1] SWAT shows featuring Dallas, Detroit, and Kansas City (Missouri) gives us some idea how society reacts to police militarization. The shows' popularity implies that military clothes and equipment do not fill citizens with the fear and outrage toward police as Kraska and Paulsen (1997) suggested. Furthermore, agencies use pictures featuring militaristic uniforms and equipment used by SWAT and other special operations teams as recruiting tools. Special operations units, which also include helicopter units, mounted units, motorcycle officers, and K-9s[2] are displayed at community fairs.[3] In this way, police take advantage of police militaristic aesthetics to attract potential police candidates from diverse communities. Perhaps Bieler (2016) was correct when he stated that both sides of the debate have merit. Certainly, context of the encounter between police and citizens matters. Citizens who find themselves in an active shooter situation would likely prefer heavily armed and trained officers to respond rather than officers in civilian attire. Yet, heavily armed officers responding to a peaceful demonstration would surely elicit the opposite reaction (Institute for Intergovernmental Research, 2015).

In fact, even small changes in the police uniform matter to citizens (Johnson, 2005; Simpson, 2017). Certainly, it matters to lawmakers concerned with images of "[H]eavily armed police officers confronting unarmed civilians, often with military grade weapons and equipment..." (Turner & Fox, 2017, p. 1). Unfortunately, there are only a few scholars who have examined correlates of citizens' perceptions of police legitimacy vis-à-vis officer appearance; fewer still have tested the effect (moderation or mediation) of militaristic clothing on those perceptions. Of the available research, there is evidence that uniforms and equipment do, in fact, have significant effects on certain outcomes on police citizen interactions and crime (Bieler, 2016; Bove & Gavrilova, 2017; Simpson, 2017).

Singer and Singer (1985), for example, have observed the perceptions of police based on attire. From a sample of 72 young women, they found that police uniforms have significant effects on interpersonal responses. Police officers in uniform were perceived by participants as more competent, reliable, intelligent, and helpful compared to officers wearing civilian clothing. Simpson (2017) provides additional support for Singer and Singer's (1985) findings. Additionally, Johnson (2001) concluded that police uniforms provide powerful clues as to the wearer's authority and status. The viewer's (i.e., citizen's) reaction depends on preconceived ideas about police, yet curbs illegal activity in the presence of an officer in uniform.

Minor visual alterations to traditional police uniforms also affect citizens' perceptions of police (Johnson, 2005; Johnson, Plecas, Anderson, & Dolan, 2015; Simpson, 2017). Johnson (2005) evaluated variations in four common uniform pant/shirt combinations. Citizens in a Midwestern US city were queried about their impressions based on photos of police uniforms sans duty belt, weapon, and hat. Johnson (2005) found that very dark ensembles (i.e., black shirt/pants) were viewed as cold, aggressive, unfriendly, corrupt, and forceful. Interestingly, light-colored uniform schemes did not elicit the most favorable responses; rather study participants perceived the light-blue shirts with navy pants as most favorable. Johnson et al. (2015) examined the effect of uniform accoutrements (i.e., hats and neckties) on citizens' impressions of police. The researchers found that hats and neckties as part of the uniform had no influence on citizens' perceptions of, *inter alia*, officer friendliness, niceness, or honesty.

Recent research by Simpson (2017) examines the influence that aesthetic variations in patrol strategy and attire had on perceptions of police. Specifically, he tested patrol strategy (bicycle and foot patrol versus vehicle) and police attire (civilian clothing versus police uniform) as predictors of perceived aggressiveness, approachability, friendliness, respectfulness, and accountability of police. Simpson found that while views of the police were vastly favorable, there were important variations among the participants. Participants viewed uniformed officers as more aggressive than officers in civilian clothes while, seemingly paradoxically, they also perceived uniformed officers as more approachable. In fact, Simpson (2017) observed that participants generally perceived uniformed officers as more favorable versus officers in civilian attire. With respect to patrol strategy, study participants perceived officers as more approachable, respectful, and accountable when on bicycle or on foot versus in a patrol car. Simpson concluded that uniforms do not compromise favorable impressions due to the aggressiveness that they portray.

In sum, uniform variations and the displays of militaristic equipment affect citizens' perceptions of police. Indeed, police utilize uniforms and equipment to solicit certain responses from citizens, from a show of force to recruiting. Highlighted by events in Ferguson post-shooting, however, is that use of military equipment and tactics can create immediate negative reactions and may cause more problems than it solves. What remains open to debate is the appropriateness of police obtaining and displaying military equipment. There are also vast differences in how "militarism" is operationalized in the literature. Without a clear understanding of what it means to be "militaristic," the answer regarding appropriateness will remain uncertain.

APPEARANCE OF RACE AND POLICE BEHAVIOR

Few human characteristics found within police/citizen interactions have caused as much debate as race. In *Race, Ethnicity, and Policing: New and Essential Readings*, White (2010) suggests that there are three themes in the current literature. The first is the need to expand sources of data and examine them at varying levels of analysis. A second theme accounts for the multiculturalism of the United States and suggests broadening our definition of race beyond the Black/White dichotomy. The last theme recognizes that race has long been suspected of being a primary predictor for police/citizen interaction outcomes. A considerable body of research shows that one's race plays a major role on treatment by police, and by the criminal justice system writ large. This section of the chapter takes a closer look at race by examining the recent research and the prominence of race as a predictor of police/citizen interactions.

Certainly, disentangling race and decisionmaking at the moment of interaction is exceedingly difficult (Fridell, 2017; Todak, 2017). With this difficulty in mind, some take a more refined look at race-based police decisionmaking. Dabney and associates, for example, tested citizens' neighborhood, race, and cultural styles (e.g., hip-hop) as predictors of police behavior (Dabney et al., 2017). While they observed that race alone was not a sufficient explanation of arrest decisions, the researchers found significant differences among predictors of arrest after accounting for within-group cultural style. That is not to say police do not appreciate the importance of race on community perceptions. Police have taken great strides toward hiring minority officers (Jordon, Fridell, Faggiani, & Bruce, 2009) to increase perceptions of police legitimacy and, hence, greater cooperation with police minority-populated crime-ridden neighborhoods (Dunham & Petersen, 2017).

The discussion on race-based police decisionmaking often centers on Black/White differences between police and citizens (Paoline, Gau, & Terrill, 2016; Todak, 2017), especially in the media (Culhane, Boman, & Schweitzer, 2016; Lott & Moody, 2016; Schildkraut, Elsass, & Meredith, 2017). As they do with police militarization, academics vary in their opinions on race and racism within law enforcement. Race-centric scholarship ranges from suggesting that a white supremacist ideology permeates law enforcement and drives both police brutality and the public's reaction to it (Alang, McAlpine, McCreedy, & Hardeman, 2017), to suggestions that there may be a "reverse racism" effect taking place in deadly police/citizen encounters (James, James, & Vila, 2016)[4]. Still others posit that media reporting of police holds considerable sway over societies' perceptions of police, both positive and negative (Callanan & Rosenberger, 2011; Dowler & Zawilski, 2007; Graziano, Schuck, & Martin, 2010). On the whole, vast disparities in findings exist in studies concerning minorities in traffic stops, searches, arrests, and use of deadly force based on offender race (Dunham & Petersen, 2017; Lim, 2017 Nix, Campbell, Byers, & Alpert, 2017; Warren et al., 2006).

A considerable body of research explains, at least in part, why minority community members have negative views of the police. Public displays of police abuse anchor deep-seated notions that police treat minorities more harshly and focus enforcement actions in minority communities (Skolnick, 2007). Consider, for example, the "Driving While Black" phenomenon where the public believes that police officers are stopping and searching certain citizens because they are Black (Alpert, Dunham, & Smith, 2007; Harris, 1999). Additionally, evaluations of police behavior suggest that Blacks and other minorities receive disproportionate levels of force compared to Whites. Nix and colleagues (2017) examined crowd-sourced data from *The Washington Post* and found that of the 990 civilians shot and killed by police in 2015, Blacks were more likely to be unarmed when shot by police than Whites. Nix et al. suggest that this was important evidence of implicit bias among police.

No matter how prominent race is in research and to the media, evidence-based research has begun questioning the influence that race has on interactions and perceptions. A burgeoning body of research on race and police behavior is reevaluating suggestions of racial bias among police. For instance, Lott and Moody (2016) examined 2699 police killings across 1,500 US cities including Dallas and Philadelphia. They found that Black suspects have no greater odds of being shot by a White officer than members of any other race. Moreover, Lott and Moody's study highlights the need to view race and police use-of-force through a more focused lens than provided by bivariate regressions. Take, for example, a study by Jetelina et al. (2017) on the relationships between 11 officer/citizen racial dyads and the odds of various levels of force being used. They found that situational factors rendered most bivariate relationships insignificant. However, the odds of intermediate weapon use (e.g., pepperball saturation and TASERs) remained significant among Hispanic–White, Black–Hispanic, White–Black, and Hispanic–Black dyads.

Situational variables factor heavily in police/citizen interactions because they reflect the circumstances that police find once on the scene. Citizen demeanor during interactions with police is an extralegal factor that has garnered considerable attention (Engel, Klahm, & Tillyer, 2010; Klinger, 1994). Engel et al. (2010) found that race had no influence on arrest outcomes among more than 42,000 traffic stops recorded by Cleveland Police during an eight-month period. Verbally or physically noncompliant motorists or those who were disrespectful were more likely to be arrested than were compliant and respectful motorists. The thesis that citizen demeanor predicts arrest outcomes is not new and appears to be cemented in criminological research (Klinger, 1994). Klinger's (1994) seminal study takes the hostility thesis to task, however, and posits that conceptualization and measurement of demeanor in prior research is problematic. Rather, Klinger found criminal conduct explained the likelihood of arrest. Expounding further, he stated: "[T]he current data suggest that hostile suspects are more likely to be arrested because they are more likely to commit crimes against and in the presence of the police, not because their demeanor connotes a lack of respect for police authority" (p. 489).

In another study using Dallas Police Department use-of-force data, Jetelina, Reingle-Gonzalez, and Bishopp (2017) assessed whether or not gradual escalations of force attenuated officer injuries when faced with active aggression by citizens. They observed that officer injuries were more likely to occur when officers confronted aggressive citizens but were less likely to happen when citizens displayed a weapon. With respect to racial differences among officers, Black officers were significantly less likely than their White peers to move through the force continuum when confronting active aggression.[5] The authors speculate on why this occurred but could not fully explain the differences.

Bishopp, Klinger, and Morris (2015) have examined the relationship between a change in TASER policy and TASER use using Dallas Police Department administrative reports. This study controlled for officer race, and found that White officers were more inclined to use TASERs than their Black peers. Interestingly, the same policy was evaluated using pre/post-policy officer injury reports (Womack, Bishopp, & Morris, 2016). Officer race was not measured in this study, but researchers found that officer injury rates increased after a more restrictive policy was put into place but effects varied by patrol division. The geographical differences suggest that officer decisionmaking is a product of the location where the officer patrols. This supports Klinger's (1997) contention that negotiated rules in each patrol district (i.e., division) dictate the level of vigor with which officers respond to situations.

Analyses of variations in police use-of-force decisions show that perceptions of police are grounded more in community-level factors solely based on citizen race. Surveying residents in Cincinnati, Ohio, Cao et al. (1996) assessed the level of confidence that citizens had in police. They found that race factored heavily in measures of confidence, with Blacks having considerably less confidence in police than Whites. However, when variables such as community disorder and informal collective security were added to the model, race was no longer significant. Worrall (1999) parsed out race in a study of police efficacy and image dimensions among a nationwide sample of 1005 citizens. He found that among three confidence outcomes – police solving crime, preventing crime, and protecting citizens from crime – race was related only to citizens' perceptions of police ability to solve crime. Worrall speculated that this indicated that race is not necessarily the most important determinant of confidence in the police.

Race and high-crime locations interact to predict less-lethal force, according to Lee (2016), who examined situational and community factors affecting police use of less-lethal force. Using a sample of Stop, Frisk, and Question data from the NYPD, he found that race and community-level variables (e.g., crime-ridden neighborhood) together predicted police use of less-lethal force. Further, Lee (2016) observed that police were less likely to use less-lethal force in serious offenses, which supports similar research from Queensland, Australia (Hine, Porter, Westera, & Alpert, 2016) as well as Klinger's (1997) "police vigor" theory. While citizen race is perceived as one of the main reasons that police stop, search, arrest, or use force, empirical analyses that control for certain events (e.g., suspect demeanor, weapons, actively committing a crime) suggest that race is less important than situational variables. Unfortunately, we have an incomplete picture as there are few analyses of individual-level police uses of less-lethal and deadly force. Most are not comparable as they measure different populations, operationalize predictors and outcomes differently, and use incompatible terminology for key variables. This scenario continues to plague policing research, a likely byproduct of the lack of comprehensive national use-of-force data (Klinger et al., 2016).

This chapter echoes similar calls for the collection of national-level data that define "force", and provide clear differentiations between justified/unjustified shooting of citizens. Yet, the actual data will only tell us if similarly situated agencies experience the same level of shootings, violent crime, traffic stops, and the like. It will tell us little about citizens' perceptions of police and how those perceptions are formed. Thus, I take a step further here and suggest a national data collection effort similar to the National Crime Victim Survey. Such a survey would query citizens on their perceptions of police legitimacy, procedural justice, and feelings about certain policies (e.g., body-worn cameras, TASERs, militarized equipment). Further, a two-level mode of questioning would provide considerable information. Citizens with prior encounters with police will have two perceptions – about the interaction itself, and about

policing overall. A large body of research suggests that these two measures are strongly correlated, particularly in minority neighborhoods. Yet,
beyond perceptions of citizens from single samples, the strength of the
correlations is largely a mystery.

FINAL COMMENTS

Although SWAT and other special operations members are able to
respond to critical events, they are numerically small and rarely a part
of regular patrol. A SWAT unit is unlikely available for immediate
response when critical incidents begin to unfold, and that is especially
true in large agencies. Indeed, two events in the late 1990s highlighted the
unavailability of SWAT as well as the lack of training and weaponry of
first responders. Coffin (2007) describes the 1997 takeover bank robbery
attempt in Hollywood, California. The responding patrol officers and
detectives found themselves quickly outgunned by two men with fully
automatic assault rifles with large-capacity magazines. Responding patrol
officers and detectives were ill-equipped to control the situation. Two
years later, the school shooting at Columbine occurred. Here, officers
did what they were trained to do in critical situations in which a subject
has a gun and hostages: they set up a perimeter and waited for SWAT
(Bausman & Shaul, 2016).While patrol officers waited outside, the
gunman killed several more students before shooting himself.

   As a result of those events, Dallas, Texas, trains officers on active shooter
situations and patrol officers are allowed to carry AR-15s as patrol rifles.
Patrol rifle officers are required to go through an initial basic 40-course
instruction in addition to firing at least five rounds every month at the range
to ensure their weapons are properly sighted. In addition to the patrol rifle
program, officers have access to heavy vests, and in some cases ballistic
shields and Kevlar helmets. Up until a few years ago, such training and
equipment were once reserved for SWAT and other specialized units. Concerning perceptions of police and aesthetics, patrol officers who respond to a
critical incident may look and act like SWAT to onlookers. This also speaks
to the larger question of militarization of police, and suggests that continu-
ing police militarization research reconceptualize its operationalization
of militarization to encompass more than the size of an agency's SWAT.

   This last point is an important suggestion since research-based policy
has consequences. On July 7, 2016, Dallas city leaders wanted to prevent
a 'militaristic' appearance and officers were instructed to leave their heavy

vests, Kevlar helmets, and patrol rifles behind during an anti-police protest (Douglas & Allen, 2017). A shooter began targeting officers. When the shooting stopped, five police officers were dead and several more wounded. Hundreds of officers responded when the shootings occurred, including SWAT. It was not until several hours later and continued refusal by the shooter to surrender that Chief David Brown made the decision use a robot to kill the shooter. This incident makes a salient point concerning research and policy decisions: Lives rely on getting research and policy correct. How citizens perceive their police is vitally important to positive relationships with the community. Yet, city, county, state, and federal leadership must keep in mind that improving perceptions during volatile situations should not cost first responders' lives.

Lastly, Dallas is experimenting with a policy that is a first in the DPD history. After 136 years, male DPD officers may grow beards and goatees. Officers responded immediately, and their perceptions of their bearded peers on Facebook included "Beards are the new man bun," "Just curious, but what happens when you're on a response team and have to put on your mask, but can't seal it because 'Oh damn, I forgot I have this manly beard!,'" "It was a fantastic time to announce this just days before no shave November," and simply, "I do not like the beards in uniform." Concerning interactions with citizens, officers reported some comments from the community including "When interacting with citizens I have only had positive comments, such as 'it's about time'. These have been people from all walks of life," and "I actually had a young man at a convenience store comment on how he liked the beard because it made me seem more approachable."[6]

Interestingly, a study still under development measured citizens' perceptions of bearded officers in Canada. Brown et al. (2017) surveyed two groups of citizens' perceptions of police regarding uniformed officers with beards. They found that perceptions of police officers with beards are slightly less positive than those without beards. The jury is still out on the Dallas' beard experiment. As the author of this chapter, I rather enjoy not shaving.

References

Alang, S., McAlpine, D., McCreedy, E., & Hardeman, R. (2017). Police brutality and Black health: Setting the agenda for public health scholars. *American Journal of Public Health*, 107(5), 662–665.

Alpert, G. P. & Dunham, R. G. (2010). Policy and training recommendations related to police use of CEDs: Overview of findings from a comprehensive national study. *Police Quarterly*, 13(3), 235–259.

Alpert, G. P., Dunham, R. G., & Smith, M. R. (2007). Investigating racial profiling by the Miami-Dade Police Department: A multimethod approach. *Criminology & Public Policy*, 6(1), 25–55.

Auten, J. H. (1981). The paramilitary model of police and police professionalism. *Police Studies: International Review Police Development*, 4, 67.

Balko, R. (2013). Overkill: The rise of paramilitary police raids in America. *Cato's Letter*, 11(4), 1–5.

Bausman, C. & Shaul, R. (2016). *Active Shooters: Patrol Tasked to Respond, but Are They Out-Gunned, Under-Equipped, And Under-Trained? And What Does This Mean for SWAT?* Mountain Tactical Institute, Retrieved December 3, 2017, from http://mtntactical.com/research/evolving-to-the-threat-law-enforcement-responses-to-active-shooters/.

Bieler, S. (2016). Police militarization in the USA: The state of the field. *Policing: An International Journal of Police Strategies & Management*, 39(4), 586–600.

Bishopp, S. A., Klinger, D. A., & Morris, R. G. (2015). An examination of the effect of a policy change on police use of TASERs. *Criminal Justice Policy Review*, 26(7), 727–746.

Bove, V. & Gavrilova, E. (2017). Police officer on the frontline or a soldier? The effect of police militarization on crime. *American Economic Journal: Economic Policy*, 9(3), 1–18.

Brown, A., Blaskovits, B., Ewanation, L., Baldwin, S., & Bennell, C. (2017, September). *Looking the part: Examining public perceptions of grooming and body modification in law enforcement.* Paper accepted for the meeting of Society for Police and Criminal Psychology, San Diego, CA.

Callanan, V. J. & Rosenberger, J. S. (2011). Media and public perceptions of the police: Examining the impact of race and personal experience. *Policing & Society*, 21(2), 167–189.

Cao, L., Frank, J., & Cullen, F. T. (1996). Race, community context and confidence in the police. *American Journal of Police*, 15(1), 3–22.

Coffin, B. (2007). WARZONE: The North Hollywood shootout, 10 years later. *Risk Management*, 54(3), 36.

Culhane, S. E., Boman, J. H., & Schweitzer, K. (2016). Public perceptions of the justifiability of police shootings: The role of body cameras in a pre-and post-Ferguson experiment. *Police Quarterly*, 19(3), 251–274.

Dabney, D. A., Teasdale, B., Ishoy, G. A., Gann, T., & Berry, B. (2017). Policing in a largely minority jurisdiction: The influence of appearance characteristics associated with contemporary hip-hop culture on police decision-making. *Justice Quarterly*, 34(7), 1310–1338.

Douglas, J. & Allen, G. (2017, November 23). Police told to leave protective gear behind. CBSDFW report. Retrieved from http://dfw.cbslocal.com/2017/06/29/police-told-to-leave-protective-gear-behind/.

Dowler, K. & Zawilski, V. (2007). Public perceptions of police misconduct and discrimination: Examining the impact of media consumption. *Journal of Criminal Justice*, 35(2), 193–203.

Dunham, R. G. & Petersen, N. (2017). Making Black lives matter. *Criminology & Public Policy*, 16(1), 341–348.

Engel, R. S., Klahm, C. F., & Tillyer, R. (2010). Citizens' demeanor, race, and traffic stops. In S. Rice & M. White (Eds.), *Race, ethnicity, and policing: New and essential readings* (pp. 287–308). New York, NY: New York University Press.

Fridell, L. A. (2017). Explaining the disparity in results across studies assessing racial disparity in police use-of-force: A research note. *American Journal of Criminal Justice*, 42(3), 502–513.

Graziano, L., Schuck, A., & Martin, C. (2010). Police misconduct, media coverage, and public perceptions of racial profiling: An experiment. *Justice Quarterly*, 27(1), 52–76.

Harris, D. A. (1999). The stories, the statistics, and the law: Why driving while Black matters. *Minnesota Law Review*, 84, 265.

Hine, K. A., Porter, L. E., Westera, N. J., & Alpert, G. P. (2016). Too much or too little? Individual and situational predictors of police force relative to suspect resistance. *Policing & Society*, https://doi.org/10.1080/10439463.2016.1232257.

Institute for Intergovernmental Research. (2015). *After-Action Assessment of the Police Response to the August 2014 Demonstrations in Ferguson, Missouri*. COPS Office Critical Response Initiative. Washington, DC: Office of Community Oriented Policing Services.

James, L., James, S. M., & Vila, B. J. (2016). The reverse racism effect. *Criminology & Public Policy*, 15(2), 457–479.

Jetelina, K. K., Gonzalez, J. M. R., & Bishopp, S. A. (2017). Gradual escalation of use-of-force reduces police officer injury. *Injury Prevention*, http://dx.doi.org/10.1136/injuryprev-2016-042198.

Jetelina, K. K., Jennings, W. G., Bishopp, S. A., Piquero, A. R., & Reingle-Gonzalez, J. M. (2017). Dissecting the complexities of the relationship between police officer–civilian race/ethnicity dyads and less-than-lethal use-of-force. *American Journal of Public Health*, 107(7), 1164–1170.

Joh, E. E. (2016). Policing police robots. *UCLA Law Review Discourse*, 64, 516–543.

Johnson, R. R. (2001). The psychological influence of the police uniform. *FBI Law Enforcement Bulletin*, 70, 27.

(2005). Police uniform color and citizen impression formation. *Journal of Police and Criminal Psychology*, 20(2), 58–66.

Johnson, R. R., Plecas, D., Anderson, S., & Dolan, H. (2015). No hat or tie required: Examining minor changes to the police uniform. *Journal of Police and Criminal Psychology*, 30(3), 158–165.

Jordan, W., Fridell, L., Faggiani, D., & Kubu, B. (2009). Attracting females and racial/ethnic minorities to law enforcement, *Journal of Criminal Justice*, 37(4), 333–341.

Kappeler, V. E. & Kraska, P. (2015). Normalising police militarization, living in denial. *Policing and Society*, 25(3), 268–275.

Klinger, D. A. (1994). Demeanor or crime? Why "hostile" citizens are more likely to be arrested. *Criminology*, 32(3), 475–493.

(1997). Negotiating order in patrol work: An ecological theory of police response to deviance. *Criminology*, 35(2), 277–306.

Klinger, D. A. & Grossman, D. (2001). Who should deal with foreign terrorists on US Soil: Socio-legal consequences of September 11 and the ongoing threat of terrorist attacks in America. *Harvard Journal of Law and Public Policy*, 25, 815.

Klinger, D., Rosenfeld, R., Isom, D., & Deckard, M. (2016). Race, crime, and the micro-ecology of deadly force. *Criminology & Public Policy*, 15(1), 193–222.

Kraska, P. B. (2007). Militarization and policing – Its relevance to 21st century police. *Policing: A Journal of Policy and Practice*, 1(4), 501–513.

Kraska, P. B. & Cubellis, L. J. (1997). Militarizing Mayberry and beyond: Making sense of American paramilitary policing. *Justice Quarterly*, 14(4), 607–629.

Kraska, P. B. & Kappeler, V. E. (1997). Militarizing American police: The rise and normalization of paramilitary units. *Social problems*, 44(1), 1–18.

Kraska, P. B. & Paulsen, D. J. (1997). Grounded research into US paramilitary policing: Forging the iron fist inside the velvet glove. *Policing and Society: An International Journal*, 7(4), 253–270.

Lee, J. (2016). Police use of nonlethal force in New York City: Situational and community factors. *Policing and Society*, 26(8), 875–888.

Lim, H. (2017). Police bias, use of deadly force, public outcry. *Criminology & Public Policy*, 16(1), 305–308.

Lott, J. R. & Moody, C. E. (2016, November 29). Do white police officers unfairly target black suspects? *Social Science Research Network*. Retrieved from https://cargogunclub.org/files/John%20Lott%20Crime%20Study.pdf.

Merchant, N. (2015). *Suspect killed after attack on Dallas Police headquarters*, Associated Press report, Fox4 News, www.fox4news.com/news/suspect-killed-after-attack-on-dallas-police-headquarters.

Miller, T. R., Lawrence, B. A., Carlson, N. N., Hendrie, D., Randall, S., Rockett, I. R., & Spicer, R. S. (2017). Perils of police action: A cautionary tale from US data sets. *Injury prevention*, 23(1), 27–32.

Nix, J., Campbell, B. A., Byers, E. H., & Alpert, G. P. (2017). A bird's eye view of civilians killed by police in 2015. *Criminology & Public Policy*, 16(1), 309–340.

Paoline, E. A., Gau, J. M., & Terrill, W. (2016). Race and the police use-of-force encounter in the United States. *The British Journal of Criminology*, https://doi.org/10.1093/bjc/azw089.

Paul, J. & Birzer, M. L. (2004). Images of power: An analysis of the militarization of police uniforms and messages of service. *Free Inquiry in Creative Sociology*, 32(2), 121–128.

President's Task Force on 21st Century Policing. (2015). *Final Report of the President's Task Force on 21st Century Policing*. Washington, DC: Office of Community Oriented Policing Services.

Schildkraut, J., Elsass, H. J., & Meredith, K. (2017). Mass shootings and the media: Why all events are not created equal. *Journal of Crime and Justice*, doi.org/10.1080/0735648X.2017.1284689.

Schmidt, C. J. & Klinger, D. A. (2005). Altering the *Posse Comitatus* Act: Letting the military address terrorist attacks on US soil. *Creighton Law Review*, 39, 667.

Simpson, R. (2017). The police officer perception project (POPP): An experimental evaluation of factors that impact perceptions of the police. *Journal of Experimental Criminology*, 13(3), 393–415.

Simpson, R. & Hipp, J. R. (2017). What came first: The police or the incident? Bidirectional relationships between police actions and police incidents. *Policing and Society*, https://doi.org/10.1080/10439463.2017.1405957.

Singer, M. S. & Singer, A. E. (1985). The effect of police uniform on interpersonal perception. *The Journal of Psychology*, 119(2), 157–161.

Skolnick, J. H. (2007). Racial profiling – Then and now. *Criminology & Public Policy*, 6(1), 65–70.

Thielmann, S (2016). Use of police robot to kill Dallas shooting suspect believed to be first in US history. *The Guardian*. Downloaded December 1, 2017 from www.theguardian.com/technology/2016/jul/08/police-bomb-robot-explosive-killedsuspect-dallas.

Todak, N. (2017). *De-escalation in police–citizen encounters: A mixed methods study of a misunderstood policing strategy*, PhD dissertation, Arizona State University.

Turner, F. W. & Fox, B. H. (2017). Public servants or police soldiers? An analysis of opinions on the militarization of policing from police executives, law enforcement, and members of the 114th Congress US House of Representatives. *Police Practice and Research*, https://doi.org/10.1080/15614263.2017.1371600.

Volpp, J. M. & Lennon, S. J. (1988). Perceived police authority as a function of uniform hat and sex. *Perceptual and Motor Skills*, 67(3), 815–824.

Warren, P., Tomaskovic-Devey, D., Smith, W., Zingraff, M., & Mason, M. (2006). Driving while black: Bias processes and racial disparity in police stops. *Criminology*, 44(3), 709–738.

White, M. (2010). Introduction to Part III in Rice, S. & White, M. (Eds.), *Race, ethnicity, and policing: New and essential readings*. New York, NY: New York University Press.

White, M. D., Gaub, J. E., & Todak, N. (2017). Exploring the potential for body-worn cameras to reduce violence in police–citizen encounters. *Policing: A Journal of Policy and Practice*, https://doi.org/10.1093/police/paw057.

Womack, V. G., Morris, R. G., & Bishopp, S. A. (2016). Do changes in TASER use policy affect police officer injury rates? *Police Quarterly*, 19(4), 410–434.

Worrall, J. L. (1999). Public perceptions of police efficacy and image: The "fuzziness" of support for the police. *American Journal of Criminal Justice*, 24(1), 47–66.

Wu, Y., Sun, I. Y., & Triplett, R. A. (2009). Race, class or neighborhood context: Which matters more in measuring satisfaction with police? *Justice Quarterly*, 26(1), 125–156.

Endnote

1 Originally named the Arts & Entertainment Network, A&E is an American cable television channel that presents documentaries, biographies, and reality shows.

2 Members of these units fit the broad definition of 'militarization' (Bove & Gavrilova, 2017; Kraska 1997). They dress in dark BDUs, use specialized weapons or equipment supplied by the military, or work closely with federal agencies including the military on certain operations.

3 In Dallas, "Chief on the Beat" Crime Prevention Safety & Health Fairs hosted by the DPD Community Affairs team are regularly held at community events throughout the city.

4 James et al. (2016, p. 1) found that "officers were slower to shoot armed Black suspects than armed White suspects, and they were less likely to shoot unarmed Black suspects than unarmed White suspects."

5 The Dallas Police Department General Orders (901.04) presents a linear use-of-force policy. At the lower end, officers use physical presence and verbal control. If the event warrants it, officers can go through the use-of-force continuum up to and including deadly force (for more detailed description of the Dallas Police Department's use-of-force continuum, see Bishopp et al., 2015; Womack et al., 2016).

6 The comments were from members of a private Facebook account used by Dallas Police officers. The author received permission to publish the comments from the officers who posted them.

PART IV

IDENTIFYING TERRORISTS, MISTAKENLY OR NOT, BY APPEARANCE

EDITORIAL COMMENTS

We, the public and the crime control system, make numerous, grievous errors in identifying and failing to identify terrorists and, frequently, these errors are based on appearance bias. From public reports to airline security practices to governmental policy, we make false assumptions about who terrorists are and are not. Of course behavioral cues play a role, as they do in all crime scenarios, but the first-glance visual impression is remarkably important in identifying terrorists and terrorist activities.

Mainly and contemporarily, media stories focus not only on terrorism of the "foreign" (to the United States and Europe) variety such as criminal acts carried out by the Islamic State, but also on "homegrown" terrorism (terrorism carried out by nativist Caucasians). While we are told in present-day US that terrorism is mainly carried out by Islamic extremists and, for that reason, immigration should be restricted for a wide range of Middle Eastern countries, the fact is that most of the terrorism experienced in the United States is deployed by White "homegrown" terrorists. Data from the Anti-Defamation League "confirms that over the last decade, native-born white supremacists and others identifying with far-right movements have been responsible for the vast majority of extremist-related murders in the United States" (Greenblatt, 2018: 20). Over 70 percent of extremist killings are associated with domestic (US) right-wing extremists as against only 26 percent of the killings are committed by Islamic extremists (see Image 9).

Terrorism by nativist Caucasians occurs worldwide. Examples picked from the mainstream news on a given day in the Autumn of 2017 show

IMAGE 9. Skinhead with tattoos (Getty Images)

(1) a case of a Swastika-wearing man on the streets of Seattle (who, incidentally, was beaten up by a fellow pedestrian), (2) a German police officer being investigated for wearing a far-right patch on his uniform), (3) a Nazi eagle statue being displayed in Uruguay, and (4) an activist gaining approval to burn a flag bearing combination Nazi and US Confederate symbols (Associated Press, 2017a; Associated Press, 2017b; Clarridge, 2017; Haberkorn, 2017).

In Chapter 10, Daniela Pisoiu describes the recent debates linking terrorism to clothing assumed to be related to IS (Islamic State). She interviewed people who wear terrorist-looking clothing, some of whom are legitimate members of a terrorist organization and some who just want to look "cool." Apparently, some young people, mainly men, adopt certain styles of clothing to look like terrorists because they like the look. Real terrorists, those steeped in Islamic religion and who take terrorist philosophies and activities very seriously, resent the faux terrorists and the commercialization of the terrorist look.

In my own musings on burkas and burkinis, given that burkas and burkinis ("bikinis" that cover a great deal more than what bikinis usually cover) are worn by women, we have here a focus on gender differences intersecting with terrorist appearance. We usually assume that women are less likely to be criminals or terrorists than men. Yet, the French police were at one point forcing burka-wearing women to disrobe in order to show that they were unarmed. An immediate question is: were the French police really looking for weapons or were they intimidating female suspects or were they merely scoping out the women's bodies?

In 2017, burka (also spelled burqa) bans spread worldwide. The face-covering garments, publicly worn by Muslim women, had already been banned in some societies but is now prohibited in Canada, Austria, France, Belgium, Germany, and Bulgaria (Stack, 2017). Think about this: it is an article of clothing, worn to signify religious affiliation, yet its wearing is prohibited as an identifier of terrorism. Yes, it is possible to see the ban as a means of banning a disguise. It can also be seen as a means of forcing women to dis-identify their adherence to their religion having nothing to do with terrorism.

To be sure, there has been a shift in ISIS roles with French Jihadists including more women, and that concern is growing as radicalized European women plot terrorist attacks (Rubin & Breeden, 2016). But that does not rationalize first responders (1) assuming that burka-wearing women are terrorists or (2) peeking under burka-wearing women's clothing. Nor does it necessitate banning the sale of burkas, citing "safety" concerns, as Morocco has done (Alami, 2017). Not that men escape notice if they sport "abnormal" beards or otherwise appear "terrorist." The western province of Xinjiang (China) has banned women's wearing of veils as well as men's growing long beards ("names") since these appearance features are thought to represent extremism. Indeed, at the Chinese border town of Horgos, all Islamic garb and grooming styles are prohibited (Higgins, 2018). Definitions of "terrorist" clothing are vague, but it seems that the concern on the part of those identifying terrorists is *coverage*, as though something dangerous might be hidden under the clothing. The niqab is a veil that covers the face and the burka covers the face and the body (Smith, 2017).

The United States presently (in 2018, as I write this) discriminates against Muslims, going on the anti-Muslim assumption that adherents to this particular religion are necessarily terrorists. Numerous examples abound but, to name one instance, the US Supreme Court has agreed to "decide whether high-ranking George W. Bush administration officials . . . may be held liable for policies adopted after the September 11 [2001] attacks" (Liptak, 2016: 13). Apparently, there was no effort to distinguish between genuine suspects and Muslim immigrants; the plaintiffs were subjected to beatings, strip searches, and other abuses, owing to religious and racial profiling.

In Chapter 11, Mark Hamm describes not only appearance as has been ordinarily discussed in this volume but also another important aspect to visual cues, behavior. He does not make the case that behavioral cues and demeanor outweigh physical appearance cues but that these two visual indices work together to alert terrorist trackers. Throughout his career, Hamm has focused on white US citizens, mainly white men, as terrorists and the behavioral and appearance traits as clues to their terrorist intentions. Known for his work on US white supremacists and survivalists (for example, 2002, 1997, 1994), his new work investigates how terrorism as a philosophy is spread within the US prison system (2017). In his analysis, we find that a "mask of charisma," a carefully displayed face and demeanor, is a useful tool for recruiting terrorists.

Hamm is not the only scholar to consider visual, behavioral cues as an indicator of criminal intent. Brown (2017) describes how

immigrants from a predominantly agrarian society must adapt and restrain their bodies . . . to meet the demands of American social institutions. Immigrants' ability to move their bodies in socially prescribed ways affect three crucial aspects of the incorporation [to US society, how well they "fit in"]: identity formation, economic mobility, and transnational practices. Immigrants who struggle to execute the host society's normative bodily movements. . .

will have a hard time fitting in and will stand out to the observer as an immigrant and thus as suspicious (p. 14; see also Ulibarrí's work on behavioral and demeanor cues presented in Chapter 5). Bodily, physical movements and gestures can serve as a signal of foreignness (Brown, p. 25). People give themselves away as foreigners in their management of ATM machines, telephones, and other cultural accoutrements and, as a result, make their personal safety and their economic security more vulnerable (p. 26); they are more likely to be excluded from American society when they cannot adopt bodily socializations needed to blend (see also Bourdieu, 1984, on observable distinctions and judgments of taste). Citing Brown's remarks on Bourdieu, we learn that the body "bears the imprint of the social structure in which it originated . . . with important implications for individuals' life chances" (p. 26). This judgment by Bourdieu would apply to many in this present study of appearance bias, such as refugees, terrorists, and undocumented immigrants.

Broadening our look at appearance and terrorism, consider Stephen Muzzatti's (2017) work on terrorism and counterterrorism in popular culture. Muzzatti focuses on the *image* of terrorism. Related to the above arguments about seeing terrorism and terrorists everywhere since September 11, 2001, Muzzatti makes a distinction between fictional depictions of fantastical terrorism before and after 9/11. Here, I am reminded of the visibility–invisibility contrast raised in my editorial comments for Part II. Indigenous peoples are identifiable by their physical traits and are gravely overrepresented in criminal and victim populations but, at the same time, they are more invisible than the White populations that surround them. This invisibility works for and against them: visibility makes them prone to intervention by crime control agencies while invisibility makes them vulnerable to hidden abuses. In Muzzatti's argument, terrorism is front-and-center visible even when it is not present.

The pre-9/11 depictions of terrorism and counterterrorism, as part of the US media's cultural production, focused on terrorism as it occurred "somewhere else" (not in the United States) and the conduits were several (news reports but also entertainment genres like political thrillers as well as stories about war, romance, sci-fi, and suspense). The post-9/11 portrayals of terrorism and the War on Terror put forward by the George W. Bush administration had a significantly changed narrative, with the image of terrorist threats now being ubiquitous. Terrorism can happen anywhere in any venue (schools, sporting arenas, shopping malls, or any number of "more mundane parts of the US landscape"), with the main point being that "no one is safe from terrorism" (Muzzatti, p. 2). That may mean that we see it, searching for visible cues, even when it isn't there.

Moreover, the new narratives utilize "fetishized presentations of military, national security, and law enforcement agents with state-of-the-art weaponry dispatching terrorists with deadly force" without supplying an "alternative to resolving conflicts other than the use of state violence" (Muzzatti, p. 2). I have two points to make here. Refer to Chapter 9 in which Stephen Bishopp portrays the various forms of police appearance, for instance weaponry, as a means of intimidating would-be criminals and the public. The second point pertains to the following chapters on terrorism: if terrorism is everywhere and terrorists are everywhere, we must be suspicious of anyone who doesn't *look like us*, assuming that *we* do not look like those presently depicted as terrorists, for instance, Muslims. One of the grandest fallacies of terrorism as it occurs in the United States is that we are vulnerable to people who do not look like "us" when, in truth, we have always have been far more vulnerable to native-born White Christian men behaving as terrorists than to any other racial or religious category.

Relatedly, consider the visible symbols of terrorism as they appear internationally and within the United States. Staples (2018) reminds us that symbols exalting the Confederacy (statues of Confederate heroes, Confederate place names) are still in abundance in the US South. This is occurring at a time when "white supremacists are rallying to the Confederate cause and sowing hate from coast to coast" (p. 22). Staples further (2017) reminds us that the US Confederate flag, representing the Southern United States' pro-slavery position during the Civil War and still representing white supremacists' ideals, has been replaced in some venues by the Nazi swastika. The Confederate flag has fallen into disfavor among diversity-minded people after it and other Confederate symbols were proudly displayed by Dylan Roof, the killer of nine Black worshippers in a church in South Carolina. After Roof's mayhem, some but not all people in the Southern US rethought their displays of Confederate memorabilia such as the flag but also statues honoring Confederate soldiers and officers.

However, today the White power survivalists and their "raving skinhead counterparts" are rebranding themselves (Staples, 2017: 24). They are wearing business attire and trying to sound reasonable (some of them), but they are still engaging in White supremacist protest against removal of Confederate symbols by substituting "toxic symbolism of the Third Reich"; indeed, "the Confederate flag can legitimately be seen as an alternate version of the Nazi emblem" (p. 24). Apparently, Germany is more advanced than the United States in terms of coming to grips with the wrongness of supremacy since Germany, after World War II, abandoned the public display of the swastika. Terrorists in the US, however, openly parade with both Nazi and Confederate emblems.

QUESTIONS

Given the sexism across all cultures, is there bias against "terrorist"-appearing women that outweighs bias against "terrorist"-appearing men, or is the reverse true?

After you read Pisoiu's chapter, compare her conclusions to my earlier remarks about hip-hop clothing and grooming as displayed by Blacks and its effect on police decision to arrest (see Dabney, Teasdale, Ishoy, Gann, & Berry, 2017). If wearing certain types of clothing attracts unwanted attention, such as law enforcement intervention, why do it? Does the desire for a "bad" impression outweigh the hazards of social control intervention?

Per Pisoiu's work, is it possible that, with commercialization of terrorist-looking clothing, such clothing will lose its "badness" and thus its popularity?

Per my comments above and Mark Hamm's work, if, since the election of Donald Trump, there has been an increase in and legitimation of White supremacy in the United States, what can be done to reduce this activity and this attitude? Bear in mind that the US Constitution guarantees the right to freedom of expression.

References

Alami, A. (2017, January 12). Morocco said to ban sales of the burqa, citing safety. *New York Times*, p. A10.

Associated Press. (2017a, September 22). German policeman investigated for wearing far-right patch. Retrieved from www.seattletimes.com/nation-world.

(2017b, September 22). Activist gets OK to burn Nazi-Confederate flag in protest. Retrieved from www.seattletimes.com/nation-world.

Bourdieu, P. (1984). *Distinction: A social critique of the judgement of taste.* Cambridge, UK: Cambridge University Press.

Brown, H. E. (2017). Immigrant bodily incorporation: How the physical body structures identity, mobility, and transnationalism. *Social Problems*, 64, 14–29.

Clarridge, C. (2017, September 22). Swastika-wearing man punched on Seattle street, removes swastika, police say. Retrieved from www.Seattletimes .com-seattle-news.

Dabney, D., Teasdale, B., Ishoy, G., Gann, T., & Berry, B. (2017). Policing in a largely minority jurisdiction: The influence of appearance characteristics associated with contemporary hip-hop culture on police decision-making. *Justice Quarterly*, 34(7), 1310–1388.

Greenblatt, J. A. (2018, January 22). Homegrown terrorism (Letter to the editor). *New York Times*, p. A20.

Haberkorn, L. (2017, September 22). A Nazi eagle inflames a heated debate in Uruguay. Retrieved from www.Seattletimes.com/nation-world.

Hamm, M. S. (1994). *American skinheads: The criminology and control of hate crime.* Westport, CT: Praeger.

(1997). *Apocalypse in Oklahoma: Waco and Ruby Ridge revenged.* Boston, MA: Northeastern University Press.

(2002). *In bad company: America's terrorist underground.* Boston, MA: North-eastern University Press.

Hamm, M. S. & Spaaij, R. (2017). *Age of lone wolf terrorism (Studies in transgression).* New York, NY: Columbia University Press.

Higgins, A. (2018, January 9). At Chinese border, no visas needed, no beards allowed. *New York Times*, p. A7.

Liptak, A. (2016, October 12). Justices to decide case accusing Bush officials of 9/11 abuses. *New York Times*, p. A13.

Muzzatti, S. (2016). Terrorism and counter-terrorism in popular culture in the Post-9/11 context. In H. Pontell (Ed.), *Oxford Research Encyclopedia of Criminology* (pp. 1–26). New York, NY: Oxford University Press.

Rubin, A. J. & Breeden, A. (2016, October 2). Female French jihadists signal shift in ISIS roles. *New York Times*, pp. A6, A8.

Smith, S. (2017, April 1). China bans veils and "abnormal" beards in western province of Xinjiang. Retrieved from www.nbcnews.com/news/world.

Stack, L. (2017, October 20). Burqa bans: Spreading from Europe to Canada. *New York Times*, p. A4.

Staples, B. (2017, May 22). How the swastika became a confederate flag. *New York Times*, p. A24.

 (2018, January 10). Monuments to white supremacy. *New York Times*, p. A22.

10

Dressed to Kill

Jihadi Appearance and Its Significance in Austria and Beyond

Daniela Pisoiu

The face cover ban entered in force in Austria on October 1, 2017. It forbids veiling the face, except when this is required for health reasons or on occupational grounds. Since then, several women wearing the burka, clowns, and other individuals having more or less consciously covered their faces while walking the streets of Vienna, have been fined for doing so, and it made the headlines each time. The official rationale for the implementation of the ban was the promotion of integration. Citing from the legal text, the purpose of the law is: "the promotion of integration through the strengthening of participation in society and the securing of peaceful coexistence in Austria. Integration is a process involving the whole society and whose success depends on the participation of all people living in Austria and is based on personal interaction" (BMI, 2017).

While, in principle, the law targets all types of face covering, it is significant that the text of the law was published, along with other laws, on the website of the foreign ministry. The face cover ban was part of a broader statement discussing integration-related rationales, as well as the possible effects on tourism from the Gulf States. It is also significant given the topic of this text, that the first page of the document features a veiled woman. At the time, apart from Austria, Belgium, France and one canton in Switzerland that had already implemented a similar ban, some other countries had only banned it in certain public places (the Netherlands and Bulgaria, for example).

While integration might indeed have played a role in the considerations predating these laws, the counterterrorism undertone is difficult to miss. In another context, after the June 3, 2017 attack in London, one of the measures the UK government considered implementing, besides increasing the number of counterterrorism officers and stripping terrorists of citizenship, was a burka ban (McKay, 2017). This counterterrorism reflex is in effect just an indication of deeper, underlying assumptions in counterterrorism according to which terrorists *look* a certain way and apprehending them involves, among other things, knowing and recognizing this look. If we were to compare this with the projection of the classical evildoer as a man dressed in black climbing up the chimneys of houses at night, the entire undertaking would appear rather silly. It is quite clear that in combating crime authorities do not look for specific clothes or a specific color of the skin. That said, the assumed propensity to criminality of "people from the south" or people with darker skin color is strongly evident in mainstream news. All in all however, forensic profiling is far more sophisticated than what the counterterrorism (CT) industry has so far come up with.

Making matters worse, terrorist and extremist organizations, as strategic actors, have adapted their tactics to slide through the profiling net. Initially authorities expected only men, not women, to engage in terrorist operations, in particular in the context of Islamist terrorism; thus, groups sent women through the checkpoints (see for example some classical scenes in the movie *Battle of Algiers*, 1966) or dressed as women themselves. Some of the attackers who stormed the Iranian Parliament building on June 7, 2017 were dressed as women (Erdbrink & Mashal, 2017). Toward the end of the year, five men dressed in burkas staged an attack on a government building in Pakistan (Parker, 2017). Playing on the stereotype of the dark-skinned southerner, organizations such as Al Qaeda and ISIS have specifically recruited and used Europeans, for example, in order to secure European passports and thus avoid increased scrutiny while boarding planes (Associated Press, 2014).

But terrorist organizations do not just respond to state measures, they have an agenda of their own, and they have long recognized the advantages of modern technology coupled with modern aesthetics. With the rise and fall of the infamous Islamic State (IS) organization, there has been growing awareness of the importance and impact of online and social media productions on terrorism and political violence. Such organizations have always employed means of communications for their propaganda, recruitment. and other internal organization purposes. The IS has, however, brought an unprecedented level of professionalism, manpower, and use of an aesthetic and pop-cultural arsenal to the stage. Extremist and terrorist groups have always made use of subcultural artifacts to attract new recruits and maintain internal cohesion. Living underground or as a "group of the chosen," the "avant-garde" has also always involved an alternative, closed, often absolute worldview, marked by strict rules. These features have become more obvious but also more reinforced in contemporary times.

It is also true today that individuals have become more impactful in world politics, not just as terrorists and extremists, but in other areas of political life; in so doing, they are supported, influenced, and they themselves use the internet, social media, and subcultural artifacts to achieve political objectives. Take the example of Anders Breivik: his radicalization process, but also the publicity and interpretation of his act have been facilitated by a particular mindset cultivated in extremist environments and with a heavy use of audio-visual material. But this is not just the story of lone-actors; virtually every terrorist will tell the story of particular videos or pictures that led them to join terrorist organizations, which raised the interest in the cause, which shocked and awed, etc. Organizations such as the Islamic State place such products online to recruit or use these products for training, aiming precisely at recruitment of new members. Breaking the barriers of the otherwise Spartan dress and other kinds of codes, terrorist organizations and their multipliers have managed to produce items that can fully compete with those of other extremist scenes in terms of "coolness."

Although quite evident in the many and well-known IS productions, or perhaps precisely because of this – after all, literally everybody has seen the black flag and the orange clothes at least once – the jihadi clothing style has thus far not constituted the object of intense examination. For example, the recent edited book *Jihadi culture: The art and social practices of militant Islamists* (Hegghammer, 2017) offers a rich insight in the cultural practices, poetry, music, and dream interpretation carried out by jihadi fighters in their spare time; it however dwells only a little on the matter of clothing and its significance.

THE JIHADI COOL STYLE

Perhaps counterintuitively, there is no one jihadi style, but several. Even the few individuals that we have managed to interview in Austria (see below) have slightly or even significantly different dress attires. Common to all jihadis, however, is the military style and the allure of toughness. Apart from moments of staged candor playing with cats or in a martyrdom portrait with flowers and rivers in the background, jihadi men go out of their way to show relentlessness, power, and ruthlessness. For most of them, there is no worse insult than the insinuation that they might not be "a man," or a "lesser man." As we shall see below, the importance of this value falls in line with previous or existing cultural baggage, which creates coherence in the self-narrative. Being a man means taking up challenges and standing up for one's community and family. On the other hand, this type of thinking has been exploited by movements who "use women's involvement to shame men when recruitment is sagging," as terrorism scholar Mia Bloom spotted early on (Fillion, 2011).

More importantly, what this is an indication of is how aesthetics on the one side and worldview or self-perception on the other coincide. In the subcultural literature, this has been termed *homology*, and it refers to "the symbolic fit between the values and life-styles of a group, its subjective experience and the musical forms it uses to express or reinforce its focal concerns" (Hebdige, 1994: 113). This concept was originally developed in relation to "spectacular" subcultures in music and arts, such as the Punks in this case. Recently, authors (Conti, 2017; Pisoiu, 2015) have applied it to political subcultures – jihadis among them – along with another important concept developed by Hebdige, namely *bricolage*. The latter means "the way in which prominent forms of discourse (particularly fashion) are radically adapted, subverted and extended" (Hebdige, 1994: 104). It basically refers to how subcultures take and adapt objects from the mainstream culture or other subcultures.

In his chapter "The visual culture of jihad," Afhon Ostovar (2017: 82) provides concurring arguments for the two concepts (without naming them as such):

... jihadist visual culture is based on a network of visual images, symbols, and themes widely used by the jihadist community and familiar to its supporters. Groups, media organizations, and artists deliberately draw from this "visual network" to create compositions that represent and resonate with the jihadist community. The main themes in jihadi visual culture closely correspond with the political and religious tenets of the movement itself. Images depicting austere religiosity, war, antagonism toward enemies, as well as honor, fraternity, chivalry, and justice, are all conveyed through the lens of jihadist belief and often shaped by the political context of the moment.

The author goes on to outline how simplicity of visuals and message adds to their resonance in a rather heterogeneous ethno-linguistic public. Above and beyond these observations and the concepts themselves, it is important to stress how visuals (clothes included) fit – and need to fit – not only ideology, but broader worldviews and self-perceptions, which can indeed carry more salience for the individual, especially in the beginning of their involvement. Another repository that these elements need to draw on is the broader cultural arsenal, or the "deep cultural grammar" (Johnston, 2008), which acts like a subconscious mechanism of legitimacy, but also decreases the risk of cognitive dissonance. As we shall see later, the image of the wolf through the intermediary of Jack Wolfskin attire is very present in the Austrian jihadi clothing style. (Jack Wolfskin refers to an outdoor clothing outfitter, whose logo is a wolf paw print.)

While no statistics are available on the overall number of jihadis in Austria, we know from available studies on the prison population that more than half of the individuals convicted for terrorism offences in Austria are Chechens (Hofinger & Schmidinger, 2017). In his article about the impact of deep cultural grammar on the Chechen resistance movement, Hank Johnston (2008) dedicates an entire section to the "wolf of the Caucasus." He therein shows how the wolf symbol was introduced in the nineteenth century through a Russian poem about Caucasian mountaineers, and was then adopted in the nationalist movement. This was first of all a strategic move: "What marketing professionals do for contemporary corporate logos, the historical development of the Chechen cultural text was able to do for itself automatically, namely, seize an image, claim it as its own, and reproduce it as a representation of Chechen identity for itself, for the rest of the world, and especially for its enemies" (Johnston, p. 326).

At the same time, however, the symbolism of the wolf matched several important features of the Chechen culture. Wolves live in packs, and the Chechen society is organized in clans made up of patrilineal extended families. The wolf's hunting style – attacking a prey larger than individual wolves in the pack – can additionally be compared to the Chechen fighting style: "The social structure just described was supported by a Spartan-like gendered valuation of male warrior prowess and, above all, honour and obligation to one's kin, clan, and land. Also, there was a vigilance of one's freedom and rejection of any authority that was outside family and clan structures" (ibid., p. 327).

Obviously, these deeply rooted features of social organization and allegiance also play a role in the context of the broader integration in modern Western society; it is only natural that they would be reflected to some extent in the subcultural jihadi style.

Judging by the video productions of the only Austrian jihadi involved in propaganda activities, Mohammed Mahmoud, the clothing style here is a mixture of military and traditional Afghani attire. This individual has worn a Pashtun hat virtually without interruption, ever since his first trial in Vienna in 2007–2008. The rest of his clothing has evolved from casual, to increasingly more prominent displays of Pashtun and camouflage clothing. In his famous execution video in the summer of 2015, Mahmoud wears black Pashtun clothes, a military vest with explosives, and the omnipresent Pashtun hat. This style is partially concurrent with what could be labelled the "religious style" back home, meaning again the Pashtun shirt and trousers, added to which is the "taqiyah" (the Muslim prayer hat). International productions usually picture the same combination of traditional, usually Pashtun, clothing, and military attire, in particular camouflage trousers and shirts, and the latter tends to be more pronounced. According to some authors, the intention behind this is to confer the impression of masculinity and toughness symbolized by the military apparel, thus supporting their recruitment efforts:

> One of the strongest themes projected throughout those videos is military toughness: they show young men in training camps being put through assault-course style exercises, just as they would be in a regular army or commando unit. . . . These images are very deliberately assembled to project the notion that those waging a jihad in contemporary Afghanistan and Pakistan (and beyond) actually do command an Islamic army. . . . Given the ugly reality of what's going on, it has fallen to jihadi propagandists to project the idea that their forces are strong, organised and state-like, and that task has involved multiple layers of deceit.
>
> (Semple, 2016)

Looking at another infamous executioner figure, the British Jihadi John wears a similar combination to that of Mahmoud's, with the difference being that the shirt and trousers are tighter and his face masked; he also has guns hanging on his shoulders – more like a piece of fashion then proper fighting gear – and fingerless gloves. An interesting fact is that both he and Mahmoud wear black – whereas the typical Pashtun clothes are beige. Black is generally seen as "cooler," according to our interview partners in the jihadi milieu in Austria.

The street style in Austria is usually a combination of gangsta rap and military style with pop-cultural elements, including the reappropriation of traditional Islamist symbols through the intermediary of pop culture. In a counter-narrative video series, for example, the picturing of a typical street jihadi is all in black, hoodie, jeans, and a long shirt (Hoisl, 2017). Even farther away from traditional clothing and deeper in the world of pop are ISIS propaganda productions drawing on war movies and games, such as *Call of Duty*. Here we see almost exclusively military attire and some minimal jihadi symbolism such as the black flag or the typical Arabic inscription.

HOW THEY SEE IT AND WHY

Having somewhat outlined the features, mechanisms, and available interpretations of jihadi clothing online, I turn now to the significance it has
for some of the people actually wearing it. To this end, I illustrate with
insights from several individuals interviewed in Austria for the purposes
of testing radicalization theories and understanding of how and why they
considered traveling to, or traveled to, Syria and Iraq, including the
significance of subcultural aspects such as music, clothing, and lifestyle.[1]
One of the standard questions we asked inquired into the kinds of
clothing they wore while being in the jihadi scene, how that changed over
time, and what it meant to them. In the answers that follow we see a
mixture of *strategic, motivational, cultural,* and *taste* rationales. The
reasons why they wear certain things can be more or less conscious; often
reflecting cultural scripts, this includes mainstream culture but also
imported/traditional culture; it boosts known motivations to engage in
extremism, such as status or recognition; and more often than not there is
a dire need to be "cool." Here is an example of someone outlining several
of these elements at the same time: *status, recognition,* and *taste.* The
quotation also evidences how role models presented in the propaganda
indeed also have an influence on sympathizers, in this case with respect to
the color black:

I was always dressed in black, even in summer; I was sweating, I had these long
clothes, like, they were not praying clothes, they were like invented by them like
up to the knee, such clothes so that one could not see the back whilst praying and
such or whatever; these are um um parts of the body which one must hide and um
so these were the clothes, they looked good, like I said, I had black clothes and so
forth, I really liked that. They also influenced other things by appearing so so
serious. One took them seriously when they were talking, this way of talking,
I also copied from them. And how they, when they debated, how they debated,
with which arguments, how they answered to which argument and so forth, also
verbally they were, so how they spoke, how they talked, how they discussed, they
were role models because they had a lot more knowledge and one asked them
when the Imam for example was not there or not reachable. So in these kinds of
things they were role models.

(Interview 15)

The interviewee here is on the one hand attracted to the status and
recognition of older people in that milieu, enjoyed them and tried to copy
them, including in style. On the other hand, it is the aesthetics alone that
plays a role. While he does mention that there is a religious (original)
significance to the clothes, the knowledge thereof is superficial and

certainly less important by comparison, thus the "whatever." Another person, interviewee 6, recounted how he dressed in both styles: the *Sunna* clothes (Islamic coat and headgear for men) and the *jellabiya*, but also the flag and the ISIS T-shirts, and posted photos of himself on social media. The *jellabiya* is a traditional Sudanese and Egyptian long shirt or robe, similar to the Arab *thawb*.

Interviewee 15 is somewhat in between the religious and the street style. The following example is clearly of the former type; consequently, his line of argumentation is *abiding rules*. Asked how he would describe his and appropriate clothing more generally apart from the beard and headscarf, another interviewee says:

Yes, they say about the Prophet SAW [peace be upon him] that the one who um has his clothes grinded will not enter paradise so by analogy, so, arrogant, in the past people have, um, 600 years after Christ ... grinded their clothes, and even had servants that carried their clothes, no? In hindsight, and this in any case does not fit with a creature who, yes, boasts in front of others. And that's why it was said that one, what one has on should try to, um, keep above the ankles, what one calls here trousers at half-mast is actually in terms of lifestyle according to the laws of Islam.

(Interview 15)

We have here the broader precept of "modesty," which can go beyond the jihadi or even Islamic fundamentalist scenes, and also the element of "above the ankles," which does not. There is however another dynamic occurring around this feature, which is appropriation by the mainstream. As we shall see below, certain fashion styles also involving trousers above the ankles cause confusion and even outrage in the jihadi scene. But for now, going for a moment even farther away from the fixation on clothes, there are of course examples where concern for attire is minimal. For example, interviewee 9 says: "Concerning clothing, one should try to wear wide clothes, so that one cannot recognize the body. With me, nothing changed [as compared to the time before]." It might be important here to mention that gangsta rapper clothes are in and of themselves rather "baggy," so in principle one need not apply significant changes when transitioning from a gang or petty crime career, for example, to jihadism.

Thinking about the visual evolution of former gangster and rapper Deso Dogg from Germany, his appearances did not initially feature major changes, with the exception of a Palestinian headscarf. Photos taken during his previous rap career already featured him with black clothes and camouflage. It was only later, as he arrived in Syria and started producing propaganda videos, that he slowly started appearing in more traditional clothes, which, might in fact have been easier to procure in Syria than hoodies and sports pants.

Similar to other subcultures, certain elements of clothing can also serve as a *code* for belonging to a certain group, not unlike, for example, skinheads and bomber jackets. Interviewee 15 explains for example:

... one thing I have to say about this, I don't know if anyone is interested or whatever, Jack Wolfskin stuff were the fashion there, even now one can, so one can orient oneself [by this] when one sees a Muslim with full beard, so, black things on, has a Jack Wolfskin jacket and trousers or only trousers, one could assume 50–50 that he is an IS sympathizer, because these are the top signs among each other also, it was among one another like this that Jack Wolfskin was a sign.

He then goes on to explain the practical meanings of this wolf-associated clothing brand: "Yes, because ... Jack Wolfskin indeed such, um, such climber stuff and so forth, they are very good in war. Shoes, trousers, underpants, T-shirts, sweaters, vests, jackets, everything from Jack Wolfskin."

The other aspect of the story was the association with the Chechen wolf. Asked why Chechen youth are so fond of this and so many use it as part of their name, interviewee 15 says:

Well um because um because a um great scholar from Saudi Arabia said that um; this was how long ago? I think it was in the seventeenth or eighteenth century, he said that the Chechens because of their courage and um their will and their um um so because they were unyielding, that one can compare them with wolves, that they are very similar to wolves; and wolves were also in Chechnya so um before he said it so house animals, typical domestic animals like cats or dogs there were wolves there yes. So Caucasian wolves so um these um um white wolves grey wolves and such...

(Interview 15)

Going farther than "taste" is the idea of appearance for appearance's sake, or *pure pop*. The individuals we have interviewed refer to this phenomenon in a rather depreciating way, as something void of content and superficial. This is in a sense not unlike the critique of "true" extreme right wingers or left wingers against the "lifestyle" ones. In the opinion of interviewee 10, simply wearing the typical jihadi pop attire does not mean, or is even at odds with "being a real man," a core jihadi value. He calls them wannabe mujahideen, wannabe martyrs, fighters, holy warriors, running around with the flag, military trousers and Jack Wolf-skin jackets. He further explains how this pop jihad in the meantime has evolved toward being exclusively pop, where the original significance and values are already lost. The association between the United States and pop culture is seen as self-evident. For an ideology that is in part built on a deep disgust toward Western culture and consumerism, this reappropriation by pop of jihadi pop is a worst-case scenario.

Interviewee 10, for example, illustrates how trousers above the ankles have already become fashion à la Swagger or YOLO (outlets for hip-hop clothing and outdoor gear, respectively). He further outlines:

Now it's also somehow, I noticed somehow this Islamic State rooted in the fashion. They already wear T-shirts like this . . . Somehow is funny, I don't know. In fact it is even creepy a bit, namely with us it was prophesized you know? *Yawn al-qiyamah* says Judgement Day. There are already signs, *Daggal*, this Antichrist comes.

(Interviewee 10)

From a more practical viewpoint, the same interviewee outlines how this ostentatious display of jihadi attire might in fact be damaging for jihadi operations, since it *attracts attention*:

And we said stop [wearing] these. *Jelebiah* these Sunna clothes, this outfit which Afghanis wear for example which is very well known, say, so that the ones who reads this understand um. We said don't wear these kinds of clothes, or they run around with military trousers, with T-shirts with Arabic writing and then proudly . . . Inconspicuous, calm, you are Muslim, you don't have to show yourself to everyone, not everyone needs to know . . . and yes – laughs – what can I say? This [guy] all of a sudden, there were cases, we wanted first [to go with the] plane of course. Of course, the easiest way. There was an idiot with us, I don't know, I think he was also Turkish. He for example was standing with such a *shahada* flag at the airport. And we had of course our women with us, two three *Niqabis* and of course he thinks what do they want to do now? None of them is older than 18. What are they up to? Yes, also such cases.

(Interview 10)

This person himself saw no use in wearing ostentatious clothes, not even in the rather religious style, for the same reason:

I was there, I also prayed there, I listened to the lectures but I never ran around with such clothes, I did wear this prayer hat so on *Juma* always. But there are people who run around 24 hours a day with these togs. I've never done such a thing, maybe I wore it at Ramadan or on at the *Juma* prayer, dressed nicely like this at the Friday *Juma* prayer. Otherwise like this, but 24 hours running around with it, what's in it for me? Maybe at the time one did this, but now I don't want to raise attention at all, people, there is dangerous pseudo-knowledge at the time in the media, there is a lot of agitation against Islam at the moment. . .

(Interview 10)

Interviewee 10 is further down the line of radicalization, when the time comes to match words with deeds. This positionality creates difficulties in terms of appearance, since the positive-value baggage associated with wearing certain clothes contradicts practical security considerations. In this stage, the individual basically needs to separate himself from the radical milieu and thus put up with its scorn. As a solution to this cognitive dissonance, this individual chooses to actively diminish the value of external display of faith and put forward an argument of the type that deeds are better than words:

I'm saying really, a big mouth, a real barking dog, it was a Bosnian. And I said to him, he says like Syria Syria, this and that you know, he told me something like, he used an Arabic word like um I don't know … not that I am an unbeliever but, I don't know, it came out like, not apostate. Not hypocrite, another expression, I don't know anymore, an Arabic one. It is not well known either. It doesn't matter, I felt so insulted, like I am not a man basically. I told him clearly in his face, as opposed to you barking dog, I said to him like this word for word. If I go I don't say it to everyone. I don't run around with such clothing either and scream jihad jihad with these Arabic [words] which are written there *shahada* that's what is says, it is also not something bad what it says, just *Lā ilāha illā 'llāh Muḥammadun rasūlu 'llāh* so there is no other God apart from God and Moham-med was his first prophet. There is nothing special written there, so I don't know what's supposed to be so brutal about it, what people think. Um yes I say to him literally when I go I go but I don't run around and say to everybody, what is this? He barks like a dog. Raises attention and such …

(Interview 10)

WHAT DOES THIS TELL US ABOUT RADICALIZATION?

The consumption and production of subcultural artifacts seems to be an important element of the radicalization process. We are nevertheless still far from understanding how these interactions work, how radicalization expresses itself in subcultural products and how the latter influences individual radicalization processes. As a notable exception, we have gained a fuller and more nuanced understanding of the ways in which music affects individual radicalization through the work of Mark Hamm (1993). In terms of visuals, however, and in particular clothes, systematic studies are still necessary. Based on this incipient analysis, which is by no means representative, I can however already draw some insights with respect to the radicalization processes of jihadis in Austria. First, a con-nection can be made to theories outlining the importance of non-material gain such as status, recognition, and empowerment or self-esteem

(Horgan, 2005; Kruglanski et al., 2014; Pisoiu, 2012). It is apparent from the interviews that wearing particular value-laden clothes contributes to an increased sense of empowerment. We could also see how individuals would try to copy the clothing style of others who already enjoy status and recognition.

Another aspect, which has been so far not sufficiently addressed in the classical radicalization literature, is the issue of taste. We know from the broader research on extremism that merely "liking" certain music or clothing can act as a facilitating factor or a bridge toward membership in a scene (see, for example, Wörner-Schappert, 2017: 125). Also, some individuals would only stay on "for the fun," rather than out of ideological conviction. It seems, however, that also with other, more regular and thoroughly ideological members of these scenes, taste is not insignificant. Still along the dividing line between the lifestyle vs. the professional extremists, a connection can also be drawn to a dilemma outlined in the broader terrorism literature, namely the tension between publicity and secrecy (Crenshaw, 2011). Generally, for a terrorist organization to survive and grow, it needs visibility through acts; it needs to show that it is capable of acting. This however reduces the degree of secrecy and can potentially jeopardize its existence. We have similarly seen how, for individuals who are already in the stage of thinking about concrete deeds, too much attention triggered by ostentatious clothing can be a problem. Terrorist organizations do explicitly allow for deviations from the rules concerning clothing, but also for drinking or smoking, if this is necessary in order to "blend in" and ensure the success of the operations. Also in the case of Boko Haram (a jihadi organization in Nigeria and other neighboring countries) where Western education is forbidden, and which is known to be one of the stricter organizations in terms of clothing prescriptions, it was found that fighters were allowed to disguise themselves by wearing other, regular clothes, in order to carry out certain attacks (Nwigwe, 2018: 8).

Finally, another debate, which has only been initiated in recent years, is the nexus between criminality and terrorism. Two separate studies have for example found more than half of their samples of IS recruits have had criminal pasts (Basra, Neumann, & Brunner, 2016; Heinke, 2017). At the time of this writing, we do not have more concrete information about how this transition occurs and what mechanisms are at play. Drawing on the insights from this chapter it could nevertheless be safe to say that the typical IS mix of gangsta rap plus military style facilitates a low-cost transition from petty criminality to terrorism. In other words, individuals can transition without much change in appearance.

CONCLUSION AND OUTLOOK

This chapter has been a first attempt to gain a deeper insight of the significance of jihadi clothing for the ones who wear it and for radicalization more broadly. In particular, I have attempted to indirectly show how the most obvious or the most publicly exploited items such as the burka are not necessarily the most relevant or impactful elements when it comes to individual radicalization. In terms of outlook, I would like to close by drawing attention to the phenomenon of commercialization of jihadi clothing. This trend has already been noted by authors looking more broadly at jihadi merchandise online. Examples would include hoodies and T-shirts with two fire-and-water walls with, in the middle, a face covered in a Palestinian scarf along with an IS headband attached on the forehead, as well as more classical Hamas and Hezbollah symbols on hoodies (Culzac, 2014). Also in the German-speaking countries we have observed the emergence of unofficial "Islamic shops" or providers of "Islamic merchandise" in more or less open spaces. For example, on social media there are advertisements for sprays, shampoos, oils, and of course clothing. On a posting on Telegram we find instructions about how the hijab should look:

The requirements for an appropriate hijab: first, it must be heavy (thick) and not transparent; second, it must be loose-fitting; third, it must cover the whole body; fourth, it must not jump in the eye; fifth, it must not resemble the clothing of kuffar women or clothing for men; sixth, it must not be a piece of clothing that attracts looks; seventh, it must not be perfumed (perfume or incense).

On a website dedicated exclusively to merchandise, we find perfume, prayer carpets for children, niqabs, and serpent oil (which is said to help strengthen the roots of the hair, ensures a better blood circulation, contributes to the growth of the hair and prevents hair from falling out, and moisturises dry hair without shine), as well as burkas, khimar (long veil) sets, trousers for children in military colours, and shirts and harem pants for men.

In the typical extremist scene, such merchandise is meant to keep the machinery running and be attractive to potential recruits. Additionally, we also have the appearance of manufacturers who tap into this source of inspiration to simply sell clothes. Related to this, and this is the second aspect here, the merchandise appeals less to the significance of the symbols as such, and more to the "coolness" of the entire package. How the respective publics indeed interpret these items can only be reliably established by means of interviews. Yet it is already known from the interviews captured here how the attractiveness of these objects works, namely largely divorced from ideology, with a trace of "extremist" significance as simply "coolness." Jihadi subcultural production, in other words, is already on the way to being commercialized, just like other subcultures before it; jihadi subculture has reached its maturity.

References

Associated Press (2014, September 15). Al-Qaeda recruiting European jihadists in Syria to attack US planes, say American officials, *The Telegraph*. Retrieved from www.telegraph.co.uk/news/worldnews/middleeast/syria/11097660/Al-Qaeda-recruiting-European-jihadists-in-Syria-to-attack-US-planes-say-American-officials.html.

Basra, R., Neumann, P. R., & Brunner, C. (2016). *Criminal pasts, terrorist futures: European jihadists and the new crime-terror nexus*. London: International Centre for the Study of Radicalisation and Political Violence.

BMI. (2017). Bundesministerium für Inneres, Bundesgesetz über das Verbot der Verhüllung des Gesichts in der Öffentlichkeit (Anti-Gesichtsverhüllungsgesetz – AGesVG). Retreived from www.bmeia.gv.at/reise-au fenthalt/einreise-und-aufenthalt-in-oesterreich/vollverschleierungsverbot-in-oesterreich/.

Conti, U. (2017). Between rap and jihad: Spectacular subcultures, terrorism and visuality. *Contemporary Social Science*, 12(3–4), 272–284.

Crenshaw, M. (2011). *Explaining terrorism: Causes, processes and consequences*. Abingdon, UK: Routledge.

Culzac, N. (2014, June 24). Dress like a jihadist: Isis and terror-related merchandise flogged online and in Indonesian stores. *The Independent*. Retrieved from www.independent.co.uk/news/world/middle-east/dress-like-a-jihadist-isis-and-terror-related-merchandise-flogged-online-and-in-indonesian-stores-9560230.html#gallery.

Erdbrink, T. & Mashal, M. (2017, June 7). At Least 12 Killed in Pair of Terrorist Attacks in Iran. *New York Times*. Retrieved from www.nytimes.com/2017/06/07/world/middleeast/iran-parliament-attack-khomeini-mau soleum.html.

Fillion, K. (2011, January 24). In conversation with Mia Bloom: On the rise in female suicide bombings, how women cause more damage and why they do it. *Macleans*. Retrieved from www.macleans.ca/general/macleans-interview-mia-bloom/.

Hamm, M. S. (1993). *American skinheads: The criminology and control of hate crime*. Westport, CT/London: Praeger.

Hebdige, D. (1994). *Subculture: The meaning of style*. London/New York: Routledge.

Hegghammer, T. (2017). *Jihadi culture: The art and social practices of militant Islamists*. London/New York: Cambridge University Press.

Heinke, D. H. (2017). German foreign fighters in Syria and Iraq: The updated data and its implications. *CTC Sentinel*, 10(3), 17–22.

Hofinger, V. & Schmidinger, T. (2017). Endbericht zur Begleitforschung Deradikalisierung im Gefängnis, Wien: Institut für Rechts- und Kriminalsoziologie. Retrieved from www.irks.at/assets/irks/Publikationen/Forschungsbericht/ Endbericht_Begleitforschung_2017.pdf.

Hoisl, T. (2017). In dieser Videoserie schwört ein ehemaliger IS-Sympathisant aus Wien dem Dschihadismus ab. *Vice*, September 6. www.vice.com/de_at/article/ xww4vq/in-dieser-videoserie-schwort-ein-ehemaliger-is-sympathisant-aus- wien-dem-dschihadismus-ab.

Horgan, J. (2005). *The psychology of terrorism*. London/New York: Routledge.

Johnston, H. (2008). Ritual, strategy, and deep culture in the Chechen national movement. *Critical Studies on Terrorism*, 1(3), 321–342.

Kruglanski, A. W., Gelfand, M. J., Bélanger, J. J., Sheveland, A., Hetiarachchi, M. & Gunaratna, R. (2014). The psychology of radicalization and deradicalization: How significance quest impacts violent extremism. *Advances in Political Psychology*, 35, 69–93.

McKay, H. (2017, June 4). London terror attack: British officials eye burka ban and stripping citizenship. *Fox News*. Retrieved from www.foxnews.com/world/ 2017/06/04/london-terror-attack-british-officials-eye-burka-bans-and-strip ping-citizenship.html.

Nwigwe, C. (2018). Fashioning terror: The Boko Haram dress code and the politics of identity, fashion theory. *The Journal of Dress, Body and Culture*, DOI: 10.1080/1362704X.2017.1420301.

Parker, N. (2017, December 2). Gunmen in burkas massacre nine and wound 35 in Pakistan terror attack. *The Sun*. Retrieved from www.thesun.co.uk/news/ 5048629/gunmen-in-burkas-massacre-nine-and-wound-35-in-pakistan/.

Pisoiu, D. (2012). *Islamist radicalisation in Europe. An occupational change process*. London: Routledge.

(2015). Subcultural theory applied to jihadi and right-wing radicalization in Germany. *Terrorism and Political Violence*, 27(1), 9–28.

Semple, M. (2016, January 16). Black flags and balaclavas: how jihadists dress for imaginary war. *The Conversation*. Retrieved from http://theconversation.com/ black-flags-and-balaclavas-how-jihadists-dress-for-imaginary-war-36152.

Wörner-Schappert, M. (2017). Fallbeispiel: Musik – Propagandawaffe im Internet. In Glaser, S. and Pfeffer, T. (Eds.), *Erlebniswelt Rechtsextremismus: modern – subversiv – hasserfüllt*
Hintergünde und Methoden für die Praxis der Prävention, pp. 118–128.

Endnote

1 The interviews were conducted in the context of the project *Life-worlds of Austria jihadis. A milieu study*, ongoing at the time of writing and financed by the Austrian Federal Ministry of Defence.

II

Charisma, Prisoner Radicalization, and Terrorism

The Role of Appearance

Mark S. Hamm

Folsom Prison occupies a special place in the history of American penology. Built with granite rock by inmate labor in the late 1870s, Folsom State Prison is nestled against a series of dry, rolling hills along the American River some thirty miles east of Sacramento in a town appropriately named Repressa, California. Folsom's list of notable convicts reads like a Who's Who of American crime. They include Charles Manson, the Hell's Angels founder Sonny Barger, the Black Panther Eldridge Cleaver, the prison revolutionary George Jackson, the LSD guru Timothy Leary, the serial killer Edmund Kemper, the spree killer Erik Menendez, and the rap mogul Suge Knight. Its legacy of violence is incandescent. Over the years convicts have killed and maimed an untold number of guards, and hundreds of prisoners have died at the hands of other inmates. As late as 2017, the Folsom warden reported an estimated 280 stabbings at the prison each year. To control the violence, each year guards fire some four hundred rounds at inmates with semiautomatic rifles. On a normal day, at least five inmates are assaulted with makeshift weapons (Mueller, 2017). As a result, Folsom Prison has been touted in national news reports as "the bloodiest joint in America." One inmate described Folsom "the citadel of suffering. It is gray – a dull, lifeless gray ... An oppressive sense of doom radiates outward from the blocks of stone" (Hartman, 2009: 34). Other inmates simply call Folsom "the end of the world."

In the eyes of most people, though, the prison is known for a legendary cultural event that occurred there on the morning of Saturday, January 13, 1968: the making of *Johnny Cash at Folsom Prison* – Cash's live concert played before a thousand prisoners in the dining hall. The historic show featured such laments on confinement and regret as "Folsom Prison

Blues," "Dark as a Dungeon," "I Got Stripes," "Busted," "Cocaine Blues," the mournful "I Still Miss Someone," and "Green, Green, Grass of Home" – each song greeted with uproarious applause. Cash closed the show with "Greystone Chapel," a cry of sin and redemption written by a Folsom prisoner named Glen Sherley, who sat nearby the stage. "There's a Greystone Chapel here in Folsom," Cash sang: "A house of worship in this den of sin." "Cash was singing from inside the place where American law and order and American hell met," wrote the music critic Mikal Gilmore of the concert, "and nobody else in popular music could match him for radical nerve or compassion" (Gilmore, 2008: 197).

All songs are more important than their literal content. Along with his authentic concern for life's losers, what made Johnny Cash the towering figure that he was and explains why he was able to win over the hearts and minds of a thousand felons living at "the end of the world," was his minimalist approach to American folk music. Backed by simple guitar, bass and drums forming his trademark *boom, chuck-a-boom* sound (*I hear that train a comin' rollin' round the bend/I ain't seen the sunshine since I don't know when/Well I'm stuck in Folsom Prison and time keeps dragging on/While a train keeps a rollin' on down to San Antone*), Cash sang in a lonesome baritone that could wrench power and feeling from the darkest of places. But there was something more to Cash's appeal: his amazing presence. This is Johnny Cash, leaning against the East Gate at Folsom an hour before taking the stage on that winter morning back in 1968, looking like a man worthy of his place on Mount Rushmore (see Images 10 and 11).

At Folsom Prison, Johnny Cash's compassion, his unpretentious musical style, and his incredible appearance coincided in a manner that went far beyond the cliché common to other entertainers of the day. Released in the summer of 1968, *Johnny Cash at Folsom Prison* would go on to sell millions and become one of popular music's essential albums. Not only did the album represent a milestone for Johnny Cash the performer but it established Cash as the nation's leading public figure on prison reform, drawing the support of such powerful law-and-order hard-liners as Richard Nixon, Ronald Reagan, and the Reverend Billy Graham. Testimony to his influence is found in the recollections of a music critic from the *Los Angeles Times*, Robert Hilburn, who accompanied Cash at the 1968 Folsom concert and would later become his biographer:

The subject matter he chose to write about, values of American life, the underdog – we're all underdogs in some way. We all respond to that. We all felt he was talking

IMAGE 10. Johnny Cash at Folsom Prison, album cover (Getty Images)

IMAGE 11. The forbidding image of Folsom Prison (Getty Images)

to us. Whether it was a prison, a Native American reservation, everyone felt he was one of them. And so, he was speaking to the heart of America, somehow, and it came through . . . Johnny Cash had a mission, and he had a charisma.

(Hilburn, 2013)

CHARISMA AND TERRORISM

A turning point in my thirty-year career as a terrorism researcher occurred in 2004 when Moroccan and Spanish jihadists bombed commuter trains in Madrid. More than two hundred people were killed and over a thousand were wounded, marking the deadliest terrorist attack in modern Spanish history. Investigators discovered that the attack was waged by what a leading terrorism scholar would call "a loosely-affiliated cluster of childhood friends, neighborhood homeboys, siblings, cousins, petty criminals, drug dealers and former prison cellmates" (Atran, 2010: 206). In early 2006, I was contacted by representatives of the US Department of Justice who asked if I was interested in conducting a study of prisoner radicalization with the goal of estimating America's vulnerability to a Madrid-style attack by former prison inmates. There was good reason for their concern. A fringe group of Sunni Muslims called Jam'iyyat Ul-Islam Is-Saheeh (the Assembly of Authentic Islam, or JIS) had recently been arrested by the FBI in a "fully operational plot" to attack US Army recruiting centers, Israeli government facilities, and synagogues in Los Angeles on the symbolic date of September 11, 2005. The JIS plot was led by an inmate at California's New Folsom Prison, named Kevin James.

I accepted the government's offer and began a series of interviews with inmates who had experienced a conversion to a non-Judeo-Christian religion while in prison, with a special focus on inmate leaders at Folsom Prison and New Folsom Prison. I conducted approximately 140 hours of interviews with thirty prisoners, along with several dozen interviews with prison chaplains, gang intelligence officers, wardens, and FBI analysts. Inmate interviews were done inside prison chapels, with no guards, chaplains, or other inmates present. More than a dozen interviews were conducted inside Greystone Chapel. The prisoners ranged in age from 19 to 63, and their ethnicities included African-American, Latino, Native American, and Caucasian. All the prisoners were serving time for violent crimes, ranging from aggravated assault, kidnapping, and armed robbery to homicide. Most came from urban areas and were involved in gangs prior to their incarceration. About two-thirds belonged to prison gangs. Prisoners had undergone conversions to Islam (traditional and American versions such as the Nation of Islam), Native American faiths, Black Hebrew Israelism (a black supremacy group), and those preferred by white supremacists (Odinism/Asatru, Teutonic Wicca, and Christian Identity).

My overarching finding was that radicalization can and does take place in large, overcrowded maximum-security prisons. As one Shiite prisoner told me at the height of the Iraq War, "People are recruiting on the yard every day. It's scandalous. Everybody's glorifying Osama bin Laden. But these Muslims come to Islam with the same gang mentality they had on the streets. Same red rags, same blue rags [symbols of the Crips and Bloods]. The mentality is pure ignorance driving terrorism"

(Hamm, 2013: 53). Radicalization is based on a prison gang model whereby inmates adopt extreme views through a process of one-on-one proselytizing by charismatic leaders.

Charisma is one of the most frequently used but underexplored concepts in the criminology of collective violence. The term was introduced to sociology by Max Weber in 1922 as part of his ideal-typical classification of authority figures in German society – presciently written a decade before Hitler seized power. Weber defined charisma as:

A certain quality of an individual personality by virtue of which he is set apart from ordinary men and treated with supernatural, superhuman, or at least specifically exceptional powers or qualities. These are such as are not accessible to the ordinary person, but are regarded as of divine origin or as exemplary, and on the basis of them the individual concerned is treated as a leader.

(Weber, 1968: 48)

For Weber, then, charisma was created in a relationship between a community and a leader who had a vision for what the world should be. Charisma was a divine gift that evoked the loyalty of community members afflicted by a crisis so great as to defy resolution by established authorities or institutions. A charismatic person can alleviate the crisis and restore equilibrium to the community, which explains why followers form a bond with their leader. Charismatic authority is therefore validated by *others*. This person's capabilities are a function of his or her unique talents; indeed, the charismatic leader's authority derives solely from those talents.

Psychologists have also emphasized the role of talent in their discussions of charisma. Fried (2004), for example, points out that the characteristics of a leader's talents will always turn on the nature of the crisis facing a community. Therefore, if the crisis involves spiritual decay, the leader's gifts will be in religion. If the crisis involves disease or famine, the gifts tend to be organizational. If the critical problem involves political conflict, the gifts will be in the realm of oratory. And if the conflict leads to violence, the leader is likely to be gifted in military tactics.

Sociologists of religion have employed Weber's model by arguing that new religious movements tend to have leaders who wield considerable charismatic authority and are believed to have special powers or knowledge. Charismatic leaders are unpredictable, according to Barker (1999), because they are not bound by tradition and they may be accorded by their followers the right to control all aspects of their lives. In these cases, the leader may lack any accountability, require unquestioning obedience, and encourage a dependency upon the movement for personal resources that have nothing to do with the movement's religious goals. If leaders fail to adequately address these issues, it can lead to a dysfunctional group dynamic that encourages violence (Dawson, 2004).

Within the terrorism literature, charismatic leadership is treated less formally and is based almost entirely on anecdotal evidence derived from case studies; often, the role of charisma is ignored by terrorism researchers (Hoffmann & Dawson, 2013). Robert Mathews, leader of the near-mythical American neo-Nazi terrorist group known as the Order (responsible for a series of assassinations and armored truck robberies during the 1980s), is typically described as a charismatic figure by terrorism scholars (Hamm, 2007). "It was the way he carried himself," recalled a confederate, almost rhapsodizing about Mathews's physical appearance, "sinuously, as though at any moment he were poised to leap – a graceful leap to some strange place" (Martinez, 1999: 53).

Research on the question of how physical appearance influences charismatic leadership inside prisons, and how it affects the occurrence of terrorism, is virtually non-existent. Crucial to filling this lacuna is an understanding of the prison environment in which radicalization takes shape.

INMATE APPEARANCE IN A FAILED PRISON

Folsom Prison is severely overcrowded, with more than 4,000 inmates living in spaces designed to hold 1,800 (for sources on statistics in this section, see Hamm, 2013: 108–109). Most of the inmates are African-American and Latinos, mainly from big cities (60 percent from Los Angeles) and mostly unemployed prior to incarceration. About two-thirds have been locked up before. Over half read at or below the third-grade level or are "marginally literate" by normal educational standards. Every cell at the prison is double-bunked by race, and another five hundred inmates are double-bunked by race in hallways (called "bad beds"), leading to the dining hall where the Man in Black had recorded his work of genius.

An estimated 80 percent of the prisoners have histories of intravenous drug abuse, and they continue to share tainted needles while incarcerated. Mental illness is extensive, and the suicide rate is twice the national average. An unimaginable 40 percent of the prisoners are infected with hepatitis C – a condition that, under California penal policy, cannot be treated until an inmate's liver begins to malfunction. The prison's medical facility is under federal receivership after the courts ruled that it violated constitutional standards of cruel and unusual punishment. In a Supreme Court case upholding the judgment, *Brown v. Plata*, Justice Stephen Breyer described conditions in California prisons as "horrendous," citing evidence of prisoners "found hanged to death in holding tanks where observation windows are obscured with smeared feces, and discovered catatonic in pools of their own urine after spending nights locked in small cages" (Liptak, 2010).

Funding for rehabilitation and work programs has been slashed to pieces at Folsom, so prisoners spend their days doing little more than lying in bed or walking the yard and bangin' Crip, Blood, Mexican Mafia, Aryan Brotherhood. Overcrowding has paralyzed wardens from transferring troublemakers out of the population, increasing gang tensions. Seven out of ten inmates released from the prison return within three years, representing the highest recidivism rate in the nation. The state's prison commissioner described the place as a "powder keg" at risk of exploding (Steinhauer, 2006).

This powder keg of incarceration can be summed up in two photographs. One illustrates the structural problems at Folsom. The other illuminates a corresponding human factor that becomes the overriding catalyst to violence (see Image 12).

Image 12 shows the conditions of confinement caused by overcrowding at Folsom and other California state prisons, where inmates are stacked like cordwood on row after row of double bunks – with only a few feet of floor space separating one bunk from another – and no meaningful activity to sustain them. John Irwin (2007) called this the

IMAGE 12. Prison overcrowding (Getty Images)

warehouse prison. The inmates are idle and racially segregated into *cultural communes*, which heighten the emphasis on ethnic identities. A consequence of warehousing, the cultural commune is a deviant social contrivance through which its members displace their anger and rage. They displace it outwardly toward rival communes, downwardly toward communes of the weak and wretched, and upwardly toward authorities responsible for their miserable situation. In his majority opinion in *Brown v. Plata*, Supreme Court Associate Justice Anthony Kennedy argued that California prisons are criminogenic, that is, likely to produce crime (Hamm, 2013). Criminologists who study failed prisons need only to look at Folsom for a model. Folsom Prison has entered the Dark Ages of American penology – a place where convict preachers trawl for new recruits from the legions of dead souls. It is the perfect storm for prisoner radicalization.

The harrowing Image 13 shows what can happen to inmates under such conditions of confinement. The mugshot displays a gang member at Folsom Prison with an elaborate mark of a swastika tattooed in a ring around his neck. His nose is broken from a fistfight, and his eyes are ulcerated from the ravages of methamphetamine and hepatitis C. His appearance implies sheer danger. He did not look like this when he entered prison but adopted the menacing appearance to survive.

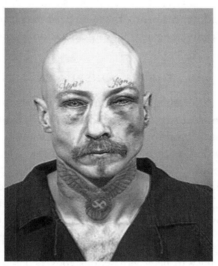

IMAGE 13. Image of prisoner, booking photo, courtesy of California Department of Corrections and Rehabilitation

In Erving Goffman's (1959) terms, the appearance represents a mask the inmate wore to control the impressions that other convicts formed about him.

Yet my ethnography revealed further insight into the inmate's appearance. The prisoner is also a devout Wiccan, a prayer leader, and a mentor to younger inmates, most of whom also have Nazi tattoos. He is slight of build, soft spoken, intelligent, and well-behaved, suggesting a disconnect between appearance and danger. Viewed from the perspective of Folsom's cultural communes, the inmate may bear signs of beauty, even charisma given his status as a religious leader in the maximum-security mix. In her introduction, Bonnie Berry reminds us that beauty is in the eye of the beholder, and "beholders often agree on what constitutes good looks." In the free world, the inmate would be considered a monster based upon prevailing assumptions about visual images of criminality. It is a different story among the Aryan Brothers and Nazi Low-Riders of a failed prison. Context matters.

But most importantly, the inmate is in prison on a drug charge and has not murdered anyone. Nor has he plotted to commit an act of terrorism. This is due in no small measure to the chaplains who run Greystone Chapel. Over the years they have developed a culture of religious tolerance and mutual respect among inmates of all faiths at the prison – Christians, Muslims, Jews, Native Americans, and even white pagans covered with tattoos of the German Reich. Essentially, the collective commitment of chaplains and prisoners to authentic religious transformations makes Greystone Chapel the safest area in an otherwise perilous place. And this, in turn, has served as a prophylactic against radicalization leading to terrorism.

THE JIS CONSPIRACY

Something quite different is going on at New Folsom Prison, an ultra-modern maximum-security complex adjacent to Folsom. Built in 1986 as part of California's multibillion-dollar construction boom, it is also severely overcrowded, with more than half of the 3,300-man population living in double bunks. New Folsom is another failed prison, replete with violent gangs, racial segregation, rampant suicide and drug abuse, epidemic levels of hepatitis C, and a near-total lack of treatment. Yet in stark contrast to Folsom, there is no overarching authority to ensure religious tolerance at New Folsom. As New Folsom's head chaplain put it to me:

Chaplains are too busy to help with serious conversions due to overcrowding. Chaplains are hired here simply for compliance and nobody's in charge. There's an element of evil in this prison due to the stupid, brain-dead mentality of the [department]. The administration is in chaos, there's no stability. Inmates who come here are all pressed into a gang because there are no safety measures to avoid violence in the yards. Chapels are used by gangs mainly to do gang business. There's no state-sponsored effort to save the inmates. Most of them sit around making knives at night. This makes the prison a petri dish just waiting to foment terrorism. The same mentality that drives prisoners drives the suicide bombers in Iraq.

(Hamm, 2013: 118)

These problems are especially significant when it comes to Islam. Because the religion has no central authority akin to the papacy, for example, matters of Koranic interpretation are left to the individual. When questions of interpretation do arise, Muslims turn to prayer leaders, or imams, who provide respected answers through teaching. When there are no imams to assume this teaching role in prison, then religious searchers in prison become susceptible to other inmates who operate on their own, some of whom hold radical views that may include the use of terrorism.

Kevin James created JIS for this very reason. James grew up in South Central Los Angeles during the crack epidemic of the 1990s. He found kindred spirits in the 76th Street Hoover Criminals, one of the city's numerous Crip factions, and was sentenced to prison on a robbery charge in 1995 at age 19. Only days into his prison term, James was introduced to the Nation of Islam. "I decided to take my life seriously then," he recalled. "The Muslims were the only ones on the yard who [had] achieved a sense of peace out of chaos" (Hamm, 2013: 129). In 1997, James was transferred to the California State Prison at Tehachapi where he converted to Sunni Islam but became disillusioned with its teachings. It was at this point, according to the FBI, that James founded the group Jam'iyyat Ul-Islam Is-Saheeh (JIS), based upon his idiosyncratic interpretation of Salafi texts, which he had acquired from other inmates.

James underwent a serious religious transformation to the Salafi–Jihadist calling, leading him to adopt a nihilistic worldview against apostates, or nonbelievers, and came to view adherents of orthodox Islam as traitors of the "true" faith. Accordingly, he began recruiting other inmates into a conspiracy to wage holy war not only against the US government but also the Nation of Islam, Shiites and Muslim prison guards. Each recruit was required to swear an oath of obedience to James. He focused his recruitment efforts on convicts with backgrounds like his own. Just as Goffman (1963) noted that religious conversions insulate true believers against the psychological assaults of the total institution, James would shelter his converts from the dangers of mass incarceration, redeeming them from the humiliation of what Goffman called the *spoiled identity*. Central to James's recruitment strategy was the African tradition of mythmaking, and a lot of shuck and jive.

Among the inmates at Tehachapi, James referred to himself "Ash Shakyh Sudani," meaning that he was an imam from the Sudan, even though he had never been to the Sudan and had not traveled abroad. To attract recruits, James bragged about his experiences as an active jihadist, but his criminal profile was limited to petty theft and robbery. James presented himself as a Koranic scholar, yet he had never set foot inside a mosque. Moreover, JIS was a synthetic jailhouse religion fashioned by Kevin James based upon his limited understanding of Islam combined with gang tactics he had learned from the streets. Using prison "kites" (or small bindles of rolled paper), James secretly distributed a handwritten document to other inmates entitled "JIS Protocol," which included a justification for killing "lawful targets," including non-Muslims. Even James would discredit the religious value of JIS by later admitting that the Protocol was never meant for "the real world." Rather, it was intended for consumption only among people of his world – the black convicts of California. In late 2002, officials caught wind of James's agitation and transferred him to New Folsom Prison.

By this time, James had become a prisoner of considerable charismatic bearing. "The only thing I can say about Kevin James," said a New Folsom employee, "is that he's all man. Guys in prison are under a lot of pressure and he never appeared to buckle" (Hamm, 2013: 131). A journalist, who interviewed James, described him as "articulate, calm, sedate, and well-read in the Koran. Quite honestly, I was impressed by him." James is remembered at New Folsom as a slight, soft-spoken inmate with large cornrows running back from his forehead, an untrimmed goatee, and tattoos of crescents on his neck and "Allah" (in Arabic) covering "7" and "6" tattoos on his forearms (for 76th Street Hoover Criminals). Yet what was most striking about James's appearance was a prayer bump, a *zabidah* (Arabic for raisin) in the middle of his forehead, the sign of dedication and piety caused by grinding one's forehead into the ground during Muslim prayers. James's raisin protruded from his forehead, a mark of the most pious, which would first be seen on the forehead of al-Qaeda leader Ayman al-Zawahiri in 2006 (see Image 14). In short, Kevin James socially constructed a mask of charismatic authority

IMAGE 14. Kevin James, prisoner with pronounced "raisin" on forehead. Photo courtesy of Eric Longabardi, April 2009

designed to lure other inmates into an al-Qaeda-inspired terrorist attack against the United States.

Yet what really matters – especially from the standpoint of preventing terrorism – is whether someone with such a radical appearance exhibits behavioral cues of political violence like "over-arming" themselves with weaponry or "over-sharing" extremist beliefs with others (Hamm & Spaii, 2017). James displayed an abundance of both traits, but prison authorities never intervened to provide James with an offramp to his radicalization. ("Chaplains are too busy to help with serious conversions due to overcrowding.")

By 2005, James had distributed the JIS Protocol to numerous Califor-nia prisons using kites and regular prison mail, reaching dozens of pris-oners. At New Folsom, JIS numbered about fifteen at this point, and James had recruited several other young Muslims from Los Angeles into JIS by using a smuggled cellphone and his connections with the Hoover Criminals. At James's behest, they began robbing gas stations to fund a jihad. The signals for a forthcoming attack were obvious to anyone who cared to look. At New Folsom, James used his growing reputation to expand JIS's recruitment program by introducing opportunities for inmates to participate in guerrilla training while inside prison. James's violent discourse was conducted, in part, under the guise of religious worship, such as it existed at New Folsom. A gang intelligence officer, who used to shake down James and his JIS brothers for weapons as they entered the chapel for Jumna services, recalled walking into a service one

Friday evening to discover James and his followers engaged in martial arts. At another time, JIS members were caught with razor blades during a training session. This is the thing about prisons: when they fail everything fails, including security.

Postscript

JIS proved to be long on leadership but short on criminal skill. Its members in LA were arrested after one of them left his cellphone behind during a gas station robbery. The phone contained Kevin James's cellphone number. "This is a case in which a terrorist cell grew out of a prison cell," announced the FBI director, Robert Mueller. "Despite the fact that they had no connection to al-Qaeda leaders, they had adopted their cause" (Hamm, 2013: 141–142). James was arrested at New Folsom and later sentenced to sixteen years in federal prison where he was isolated in a special unit for terrorists.

CONCLUSIONS

This chapter has offered some observations on how physical appearance influences charismatic leadership inside prisons, and how charismatic leaders may affect the incidence of terrorism. Recent terrorism scholarship has called for detailed case studies involving the "systematic documentation and comparative analysis of the role of charismatic authority" in the radicalization process (Hoffmann & Dawson, 2013: 363). In this vein, two general conclusions can be gleaned from the research.

First, although Weber's model of charismatic authority has never been applied to case studies of radicalization based on prison ethnography, the model does have relevant analytical value. At a basic level, Weber argued that charisma is a quality attributed to individuals who are thought to possess exceptional talents, particularly to influence and inspire others, which are not accessible to most people. This was suggested in the white supremacy case at Folsom Prison where a menacing-looking inmate rose from the squalor to assume a leadership role among Wiccan inmates by becoming a prayer leader and a mentor to younger cons. It was seen at New Folsom Prison where, through deviant but creative means of leadership, Kevin James established his own brand of "Prison Islam," which attracted numerous followers, not only from the prison but the community as well. In both case studies, leaders evoked the loyalty of followers afflicted by a crisis so great as to defy resolution by established authorities. The failed prison – with its chronic overcrowding, mismanagement, violence, racism, disease, drugs, and lethargy – explains why prisoners committed themselves to an inmate leader in the first place. And both leaders evinced talents in interpersonal relations – not through public oratory but through more intimate persuasion. Weber's conceptualization of charisma as a "divine gift" is certainly relevant to JIS's recruitment strategy. (Such heavenly notions would not apply to Wiccans since they do not recognize an omnipotent being.) A defining feature of creating and sustaining networks of personal affiliation within the global Salafist movement is a bond that forms between teachers and their students (Sageman, 2004). By lying to recruits about his religious experiences in the Sudan, by clandestinely sending them the JIS Protocol justifying sacred murder, by requiring them to take an oath of loyalty to him and teaching them guerrilla tactics, and by grinding his forehead into the ground until his raisin protruded, James bonded with followers by presenting himself as a Salafist authority who was fighting a godly war, giving him special status relating to the divine.

Second, by drawing attention to appearance, the case studies provide a novel way of thinking about charisma. In terrorism research, charisma is commonly used as a colloquialism or as a literary device (Hoffman & Dawkins, 2013). When charisma is used in such a subjective fashion, the concept fails to explain why certain leaders emerge from the pack of aspiring leaders, or why leaders gain authority over their followers. In other words, charisma is functional, as Weber stipulated, and functionality cannot be explained through idioms. To be useful, terrorism studies of charisma must delineate the social scientific themes implied by the term and explain how they lead to the creation of social bonds. For it is through these means that people internalize radical messages espoused by their leaders (Sageman, 2004). In their interviews with al-Qaeda-inspired terrorists in Britain, Europe, and Canada, Bartlett and Miller (2012) found that the path toward violent extremism is often driven by emotional, rather than religious, factors. Terrorists are frequently swayed by a "jihadi cool" influence in videos and the presence of a charismatic leader. "For religious figures to be granted legitimacy," the authors conclude, "appearance and personal experience [are] as important as formal religious knowledge" (Bartlett & Miller, 2012: 15).

I have come to the same conclusion. For charisma to be fully under-stood within the context of radicalization, however, it must be explained descriptively through a visual criminology, one that engages with the ascendant power of spectacle, where ethnographic bounty is framed in photographs, films, and mugshots.

References

Atran, S. (2010). *Talking to the enemy: Faith, brotherhood, and the (un)making of terrorists*. New York, NY: Ecco.

Barker, E. (1999). *New religious movements*. New York, NY: Bernan Press.

Bartlett, J. & Miller, C. (2012). The edge of violence: Toward telling the difference between violent and non-violent radicalization. *Terrorism and Political Violence*, 24, 1–21.

Dawson, L. L. (2004). Crises of charismatic legitimacy and violent behavior in new religious movements. In D. G. Bromley & J. G. Melton (Eds.), *Cults, religion and violence* (pp. 80–101). Cambridge, UK: Cambridge University Press.

Fried, W. (2004). Charisma: Belief, will and the power of the gifted. *Round Robin* (Newsletter of the Psychologist Psychoanalysis Practitioners, American Psychological Association), 39, 1–18.

Gilmore, M. (2008). *Stories done: Writings on the 1960s and its discontent*. New York, NY: Simon & Schuster.

Goffman, E. (1959). *The presentation of self in everyday life*. Garden City, NY: Doubleday.

(1963). *Stigma: Notes on the management of spoiled identities*. Englewood Cliffs, NJ: Prentice Hall.

Hamm, M. S. (2007). *Terrorism and crime: From Oklahoma City to Al-Qaeda and beyond*. New York, NY: New York University Press.

(2013). *The spectacular few: Prisoner radicalization and the evolving terrorist threat*. New York, NY: New York University Press.

Hamm, M. S. & Spaaij, R. (2017). *The age of lone wolf terrorism*. New York, NY: Columbia University Press.

Hartman, K. E. (2010). *Mother California: A story of redemption behind bars*. New York, NY: Atlas.

Hilburn, R. (2013). Biography doesn't hold back on darkest years of "Man in Black." NPR, October 29.

Hoffmann, D. C. & Dawson, L. L. (2013). The neglected role of charismatic authority in the study of terrorist groups and radicalization. *Studies in Conflict & Terrorism*, 37: 348–368.

Irwin, J. (2007). *The warehouse prison: Disposal of the new dangerous class*. New York, NY: Oxford University Press.

Liptak, A. (2010, November 30). Supreme Court hears arguments on California prison crowding. *New York Times*, p. A16.

Martinez, T. (1999). *Brotherhood of murder*. New York, NY: to Excel.

Mueller, G. (2017). (Warden of Folsom Prison) *Folsom state prison*. The History Channel, March 5.

Sageman, M. (2004). *Understanding terror networks*. Philadelphia, PA: University of Pennsylvania Press.

Steinhauer, J. (2006, December 11). Bulging, troubled prisons push California to seek a new approach. *New York Times*, p. A18.

Weber, M. (1968). *On charisma and institution building*. S. N. Eisenstadt (Ed.), Chicago, IL: University of Chicago Press.

PART V

VERY VISIBLE DIFFERENCES

Orientation, Disability, Freaks, and Clowns and Their Relationship to Crime and Victimization

The literature on appearance bias, as covered in the Introduction to this text, illustrates that commonplace or ordinary looks are more acceptable than unusual or stand-out looks. The three chapters in this final section refer to unusual appearance traits that can lead to criminal victimization or to social control engagement; either way, with victimization or with sanctioning, the public and the criminal justice system are responding to those unusual traits. Of course, the disabled and the non-heterosexual are not always visibly obvious, and that fact, as we will see, is crucial to the understanding of how the disabled and the non-straight are treated by society.

Orientation

Less discussed in the literature on appearance bias and crime than, say race and crime, is the relationship between sexual orientation and criminal behavior or criminal victimization. The popular press and research literature have focused recently, since circa 2014, on issues related to orientation, at least in the United States, owing to radical changes in how society accepts or does not accept any orientation except a straight orientation. Now, because the United States has finally passed same-sex marriage laws and is at least considering (as of this writing) the right to use the bathroom of one's choice, the United States has finally, regardless of individual views about LGBTQ (lesbian, gay, bisexual, transgender, and queer) phenomena, had to grant the LGBTQ community many of the same equal rights as the straight community. The United States and other cultures still have a long way to go in granting equal status to the LGBTQ community, with setbacks and progress occurring intermittently.

People are criminally suspect and treated as such because of their supposed (or real) orientation. Gay and transgender residents in the Queens section of New York City say they are singled out by the local police because of their appearance, specifically transvestism, which is assumed by the police to mean that they are involved in prostitution (Bellafonte, 2013). (To clarify, gays are not usually transvestites and transvestites are not usually gay.) It is not against the law to cross-dress or to be homosexual, obviously, but citizens who appear to be cross-dressers or gay are suspected of criminal activity. Evidence that at least some members of the Atlanta, Georgia police department are anti-gay has been uncovered, as documented by the Greenberg Traurig report (AtlantaEagleRaid.com, 2011). Two dozen Atlanta police officers were found responsible for false imprisonment and unlawful search and seizure committed against patrons of a gay bar, with no reason to suspect them of crime.

Small raids like the Atlanta gay bar do not compare to the mass shooting at "Pulse," known as "Orlando's hottest gay bar." In Orlando, Florida on June 12, 2016, Omar Mateen, a man known for his angry grudges against the LGBTQ community, entered Pulse and killed 49 people. Such attacks are indications that LGBTQ venues, representing an out-in-the-open orientation, are targeted, perhaps because they are out-in-the-open. And that is the point of Chapter 12: that which is visible and obvious causes a strong negative reaction.

Most members of the LGBTQ community look like members of the straight community. When they stand out by their mannerisms or by their clothing and grooming, or when they frequent LGBTQ venues, they face intervention from a homophobic public and the crime control system. In other words, when members of the LGBTQ community take on a contrived or exaggerated appearance, as can other members of society, they become more vulnerable to confrontation by the crime control community.

Doug Meyer (2015) and C. J. Pascoe (2012) both describe how members of the LGBTQ community can be spotted and, thus, victimized for being LGBTQ. Pascoe describes the gendered and sexualized nature of cyberbullying of gays and points specifically to a case of appearance-related bullying in which a young male appeared in a J. Crew clothing advertisement with painted toenails (p. xv). The problem seems to be gender-nonconforming appearance and behavior that leads a homophobic society to stigmatize and mistreat the LGBTQ. That is, when men and women display behavior and appearances that are "too obviously" LGBTQ, they invite violence (Meyer, p. 24).

Meyer goes further to point out that many of the appearance traits that are discussed in this text (such as minority race and lower socioeconomic status), combined with obvious LGBTQ appearance and behavior, create a *multiplicative effect*. He refers to a phenomenon called the "oppression Olympics" (p. 30), which refers to a competition among and between oppressed groups as to who has it worse than another in terms of being oppressed. Here I would add that a multiplier effect may make matters worse for those who express more than one stigmatized visible appearance trait, for instance, being gay and Black or being unattractive and gay, with the multiplicity effect possibly leading to criminal victimization. My unanswered-as-yet question is: does unattractiveness take precedence in the oppression Olympics because of its immediate visibility? Compared to other physical traits that set people apart –such as racialized features, obvious LGBTQ identity, and obvious disabilities – does unattractiveness count more toward crime control bias than any other feature?

Of course the argument could be made that members of the LGBTQ community could escape notice and thus victimization if they remained in the closet, and if they were not obviously and visibly LGBTQ. But that avoidance-type response would be identity-negating and, worse, would reinforce a homophobic attitude.

A globally helpful strategy for dealing with bias against the LGBTQ would be to support, if possible, those who are victimized by their visible appearance challenges. That goes for the United States and all other societies but particularly for those societies that exact a very harsh response to the different-looking. Chechnya's and Africa's anti-gay pogroms involving murder and cruelty require monitoring and reporting from gay rights advocates in their own and in other societies (see, for example, Kramer, 2017).

Gays were once considered so odd that they overlapped with freaks (discussed below). As Beth Macy (2016) reports, freak shows were replete with people who were thought to be odd: ethnic people, runaways, criminals, and gays. Moreover, in the nineteenth and twentieth centuries, LGBTQ were in all manner of "show business" because that was the only career open to them.

Elicka Peterson Sparks and Ian Skinner describe in Chapter 12 the gendered appearance of the police and citizens, which can result in victimization by the police and by the public. For instance, law enforcement officers, mainly men, have a masculine component to their appearance and their behavior. Hence, they expect other law enforcement officers to be masculine or even hyper-masculine. Female police officers are in a double blind since, if they appear masculine, they are chided for being "dykes" but if they appear feminine, they are seen as incapable.

Disability and Deformity

In Chapter 13, Heidi Scherer and Bradford Reyns discuss research findings from national and international samples showing that the disabled are at increased risk of interpersonal victimization. More to the point of this text, this risk is elevated as a result of visual indicators of disability, such as the use of canes, wheelchairs, and crutches. These visual signals impact how offenders assess the disabled victims' ability to resist victimization.

Clearly, a dark figure exists when measuring disablist violence. The "dark figure" is a criminological term describing what is unknown about the extent of the existence of crime. For instance, homicide is not a very dark figure since we have either a missing person or a deceased body; therefore a homicide is known to have occurred and all that remains to be discovered is who committed the homicide, the motivations, and several other factors associated with the homicide. Sexual assault, on the other hand, is a very dark figure and very much underrepresented. Victims of rape are often reluctant to report rape because they fear retaliation by the offender and humiliation by the court. Crimes against the disabled are also widely underreported and underrecorded (Thorneycroft & Asquith, 2015). Most or all societies worldwide exhibit pervasive disablism, even those societies that have proactive strategies for inclusion of the disabled into mainstream society (Thorneycroft & Asquith, p. 489). While the US Federal Bureau of Investigation finds that the disabled are less likely to be criminally victimized than members of other protected groups (minority members of race, ethnicity, religion, and sexual orientation), the crux of the matter may be the now-established fact that the disabled and their representatives are less likely to report victimization. By contrast, a self-report study from the UK Life Opportunities Survey revealed that people with disabilities are almost three (2.6) times more likely to be victims of hate crime than their nondisabled peers (Emerson & Roulstone, 2014).

This underreporting and undermeasuring is occurring because crimes against the disabled are not defined as crime; in other words, such acts are normalized. The disabled are discouraged from reporting victimization, and are advised to ignore it, and this is particularly true for those with (invisible) learning disabilities. Victimization is reconstructed as a part of everyday life for the disabled, much like, I would add, sexual harassment is for women. As Sin, Hedges, Cook, Mguni, and Comber (2009) noted, the disabled come to see themselves as second-class citizens, much as society sees them. As such, they must alter their own behavior to accommodate this view; there is not a question of the rest of society altering its behavior. The end result of this silence is, as expected, an environment in which the social structures and attitudes perpetuate criminal victimization and thus the victimization is engrained ("reproduced and sustained" per Sin et al., p. 160). The victimization becomes acceptable and normal.

Mark Sherry (2010), describing crimes perpetrated against the disabled partly based on their physical appearance, interprets these offenses as hate crimes. A disabled girl was assaulted by 12 teenage boys who urinated on her, set her hair on fire, and sexually assaulted her, making it clear that her visible disability was the reason for being targeted. The boys said, specifically, that she was the ugliest thing they had ever seen. Sherry further reports a disabled girl being bullied, in the course of being told that she is "ugly." Not uncommonly, disability and body size (obesity and shortness) are paired as reasons for victimization. Websites illustrate hatred of the mentally disabled, stating that their disability is "bad enough, but what's worse is when they are fat and ugly," and further describes them as "gruesome Quasimodoesque retards" and the like (p. 42). The height-challenged do not escape criminal victimization; in websites, they face "a great deal of hostility and antipathy." On Facebook, "midgets" are specifically targeted for scorn and derision (p. 44). In one website, social Darwinism is enlisted to rid society of those with physical impairments as "fucking eye sores" (p. 43).

We may compare disabled victims to victims of IPV (intimate partner violence) since the women in the latter scenarios are dependent and fearful of their intimate others. If the disabled or the victims of IPV report abuse, they are commonly not believed and they are commonly revictimized. (See also the above comments and the chapter on LGBTQ for an overlap with disability in terms of hiding their status.) Like many LGBTQ, the disabled, to the degree possible, attempt to "pass" and hope to avoid being "outed." The reasons are obvious: the more disabled one seems or the more non-straight one seems, the greater the likelihood of violent victimization. Recall also Part III on appearance and the crime control process. Usually, we think of the disabled as crime victims rather than criminal offenders and, for the most part, that is an accurate assumption.

However, as Thorneycroft and Asquith describe in a study of the Victorian Office of Police Integrity, regarding intervention in cases involving the disabled, the police "are more likely to associate a person with a disability as an offender rather than as a victim" (p. 499), resembling Schweik's history of the US criminal justice system's dealings with the disabled.

In her startling history on the topic of "ugly laws," Susan Schweik (2009) intersects disability, laws, and physical appearance. As discussed in the Introduction, from the time of the US Civil War (1860–1865) until 1974, the United States had in place "ugly laws" or city ordinances that permitted the arrest and punishment (often fines and confinement) of individuals considered physically unattractive. In fact, what was meant by "ugly" was disfigurement, disability, and disease. The main stated purpose for such laws was to relieve the public from the sight of repugnant members of society. The actual "offenses" for which these disfigured, disabled, and diseased were arrested were (a) being poor and (b) begging. In a circular way, repellant features (missing limbs, sores, etc.) were often the *reasons for* poverty and begging: members of society with these stigmata of illnesses and disability were denied employment and thus resorted to begging.

Public protest and unenforceability (largely due to vague criteria for ugliness) provided the reasons for the ordinances finally passing into oblivion. Today, however, similar patterns of denial to social power (such as employment) and prejudgments about criminal status exist for the poor and unattractive (Berry, 2007a, 2008). I interviewed street laborers (beggars, entertainers, and vendors) in downtown Seattle, Washington, asking them if they were confronted by the police or the public. I found that most were not bothered, bearing in mind that the setting is Seattle, which is widely regarded as a tolerant and progressive city. But of those who were confronted, they were more likely to be visibly disabled, poorly groomed, oddly attired, and have poor dentition (Berry, 2007b).

As has been pointed out in other sections, while the focus of this text is *visible* signs of physical appearance, *invisibility* can be a factor in crime and criminalization. In my editorial comments to Part II, it was noted that the invisibility of some races and ethnicities, particularly Indigenous peoples, can be life-saving or it can be life-destroying. When people are invisible because they are separated from resources, they may fall prey to illnesses or crime, and otherwise be unprotected. Such people need social services. Yet those social "services" can also mean intervention in a form that is destructive, as in deportation in cases of Mexican immigrants or brutal law enforcement in cases of Indigenous peoples. The disabled, as was pointed out to me by Paul Longmore (personal communication, 2006), can be invisibly disabled, which is generally beneficial to them because their difference is not subject to immediate bias. However, invisible disabilities can mean denial of needed services and it can mean, pertinent to this text, invasion in the form of criminal victimization if the disabled person has a learning disorder or a mental illness.

Interfacing disability and deformity with freaks, as I describe them in Chapter 14, I will remark here that the term "freak," as it refers to human oddities and as it has been used to refer to the differently abled, is a social construction. The word "freak" may offend people, especially many in the disability rights movement. Disability rights activists take strong exception to the use of words such as midget, giant, and pinhead, let alone the word freak (Bogdan, 1988). Words and phrases like "people with disabilities" are favored currently; words like "deformed," "amputee," and "anomaly" are in disfavor.

While in criminology we ordinarily conflate disability with victimization, we have an inaccurate and sorrowful public history of conflating disability with criminality. In movies, as Robert Bogdan (1988) describes it, "part of being bad *was* looking bad, and villains were marked by various disfigurements and disabilities, such as missing limbs and eyes" (p. vii, emphasis in original). He continues:

In horror films, the association of evil with disability is ... common, indeed ubiquitous. Horror film "monsters" are scarred, deformed, disproportionately built, hunched over, exceptionally large, exceptionally small, deaf, speech impaired, visually impaired, mentally ill, or mentally subnormal. In fact, the word *monster* is standard medical terminology for infants born with blatant "defects."
(Bogdan, 1988: vii)

So, the disabled can be viewed as offenders and as victims, as when disability is associated with evil (offenders) and when the disabled are mistreated as victims (Bogdan, 1988: vix).

Scary Clowns and "Freaks"

Chapter 14 deals primarily with unusual appearances (for instance deformities or albinism), which are subject to exploitation and criminal victimization. Scary clowns, or bad clowns as they are sometimes called, are the exception in that they are offenders and their unusual appearance is a matter of choice.

Scary clowns have been with us for a very long time, across cultures. As the reader will see, the phenomenon waxes and wanes, seeming to crop up in times of societal uncertainty.

Indeed, one of the main points I hope to make in Chapter 14 and throughout this book is that social trends affect and are affected by the crime–appearance nexus. As we shall see, the presence of scary clowns over the centuries varies according to what was going on in broader society at the time. The same is true in a different way about how the public views freaks. As societies evolve, there has been a greater acceptance of the physically different. Not to the degree that would be beneficial to the targets of appearance bias, nonetheless, there has been some semblance of progress in societal acceptance of the appearance-challenged.

I need not say much here in the editorial comments about freaks except to point out the obvious, that there are overlaps between "freaks" and the visibly disabled. Much of the material I found regarding freaks pertains to an earlier time when the public would pay to cast their gaze upon people with missing limbs, extra limbs, skin conditions such as albinism, unusual height (gigantism or dwarfism) and unusual weight (immense or skeletal), and so on. Today, people with such differences are perceived as disabled or simply of a different physiology. And, yes, some continue to be exploited, as in wage theft or being underpaid, but not in sideshows and circuses as they once were. However, though the contemporary picture is distinct from the past, we can learn a lot from historical examinations, and that is why this chapter is included in this book about criminal victimization of the visibly different.

As to ugliness, freakishness, and criminality, I refer the reader to the Introduction to this text and my discussion of Cesare Lombroso's "criminal man." In the late nineteenth and early twentieth centuries, criminologists linked "primitive" physiology with mental defects and with crime. Those with "asymmetrical skulls, flattened noses, large ears, enormous jaws, high cheekbones, and narrow eyes," evidencing an unevolved species of human, were clear indications of criminality (Bogdan, 2012: 116). People who look different, particularly if that difference can be perceived as unattractive, are mistakenly viewed as criminals. However, as we shall see, highly unusual-looking people are more commonly victims rather than offenders.

QUESTIONS

Referring to my question above about the "oppression Olympics," how much weight does unattractiveness have compared to an LGBTQ appearance? For example, are attractive-yet-obviously LGBTQ people less stigmatized than unattractive-and-obviously LGBTQ people? If so, does this mean that attractiveness outweighs an LGBTQ appearance?

Assuming that there is no mismeasurement problem and that scary clowns are only male, why is that? The explanation for twenty-first-century scary clowns is that they are composed of alienated disenfranchised young men. But women of all ages are also feeling alienated, so why aren't they acting out as scary clowns?

So, if freaks are not dangerous or repulsive, why are they so regarded? E.g., many bad guys in movies are deformed or otherwise human oddities. Possible answer: recall the discussion about normalcy in the Introduction to this text. Society prefers people who are attractive to be sure but certainly finds average-looking people to be acceptable. Odd-looking people are not so acceptable. This is true to the point of absurdity. In my earlier work (2007a), I referred to the late Paul Steven Miller, a dwarf, who was denied employment at a number of law firms even though he was a gifted lawyer with pedigrees from the best Ivy League universities and with numerous top-level publications. Employers would be enthusiastic about hiring him, judging from his vita, but when they met him, they told him it just wasn't going to work out. His story had a happy ending in that he was hired to serve as the head of the Equal Employment Opportunity Commission and later became a law professor at the University of Washington. Nevertheless, his history is illustrative of the bias against human oddities.

References

Bellafonte, G. (2013, April 7). When criminality becomes attached to wardrobe choice. *New York Times*, p. A24.

Berry, B. (2007a). *Beauty bias: Discrimination and social power*. Westport, CT: Praeger.

(2007b). Punishing looks: Criminalizing appearance and the American ugly laws. Paper presented at the American Society of Criminology 2007 annual meetings.

(2008). *The Power of looks: Social stratification of physical appearance*. Hampshire, UK: Ashgate.

Bogdan, R. (1988). *Freak show: Presenting human oddities for amusement and profit*. Chicago, IL: University of Chicago Press.

Bogdan, R. (with Elks, M. and Knoll, J. A.) (2012). *Picturing disability: Beggar, freak, citizen, and other photographic rhetoric*. Syracuse, NY: Syracuse University Press.

Emerson, E. & Roulstone, A. (2014). Developing an evidence base for violent and disablist hate crime in Britain: Findings from a life opportunity survey. *Journal of Interpersonal Violence*, 29, 3086–3104.

Greenberg Traurig Report. (2011, June 29). Independent report in Atlanta eagle raid confirms that APD officers broke the law, lied, destroyed evidence, and engaged in anti-gay discrimination. Retrieved from http://www.AtlantaEagle Raid.com.

Kramer, A. E. (2017, April 23). Chechnya's anti-gay pogrom: "They starve you. They shock you." *New York Times*, p. 13.

Longmore, P. K. (2006). Personal communication, September 26.

Macy, B. (2016). *Truevine*. New York, NY: Little, Brown and Company.

Meyer, D. (2015). *Violence against queer people: Race, class, gender, and the persistence of anti-LGBT discrimination*. New Brunswick, NJ: Rutgers University Press.

Pascoe, C. J. (2012). *Dude, you're a fag: Masculinity and sexuality in high school*. Berkeley, CA: University of California Press.

Schweik, S. M. (2009). *The ugly laws: Disability in public*. New York, NY: New York University Press.

Sherry, M. (2010). *Disability hate crimes: Does anyone really hate disabled people?* Surrey, UK: Ashgate.

Sin, C. H., Hedges, A., Cook, C., Mguni, N., and Comber, N. (2009). *Disabled people's experience of targeted violence and hostility*. Manchester, UK: Equality and Human Rights Commission.

Thorneycroft, R. & Asquith, N. L. (2015). The dark figure of disablist violence. *The Howard Journal of Criminal Justice*, 54, 489–507.

12

Queer Looking

Appearance and LGBTQ Citizens' Victimization and Interactions with the Criminal Justice System

Elicka Peterson Sparks and Ian Skinner

To date, there is no research exploring the explicit link between appearance and the experience of LGBTQ people with the criminal justice system, but it is almost certainly a factor that impacts these interaction to some – and likely a great – extent. In this chapter, this dynamic will be explored theoretically, drawing from studies examining the treatment of LGBTQ citizens in other spheres of public life based on appearance, as well as the culture of law enforcement.

The most significant appearance-related factor in the treatment of LBGTQ people in the criminal justice system is almost certainly the issue of gender conformity. Policing is a hyper-masculine profession that reflects traditional gender roles for men (Dowler & Arai, 2008; King, 2005; Rabe-Hemp, 2008). The culture of law enforcement is shaped by hegemonic masculinity, maintaining control through authority over women, heterosexism, and force (Rabe-Hemp, 2008). Not surprisingly, a significant body of research has detailed the difficulties of female officers in this environment, and some of that research can be used to extrapolate regarding the difficulties faced by LGBTQ people in their interactions with the police. Indeed, the bulk of evidence suggests that LGBTQ police officers face discrimination within the ranks, so it is unlikely that LGBTQ people in the general public would fare better (see Collins, 2016).

Female officers often need to adopt more masculine qualities in order to be perceived as competent by male officers, but are simultaneously criticized for those same qualities and labeled as "butch." Those with more feminine personas are frequently labeled weak (Cordner & Cordner, 2011; King, 2005; Rabe-Hemp, 2008; Stewart-Winter, 2015). This single facet of the difficulties faced by female members of law enforcement provides a wealth of insight into prevailing attitudes in the criminal justice system about gender roles and gender conformity, both of which are impacted greatly by appearance.

The treatment of lesbian, bisexual, and people in transition from female-to-male by police is undoubtedly affected by gendered aspects of appearance. If someone of the female sex fails to appear feminine "enough," it is likely that male law enforcement officers – at least straight ones – will react less positively toward them. The traditional gender role of a woman is male-oriented, and this manifests itself in appearance through easily observed feminine affectations, such as wearing make-up, dressing in a certain manner understood to be attractive to the opposite sex, having long hair, and the like. All of these ways of presenting oneself might signal gender conformity to an officer, whether this was the intention of the woman or not, and the culture of policing makes it more likely that a biological woman presenting as highly feminine (and thus perceived as being male-focused) will receive better treatment than a biological female who appears to defy those expectations.

While there is little research related to this specific area of inquiry, there are studies that are highly suggestive that gender roles play a significant role in determining treatment in the criminal justice system, particularly for LGBTQ people. Rambo (2008) highlighted a case involving Maria Perez, a woman sentenced to life after killing her ex-girlfriend. During the trial, the prosecutor spent a great deal of time de-feminizing Perez through portraying her dress and demeanor as manly and through highlighting her lesbianism. Masculinity is a key component of the criminal stereotype for appearance, and a wealth of research shows that a perception of greater masculinity results in a variety of negative outcomes in the criminal justice system. For example, a hyper-masculine physical appearance, including a muscular frame and a square jaw, results in higher rates of suspect identification (Flowe & Humphries, 2011; MacLin & MacLin, 2004; Turner, 2007) and greater perceptions of guilt for both male and female suspects (Ward, Flowe, & Humphries, 2012).

A masculine physical appearance tends to serve as a cue that activates stereotypes of criminality (Carlen, 1985; Heidensohn, 1985; Madriz, 1997; Ward, Flowe, & Humphries, 2012). Female offenders even perceive themselves as having more masculine traits than nonoffenders, particularly those who committed violent offenses, which are considered more masculine in and of themselves (Ahola, Hellström, & Christianson, 2010; Dumas & Testé, 2006; Herrington & Nee, 2005; Skorinko & Spellman, 2006; Ward, Flowe, & Humphries, 2012). The impact of this association between masculinity and criminality almost certainly has a negative effect on lesbian, bisexual, and queer women who do not conform to traditional gender norms.

Even those LGBTQ citizens who do conform to gender norms are breaking tradition norms for the relationship between men and women, and thus would likely at least perceive that they would receive harsher treatment in the criminal justice system. Support for and acceptance of the LGBTQ community tends to be closely associated with political affiliations, so this perception is not unfounded: the 2016 police magazine presidential poll showed that 84 percent of officers supported Donald Trump nationwide, compared to 8 percent supporting Hillary Clinton (Griffith, 2016, table 1).[1] Other sources show a far narrower gap in political affiliation more generally that varies greatly by rural versus urban areas, but still tends to lean noticeably to the right (Morin, Parker, Stepler, & Mercer, 2017; Swanson, 2015). Whether a particular officer is or is not conservative, they are likely to be perceived as conservative, which leads to greater distrust and fear on the part of LGBTQ citizens, regardless of their appearance. Experience further exacerbates the unease LGBTQ people feel: research consistently demonstrates that LGBTQ people face discrimination, profiling, and harassment from law enforcement officers, which is particularly bad for nonwhite LGBTQ and transgendered people, as well as LGBTQ youth (Amnesty International, 2005; Caspani, 2015; Finneran & Stephenson, 2013; Mallory, Hasenbush, & Sears, 2015; Meyer, 1980; Mogul, 2011; Nadal & Davidoff, 2015; Nadal, Quintanilla, Goswick, & Sriken, 2015; Schilt, 2010). Appearance is likely the most salient factor in law enforcement officers identifying someone as LGBTQ.

It is highly likely that gay males also receive poorer treatment at the hands of law enforcement if they do not appear masculine "enough." The more effeminate a male appears in his physicality, dress, and manner, the more he is likely to draw the disgust of law enforcement officers given the value placed on masculinity in the police subculture. Sadly, even gay men themselves discriminate against gay men who appear feminine, with attending negative effects on their own perceived desirability and self-image (Sánchez, Greenberg, Liu, & Vilian, 2009; Szymanski & Carr, 2008; Wester, Pionke, & Vogal, 2005). Sánchez et al. (2009) delineated the appearance and personality of gay men based on perceptions of masculinity and femininity as stated by a research subject:

[A masculine gay man] is tough looking, wears plaid and no colors, doesn't act demonstrative in public [while a feminine gay man] is really fashion conscious and appearance conscious, over-done facial maintenance, hugs and kisses a lot, talks with a lot of gesturing. The second most described theme for both questions related to the ability for a gay man to be "straight-acting" or to be able to pass as a heterosexual man in public. For example, one individual wrote that masculine gay men are able "not to arouse the assumption of 'gayness' from strangers," and subsequently wrote that feminine gay men exhibit "characteristics that are easily noticed [as gay] by many people who do not know the person intimately."

(p. 82)

It is likely that masculine gay men who do not self-identify as gay receive the same treatment as straight men in the criminal justice system. However, this equality of treatment is situational: if the masculine gay man has to engage with police in a gay setting, such as a gay bar or LGBTQ parade or rally, his treatment might differ despite his appearance. That said, it is likely that more feminine gay men would receive worse treatment than masculine-appearing gay men in the same situations.

The impact of the appearance of gay men mirrors sexism in the wider society, with greater value placed on the masculine over the feminine. The inverse impact of femininity over masculinity in the case of lesbians may reflect officers' discomfort with women encroaching on their more powerful position in this hierarchy, and/or discomfort with the simple violations of traditional gender roles (Dozier, 2005; Herek, 1991).

The treatment of transgender individuals in the criminal justice system is almost definitely worse, as they violate both social and physical expectations for the appearance of sex and gender. This is probably particularly true for Black and male-to-female transgender persons, who suffer from the double burden of racism and sexism in the system, as well as any nonwhite LGBTQ individuals. Judging from prior work on crossdressing, transgender people who cannot (or cannot yet) "pass" as someone of the opposite sex are more likely to suffer poorer treatment by law enforcement (Casper, 2013). The correctional system has been more responsive to addressing the treatment of transgender inmates, likely owing to the publicity focused on this issue in prisons in the popular show *Orange is the New Black* (see, e.g., Carpenter, 2017). Despite this effort, treatment is still poor in every sector of the criminal justice system, and accounts of abuse of transgender persons in the system as victims, suspects, and detainees are remarkably serious and ubiquitous (see, e.g., Amnesty International, 2005).

On the other side of the coin, LGBTQ people experience greater levels of criminal victimization than straight people, with gay men consistently found to be most likely to be victimized by hate crime perpetrators before data became available for transgender individuals (NCAVP, 2017). However, early research shows that the victimization of gay men is eclipsed by that of transgender people once data is available for this group. Self-reported levels of victimization for transgender individuals suggest that their risk is heartbreakingly high (NCAVP, 2017).

Despite growing acceptance of LGBTQ people and marriage equality in the United States, 2016 was the deadliest year on record to date for the LGBTQ community, even without counting the 49 victims in the Pulse nightclub mass shooting in Orlando (NCAVP, 2017). More than a hundred anti-LGBTQ bills were introduced in 29 states in a five-month period in 2016, and LGBTQ activists are alarmed by the increase in violence against LGBTQ people since the US presidential election (MAP, 2017). This marked increase is likely a combination of backlash from the gains made by the LGBTQ community, the increased vulnerability that comes with increased visibility, and the unusually high levels of homophobia and more generalized aggression toward people who are not White and native born in the United States exhibited during and after the election by Donald Trump (see Mason, 2001 for a discussion of visibility). As LGBTQ people become more comfortable with their appearance reflecting who they are, their treatment at the hands of the public and the criminal justice system will likely garner more attention.

References

Ahola, A. S., Hellström, Å., & Christianson, S. Å. (2010). Is justice really blind? Effects of crime descriptions, defendant gender and appearance, and legal practitioner gender on sentences and defendant evaluations in a mock trial. *Psychiatry, Psychology and Law*, 17, 304–324.

Amnesty International Staff. (2005). *Stonewalled: Police abuse and misconduct against lesbian, gay, bisexual and transgender people in the U.S.* New York, NY: Amnesty International USA.

Carlen, P. (1985). Law, psychiatry and women's imprisonment: A sociological view. *British Journal of Psychiatry*, 148, 618–621.

Carpenter, C. L. (2017). The "T" in LGBT: "Orange is the New Black" and transgender issues in corrections. *Corrections Today*, May/June, 52–56.

Caspani, M. (2015). *Police discrimination against U.S. LGBT community pervasive: Report.* New York, NY: Thomson Reuters Foundation. Retrieved from www.reuters.com/article/us-usa-lgbt-police/police-discrimination-against-u-s-lgbt-community-pervasive-report-idUSKBN0M02JM20150304.

Casper, I. B. (2013). Cross dressing and the criminal. *Yale Journal of Law & the Humanities*, 20(1), 1–30.

Collins, J. C. (2016). Retaliatory strike or fired with cause? A case study of gay identity disclosure and law enforcement. *New Horizons in Adult Education & Human Resource Development*, 28(1), 23–45.

Cordner, G. & Cordner A. (2011). Stuck on a plateau? Obstacles to recruitment, selection, and retention of women police. *Police Quarterly*, 14(3), 207–226.

Dowler, K. & Arai, B. (2008). Stress, gender and policing: The impact of perceived gender discrimination on symptoms of stress. *International Journal of Police Science & Management*, 10(2), 123–135.

Dozier, R. (2005). Beards, breasts, and bodies: Doing sex in a gendered world. *Gender & Society*, 19(3), 297–316.

Dumas, R. & Testé, B. (2006). The criminal facial stereotypes on juridic judgments. *Swiss Journal of Psychology*, 65, 237–244.

Finneran, C. & Stephenson, R. (2013). Gay and bisexual men's perceptions of police helpfulness in response to male–male intimate partner violence. *Western Journal of Emergency Medicine*, 14(4), 354–362.

Flowe, H. & Humphries, J. E. (2011). An examination of criminal face bias in a random sample of police lineups. Applied Cognitive *Psychology*, 25, 265–273.

Griffith, D. (2016, September 2). The 2016 POLICE presidential poll. *Police: The Law Enforcement Magazine*. Retrieved from www.policemag.com/channel/patrol/articles/2016/09/the-2016-police-presidential-poll.aspx.

Heidensohn, F. (1985). *Women and crime*. London: Macmillan.

Herek, G. M. (1991). Stigma, prejudice, and violence against lesbians and gay men. In J. C. Gonsiorek & J. D. Weinrich (Eds.), *Homosexuality: Research implications for public policy* (pp. 60–80). Newbury Park, CA: Sage.

Herrington, V. & Nee, C. (2005). Self-perceptions, masculinity and female offenders. *Internet Journal of Criminology*, 1–30. Retrieved from https://s3.amazonaws.com/academia.edu.documents/40016777/SELF-PERCEPTIONS_MASCULINITY_AND_FEMALE_20151115-27156-1rinivf.pdf?AWSAccessKeyId=AKIAIWOWYYGZ2Y53UL3A&Expires=1509843120&Signature=kLzdYdacoFHVPZeKCI%2BBQOCbiCk%3D&response-content-disposition=inline%3B%20filename%3DSelf_Perceptions_Masculinity_and_Female.pdf.

Ickes, W. (1993). Traditional gender roles: Do they make, and then break, our relationships? *Journal of Social Issues*, 49(3), 71–85.

King, D. J. (2005). Separate but equal: The introduction and integration of policewomen in the Bermuda police 1961–2002. *Police Practice and Research: An International Journal*, 6(3), 215–233.

MacLin, O. H. & MacLin, K. M. (2004). The effect of criminality on face attractiveness, typicality, memorability, and recognition. *North American Journal of Psychology*, 6, 145–154.

Madriz, E. (1999). *Nothing happens to good girls: Fear of crime in women's lives*. Oakland, CA: University of California Press.

Mallory, C., Hasenbush, A., & Sears, B. (2015). *Discrimination and harassment by law enforcement officers in the LGBT community*. Los Angeles, CA: The Williams Institute. Retrieved from https://williamsinstitute.law.ucla.edu/wp-content/uploads/LGBT-Discrimination-and-Harassment-in-Law-Enforcement-March-2015.pdf.

MAP (Movement Advancement Project). (2017). *Tipping the scales: The coordinated attack on LGBTQ people, women, parents, children, and health care.* Boulder, CO: MAP. Retrieved from www.lgbtmap.org/religious-exemptions-license-to-discriminate.

Mason, G. (2001). Body maps: Envisaging homophobia, violence and safety. *Social & Legal Studies*, 10(1), 23–44.

Meyer, D. (1980). *Violence against queer people: Race, class, gender, and the persistence of anti-LGBT discrimination.* New Brunswick, NJ: Rutgers University Press.

Mogul, J. L. (2011). *Queer (in)justice: The criminalization of LGBT people in the United States.* Boston, MA: Beacon Press.

Morin, R., Parker, K., Stepler, R., & Mercer, A. (2017, January 11). Police views, public views. *Pew Research Center Social & Demographic Trends.* Retrieved from www.pewsocialtrends.org/2017/01/11/police-views-public-views/.

Nadal, K. L. & Davidoff, K. C. (2015). Perceptions of Police Scale (POPS): Measuring attitudes towards law enforcement and beliefs about police bias. *Journal of Psychology and Behavioral Science*, 3, 1–9.

Nadal, K. L., Quintanilla, A., Goswick, A., & Sriken, J. (2015). Lesbian, gay, bisexual, and queer people's perceptions of the criminal justice system: Implications for social services. *Journal of Gay & Lesbian Social Services*, 27, 457–481.

National Coalition of Anti-Violence Programs (NCAVP). (2016). Lesbian, gay, bisexual, transgender, queer, and HIV-affected hate. Violence in 2016. New York, NY: Emily Waters. Retrieved from https://avp.org/wp-content/uploads/2017/06/NCAVP_2016HateViolence_REPORT.pdf.

Rabe-Hemp, C. (2008). Survival in an "All Boys Club": Policewomen and their fight for acceptance. *Policing: An International Journal of Police Strategies & Management*, 31(2), 251–270.

Rambo, K. S. (2008). *"Trivial complaints." The role of privacy in domestic violence law and activism in the U.S.* New York, NY: Columbia University Press.

Sánchez, F. J., Greenberg, S. T., Liu, W. M., & Vilian, E. (2009). Reported effects of masculine ideals on gay men. *Psychology of Men & Masculinity*, 10, 73–87.

Schilt, K. (2010). *Just one of the guys? Transgender men and the persistence of gender inequality.* Chicago, IL: University of Chicago Press.

Skorinko, J. L. & Spellman, B. A. (2013). Stereotypic crimes: How group-crime associations affect memory and (sometimes) verdicts and sentencing. *Victims & Offenders*, 8(3), 278–307.

Stewart-Winter, T. (2015). Queer law and order: Sex, criminality, and policing in the late twentieth-century United States. *Journal of American History*, 102(1), 61–72.

Swanson, A. (2015, June 3). Chart: The most liberal and conservative jobs in America. *Washington Post.* Retrieved from www.washingtonpost.com/news/wonk/wp/2015/06/03/why-your-flight-attendant-is-probably-a-democrat/?utm_term=.62efb5ee7218.

Szymanski, D. M. & Carr, E. R. (2008). The roles of gender role conflict and internalized heterosexism in gay men's psychological distress: Testing two mediation models. *Psychology of Men & Masculinity*, 9, 40–54.

Turner, N. (2007). Eyewitness perceptions: The effects of perceived likeability and masculinity on false identifications (Unpublished master's thesis). University of Portsmouth, Portsmouth, UK. Retrieved from: http://eprints.port.ac.uk/617/.

Ward, C., Flowe, H., & Humphries, J. (2012). The effects of masculinity and suspect gender on perceptions of guilt. *Applied Cognitive Psychology*, 26, 482–488.

Wester, S. R., Pionke, D. R., & Vogal, D. L. (2005). Male gender role conflict, gay men and same-sex romantic relationships. *Psychology of Men & Masculinity*, 6, 195–208.

Endnote

1 Support in the 2016 election is fraught with difficulties in terms of determining typical levels of partisanship and sexism.

13

Visible Disabilities and Risk of Interpersonal Victimization

Heidi L. Scherer and Bradford W. Reyns

Research findings from national and international samples of individuals indicate that people with disabilities experience an increased risk of interpersonal victimization in comparison to their counterparts without disabilities. This elevated risk of victimization may be the result of visual indicators of disabilities (e.g., wheelchair, cane, crutches) that can impact risk and influence how offenders perceive victims' ability to resist an attack. Utilizing data from a sample of college students, this study examines the relationship between disability and victimization risk – focusing on whether individuals with visible disabilities experience an increased likelihood of interpersonal violence (i.e., sexual violence, stalking, physical assault, intimate partner violence, and verbal threat) compared to those with invisible disabilities or no disabilities.

INTRODUCTION

The present study examined the relationship between physical appearance and crime by investigating how having a visible disability impacts risk for interpersonal victimization. Prior research suggests that persons with disabilities are victimized at rates higher than persons without disabilities (see, e.g., Harrell, 2017), but the extent and nature of these relationships are still underexplored in the empirical record. In this study, visible disabilities are associated with indicators that can be observed visually or identified based on brief communication with the individual. For instance, visual indicators of disability could include such devices as mobility aids (e.g., wheelchair and crutches), walking canes, and hearing technologies (e.g., hearing aids and cochlear implants). In addition, for an individual with a speech and language disorder, a stutter could serve as a "visible" indicator because one could be identified as having a disability as a result of brief communication with another person. With this focus in mind, the current study addressed three open issues related to the relationship between visible disability and interpersonal victimization risk.

First, this study estimated the prevalence of five types of interpersonal victimization among persons with different types of disabilities from a large probability sample of college students from across the United States. These estimates were produced using the American College Health Association's (ACHA) National College Health Assessment II Survey (NCHA II). The five types of victimization estimates reported on were for verbal threat, physical assault, sexual assault, stalking, and intimate partner violence for persons with any visible disability. Each of the estimates was compared against persons with no disability.

Second, the present study considered indicators of visible disability as risk factors for these five types of interpersonal victimization. In this context, a risk factor is a variable that increases one's likelihood or risks of experiencing interpersonal victimization. To do this, the relative odds of possessing a visible disability, an invisible disability (i.e., conditions with no visible indicators of disability), and possessing both a visible and invisible disability were calculated and compared for these five types of interpersonal victimization. In the analyses, not possessing a disability served as the reference category.

Third, the results are interpreted in light of relevant victimization theory. Specifically, we relied on target attractiveness and target congruence perspectives from victimology to frame our analyses and understand our findings. These perspectives argue that certain individuals face heightened risks for victimization because they are especially attractive targets for offenders or have characteristics that align with the desires of offenders (Felson & Clarke, 1998; Finkelhor & Asdigian, 1996; Wilcox & Cullen, 2017). Other theoretical perspectives centered on victim vulnerability and social indifference also were used to understand and interpret the increased risk of victimization among those with visible disabilities (e.g., Calderbank, 2000; Curry, Hassouneh-Phillips, & Johnston-Silverberg, 2001; Mays, 2006).

EXTENT OF VICTIMIZATION AMONG INDIVIDUALS WITH VISIBLE DISABILITIES

Over the last two decades, there has been an increase in research estimating the prevalence of victimization among people with disabilities.

This line of research has helped to establish that people with disabilities experience more victimization than their counterparts without disabilities. For instance, data from the National Crime Victimization Survey (NCVS) indicated that people with physical, emotional, and mental disabilities had a rate of violent victimization that was over twice the rate for people without disabilities (Harrell, 2017). Further, Harrell's analyses of the NCVS data revealed that this elevated rate of victimization among people with disabilities was observed for each type of violent victimization (e.g., rape/sexual assault, robbery, aggravated assault, and simple assault) and across each sex, age, race, and ethnic group.

While much past research has utilized broad measures of disability that include people with both visible and invisible disabilities, which precludes the ability to estimate rates of victimization for individual disability types, some studies have estimated the prevalence of victimization specifically among populations with visible disabilities. These studies are valuable for illustrating that individuals with disabilities who have visible indicators have higher rates and risks of experiencing violent victimization than their counterparts without disabilities (Blum, Kelly, & Ireland, 2001; Emerson & Roulstone, 2014; Harrell, 2017). Additionally, this research indicates that in comparison to those with no disabilities, individuals with visible disabilities have an elevated likelihood to experience sexual violence (Alriksson-Schmidt, Armour, & Thibadeau, 2010; Brownlie, Jabbar, Beitchman, Vida, & Atkinson, 2007; Mueller-Johnson, Eisner, & Obsuth, 2014), intimate partner violence (Anderson & Leigh, 2011; Hahn, McCormick, Silverman, Robinson, & Koenen, 2014; Porter & Williams, 2011; Scherer, Snyder, & Fisher, 2016), stalking (Reyns & Scherer, 2017), and verbal harassment (Mueller-Johnson et al., 2014). Of particular note is that several past studies have found that having a visible disability increased risk of experiencing an interpersonal victimization even after controlling for known risk factors of victimization, suggesting that disability status has an independent effect on one's likelihood of victimization (Alriksson-Schmidt et al., 2010; Hahn et al., 2014; Muller-Johnson et al., 2014; Reyns & Scherer, 2017).

A THEORETICAL FRAMEWORK FOR UNDERSTANDING VICTIMIZATION RISK

Each of the theoretical perspectives that guide this study in some way involve a conceptualization of disability as a form of vulnerability. The underlying assumption across each perspective, then, is that vulnerability brings with it a heightened risk for interpersonal victimization. It is worth noting, however, that while vulnerability may universally increase risk, the magnitude of this effect may differ by crime type.

Target Attractiveness and Target Congruence

One of the leading theories of victimization – the opportunity perspective – explains that opportunity structures are a primary reason for differential victimization risk across individuals (see, e.g., Wilcox & Cullen, 2017). Opportunities are produced by circumstances that are favorable to some outcome – in this case, criminal victimization. According to the theory, opportunities for crime are generated by the confluence of willing offenders and attractive targets within suitable environments (see, e.g., Felson & Clarke, 1998; Wilcox & Cullen, 2017). In the context of this theory, visible signs of disability may provide a suggestion to motivated offenders that an individual is an attractive target. For instance, someone who is on crutches or in a wheelchair might be viewed as a comparatively easier target for robbery than someone who is not using mobility aids.

Target congruence theory, which is an approach that is compatible with the opportunity perspective, explains that individuals are targeted by offenders because they possess characteristics that are "congruent with the needs, motives, or reactivities of potential offenders" (Finkelhor & Asdigian, 1996: 6). According to Finkelhor and Asdigian, this means that individuals with particular characteristics are purposely chosen as crime targets by offenders. These characteristics are those that signal to offenders that the would-be victim is an especially vulnerable, gratifying, or antagonistic target.

Vulnerable targets are those that are less able to resist or deter their victimization. Signs of physical disability, then, may signal to offenders that an individual is an easy target. For example, an offender might consider someone who is blind to be less able to prevent, or respond to, their victimization. Gratifying targets possess a characteristic or quality that the offender wants to have, use, or manipulate. In other words, offenders find it rewarding in some way to target persons with a given attribute. Finkelhor and Asdigian (1996) note characteristics such as age, sex, or physical appearance as signs of gratifiability, but visible disability may also be an indicator to certain offenders of a "gratifiable" target. Finally, target antagonism refers to the how the would-be victim's characteristics antagonize the offender into targeting them. For example, individuals with a speech or language disorder might be targeted because their disability makes the offender angry or want to act in a destructive manner.

Overall, target attractiveness and target congruence have received empirical support as useful explanations of victimization in the broader victimology literature (e.g., Reyns & Scherer, 2017; Sween & Reyns, 2017). However, their utility in understanding relationships between visible disability and interpersonal victimization has not been fully explored. As such, the present research is instructive in this respect, in addition to illuminating the relationship between physical appearance and crime.

Additional Theoretical Perspectives

While target attractiveness and target congruence provide the primary theoretical lens for the present research, additional theoretical perspectives are also worthy of consideration when exploring the relationship between physical appearance and victimization. These perspectives, like target attractiveness and target congruence, center in some way on the role of vulnerability in accounting for the victimization of those with disabilities.

To begin, Calderbank (2000) has argued that there is a social indifference on the part of society surrounding persons with disabilities. In presenting three case studies of victimization and abuse of persons with disabilities, Calderbank (2000) explains that there is much ignorance, apathy, and/or denial concerning the victimization of people with disabilities, concluding that there is a "social indifference at the root of vulnerability" (p. 533). In sum, Calderbank (2000) is arguing that society and its members devalue the victimization of those with disabilities *because* they have disabilities. Using arguments similar to Calderbank (2000), Curry and associates (2001) developed an ecological model based in power and control to explain that women with disabilities are generally devalued by society, which creates a context of vulnerability. Further, they assert that women with disabilities are marginalized within a patriarchal society, which stereotypes and discriminates against their conditions. Other relevant contributors to victimization noted by Curry et al. (2001) include: poverty, dependence, fewer attachments, and a lesser ability to identify or report their victimization.

Similar to Curry and colleagues' (2001) work, feminist interpretations have also been used to understand victimization against those with disabilities. In one such example, Mays (2006) investigated the prevalence and nature of intimate partner violence against women with disabilities. Mays (2006) views disability as a social construct that has been used as a tool of oppression, and coupled with a feminist perspective, argues that domestic violence against women with disabilities is a manifestation of both sexism and "disablism" (p. 150).

METHODS

Data

This study used data from the ACHA NCHA II, which is a biannual survey that is administered to a sample of institutions of higher education across the United States and includes survey questions to gauge college students' overall health and wellbeing such as their substance abuse, victimization experiences, and mental and physical health (ACHA, 2012). Data included in this study were drawn from the Fall 2011 and Fall 2012 waves of the survey, which included 54 institutions, each of which utilized a probability-based sampling technique and varied by Carnegie classification, geographic region, and campus size (ACHA, 2014). After restricting the data to traditional-aged college students, the final sample size included 43,570 college students who were aged 18–25.

Dependent Variables

Five victimization outcome variables were examined in this analysis including (1) verbal threat, (2) physical assault, (3) sexual assault, (4) stalking, and (5) intimate partner violence. For each question, respondents were asked whether they had experienced the victimization within a one-year reference period. Sexual assault was a composite measure of three sexual victimizations including sexual touch without consent, attempted rape, and completed rape. Any respondent who reported experiencing one of these victimizations was coded as being a victim of a sexual assault. Intimate partner victimization was a composite measure of three forms of partner violence including emotional abuse, physical abuse, and sexual abuse. Any respondent who reported experiencing one of these types of abuse in an intimate relationship was coded as being a victim of intimate partner victimization. Each victimization measure was dichotomous in nature (0 = no and 1 = yes).

Independent Variables

Respondents were coded as having a visible disability if they reported having one or more of the following conditions: (1) deaf or hard of hearing, (2) blind or partially sighted, (3) mobility disability, and (4) speech or language disorder. Each of these disability types were coded as a visible disability because they are associated with indicators that can be observed visually or identified based on brief communication with the individual.

Respondents were coded as having an invisible disability if they reported having one of the following disabilities: (1) attention deficit hyperactivity disorder, (2) learning disability, (3) psychiatric condition, (4) anxiety, (5) bipolar disorder, (6) obsessive compulsive disorder, (7) phobia, (8) schizophrenia, and (9) other mental health condition.

In order to compare risk of victimization across disability status, three disability variables were created: (1) visible disability only, (2) invisible disability only, and (3) both a visible and invisible disability, while students with no disabilities served as the reference group. Nine control variables were included in the analyses. Three variables reflected risk-taking behavior including alcohol use, marijuana use, and illicit drug use. Five variables gauged respondents' demographic information namely their employment status, sexual orientation, sex, age, and race. The final control variable was year of survey administration.

Analyses

Prevalence of interpersonal victimization was estimated and Z score tests for two proportions were conducted in order to examine if there was a significantly larger proportion of victims among individuals with visible disabilities in comparison to those with no disabilities. Multivariate binary logistic regression models with adjusted odds ratios and 95 percent confidence intervals were estimated in order to examine if visible disability status shaped risk of experiencing each of the five types of interpersonal victimization.

RESULTS

Prevalence of Victimization among Individuals with Visible Disabilities

Table 13.1 presents the results estimating the prevalence of interpersonal victimization among people with visible disabilities. Consistent

TABLE 13.1. *Prevalence of Victimization among People with Visible Disabilities*

	Verbal Threat	Physical Assault	Sexual Assault	Stalking	Intimate Partner Violence
	N (%)	N (%)	N (%)	N (%)	N (%)
No Disability	8,007 (18.38)	1,135 (3.20)	2,201 (6.20)	1,835 (5.19)	3,109 (8.77)
Any Visible Disability	663 (29.34)*	154 (6.81)*	252 (11.15)*	228 (10.12)*	323 (14.29)*
Deaf or Hard of Hearing	266 (33.21)*	88 (10.95)*	94 (11.71)*	101 (12.70)*	130 (16.01)*
Blind or Partially Sighted	342 (28.69)*	88 (7.36)*	152 (12.71)*	117 (9.85)*	167 (13.92)*
Mobility Disability	106 (31.93)*	40 (11.98)*	49 (14.67)*	47 (14.24)*	47 (13.82)*
Speech and Language Disorder	136 (33.75)*	47 (11.63)*	58 (14.36)*	58 (14.54)*	69 (16.87)*

* $p < .05$; Z score tests for two proportions with no disability as the referent group.

with past research, when compared to people with no disabilities, a significantly larger proportion of individuals with visible disabilities reported having experienced each type of interpersonal victimization. For verbal threat, less than 20 percent of people with no disabilities reported having been verbally threatened while almost 30 percent of people with visible disabilities were victims of verbal threat. In particular, almost one-third of all respondents who were deaf or hard of hearing, had speech and language disorders, and mobility disabilities reported being verbally threatened, while 29 percent of those who were blind or partially sighted experienced a verbal threat.

A similar pattern emerged for physical assault; a significantly larger proportion of people with visible disabilities were physically assaulted during the reference period. Specifically, in comparison to those with no disabilities, there were twice the proportion of physical assault victims among people with visible disabilities (3 percent vs. 7 percent). Further, the prevalence of physical assault victimization was over three times higher than those with no disabilities for respondents who were deaf or hard of hearing (11 percent), had speech and language disorders (12 percent), and mobility disabilities (12 percent).

Prevalence of sexual assault was also significantly higher among individuals with visible disabilities. Approximately, 6 percent of respondents without disabilities reported having experienced sexual assault in comparison to slightly over 11 percent of those with visible disabilities. The highest rates of sexual assault was observed for those with mobility disabilities (15 percent), followed by respondents with speech and language disorders (14 percent), and those who were blind or partially sighted (13 percent) and deaf and hard of hearing (12 percent). In addition, respondents with visible disabilities also reported a larger proportion of stalking victimization than respondents with no disabilities (10 percent vs. 5 percent). Moreover, this elevated proportion of stalking victimization was evident for each of the four visible disability types, with the highest prevalence observed for respondents who were deaf or hard of hearing (13 percent), had speech and language disorders (15 percent), and mobility disabilities (14 percent). Similar findings emerged for victimization perpetrated by intimate partners, where there was a significantly larger proportion of victims among those with visible disabilities in contrast to no disabilities (14 percent vs. 9 percent). The highest prevalence of intimate partner violence was observed among respondents who reported being deaf or hard of hearing (16 percent) and those who had a speech and language disorder (17 percent).

Risk of Victimization among Individuals with Visible Disabilities

Table 13.2 presents results from the multivariate logistic regression analyses estimated to examine if individuals with visible disabilities experienced an increased risk of interpersonal victimization in comparison to individuals with no disabilities or invisible disabilities controlling for demographic characteristics and other risk factors for victimization. Across each measure of victimization, individuals with disabilities were significantly more likely to have reported experiencing interpersonal victimization than their counterparts without disabilities. In particular, in contrast to those with no disabilities, individuals with visible disabilities experienced an elevated risk of experiencing each type of victimization even after controlling for risk-taking behaviors such as alcohol and drug use. Further, those who reported having an invisible disability were also found to experience an increased risk of interpersonal victimization that

TABLE 13.2. *Multivariate Logistic Regression Results*

	Verbal Threat	Physical Assault	Sexual Assault	Stalking	Intimate Partner Violence
	AOR (95% CI)	AOR (95% CI)	AOR (95% CI)	AOR (95% CI)	AOR (95% CI)
Visible Disability	1.60* (1.40–1.82)	1.64* (1.25–2.15)	1.49* (1.20–1.84)	1.71* (1.38–2.11)	1.34* (1.12–1.60)
Invisible Disability	1.70* (1.59–1.82)	2.07* (1.82–2.35)	1.68* (1.57–1.81)	1.86* (1.70–2.05)	1.91* (1.78–2.04)
Visible and Invisible Disability	2.60* (2.26–3.00)	3.02* (2.27–4.02)	2.43* (1.91–3.08)	2.65* (2.15–3.27)	2.51* (2.11–2.98)

* $p < .05$

Note: Control variables include alcohol use, marijuana use, illicit drug use, employment, sexual orientation, sex, age, race, and year of survey; AOR = adjusted odds ratio; CI = confidence interval.

was, on average, similar or greater to the risk of victimization among those having visible disabilities.

While both individuals with visible and invisible disabilities experienced an elevated likelihood of being a victim, the greatest risk of interpersonal victimization was observed for individuals who had both a visible and an invisible disability. Across each measure of victimization, those with visible and invisible disabilities were approximately 2.5 and 3 times more likely to experience interpersonal victimization than their counterparts without disability even after known covariates of victimization were included in the analyses.

DISCUSSION AND CONCLUSION

Consistent with past research, our analyses revealed that a significantly greater proportion of individuals with visible disabilities were victimized than their counterparts without disabilities. This was observed for each measure of victimization, some of which have received little empirical attention among this population such as stalking victimization and verbal threat. Further, as was reported in past studies, this relationship was observed even after controlling for known predictors of interpersonal victimization. This indicates that having a visible disability increases one's risk, independent of risk-taking behaviors and demographic characteristics. In the context of opportunity and target congruence theories, it may be that the physical appearance of disability can signal to potential offenders that individuals with visible disabilities are more attractive or vulnerable targets than their counterparts with no visible signs of disability (see, e.g., Finkelhor & Asdigian, 1996; Wilcox & Cullen, 2017).

The greatest risk of victimization was observed for individuals who had both visible and invisible types of disabilities. Victimology theory may be particularly valuable for illuminating this finding. For instance, possessing multiple disabilities could influence one's likelihood to be exposed to motivated offenders, and be viewed as a more attractive or vulnerable target. Past research suggests that individuals with invisible disabilities may engage in risk-taking behaviors such as substance abuse and delinquency at higher rates than those with no invisible disabilities (see, e.g., Cranford, Eisenberg, & Serras, 2009; Jones & Lollar, 2008; McNamara, Vervaeke, & Willoughby, 2008). Involvement in these activities can increase one's exposure to potential offenders who may then take into account an individual's visible indicators of disability (i.e., wheelchair, cane, walking stick) when making decisions related to target selection based on perceived attractiveness, vulnerability, or antagonism.

Individuals with visible disabilities may also experience increased risk of victimization because offenders perceive them as more attractive as a result of social indifference or discrimination in society. Drawing from Calderbank's (2000), Curry et al.'s (2001), and Mays' (2006) perspectives that society devalues individuals with disabilities and their victimization experiences, increased risk of victimization against this population may be the result of offenders perceiving a lower risk of apprehension or punishment associated with victimizing individuals with visible disabilities. Taken together, the physical appearance of disability may serve to influence a diverse set of considerations on the part of potential offenders ranging from immediate factors such as the victims' ability to resist an attack and more distant factors such as the societal response to the crime.

In conclusion, future research with a focus on the role of physical appearance, disability, and victimization is needed for shedding further light on the complex causal mechanisms that may be influencing these relationships. This information would be valuable for not only theory development, but for the creation of prevention recommendations that are tailored to specific disability types rather than the broad and diverse disabilities community in general.

References

Alriksson-Schmidt, A. I., Armour, B. S., & Thibadeau, J. K. (2010). Are adolescent girls with a physical disability at increased risk for sexual violence? *Journal of School Health*, 80(7), 361–367.

American College Health Association. (2012). *American College Health Association-National College Health Assessment II: Reference group executive summary Fall 2011*. Hanover, MD: American College Health Association.

(2014). *American College Health Association-National College Health Assessment, Fall 2011 and Fall 2012*. Baltimore, MD: Mary Hoban.

Anderson, M. L. & Leigh, I. W. (2011). Intimate partner violence against deaf female college students. *Violence against Women*, 17(7), 822–834.

Blum, R. W., Kelly, A., & Ireland, M. (2001). Health-risk behaviors and protective factors among adolescents with mobility impairments and learning and emotional disabilities. *Journal of Adolescent Health*, 28(6), 481–490.

Brownlie, E. B., Jabbar, A., Beitchman, J., Vida, R., & Atkinson, L. (2007). Language impairment and sexual assault of girls and women: Findings from a community sample. *Journal of Abnormal Child Psychology*, 35(4), 618–626.

Calderbank, R. (2000). Abuse and disabled people: Vulnerability or social indifference? *Disability & Society*, 15(3), 521–534.

Cranford, J. A., Eisenberg, D., & Serras, A. M. (2009). Substance use behaviors, mental health problems, and use of mental health services in a probability sample of college students. *Addictive Behaviors*, 34(2), 134–145.

Curry, M. A., Hassouneh-Phillips, D., & Johnston-Silverberg, A. (2001). Abuse of women with disabilities: An ecological model and review. *Violence against Women*, 7(1), 60–79.

Emerson, E. & Roulstone, A. (2014). Developing an evidence base for violent and disablist hate crime in Britain: Findings from the Life Opportunities Survey. *Journal of Interpersonal Violence*, 29(17), 3086–3104.

Felson, M. & Clarke, R. V. (1998). Opportunity makes the thief. *Police Research Series, Paper 98*.

Finkelhor, D. & Asdigian, N. L. (1996). Risk factors for youth victimization: Beyond a lifestyles/routine activities theory approach. *Violence and Victims*, 11(1), 3–19.

Hahn, J. W., McCormick, M. C., Silverman, J. G., Robinson, E. B., & Koenen, K. C. (2014). Examining the impact of disability status on intimate partner violence victimization in a population sample. *Journal of Interpersonal Violence*, 29(17), 3063–3085.

Harrell, E. (2017). *Crime against persons with disabilities, 2009–2015 – Statistical tables*. Washington, DC: Bureau of Justice Statistics.

Jones, S. E. & Lollar, D. J. (2008). Relationship between physical disabilities or long-term health problems and health risk behaviors or conditions among US high school students. *Journal of School Health*, 78(5), 252–257.

McNamara, J., Vervaeke, S. L., & Willoughby, T. (2008). Learning disabilities and risk-taking behavior in adolescents: A comparison of those with and without comorbid attention-deficit/hyperactivity disorder. *Journal of Learning Disabilities, 41*(6), 561–574.

Mays, J. M. (2006). Feminist disability theory: Domestic violence against women with a disability. *Disability & Society, 21*(2), 147–158.

Mueller-Johnson, K., Eisner, M. P., & Obsuth, I. (2014). Sexual victimization of youth with a physical disability: An examination of prevalence rates, and risk and protective factors. *Journal of Interpersonal Violence, 29*(17), 3180–3206.

Porter, J. & Williams, L. M. (2011). Intimate violence among underrepresented groups on a college campus. *Journal of Interpersonal Violence, 26*(16), 3210–3224.

Reyns, B. W. & Scherer, H. (2017). Stalking victimization among college students: The role of disability within a lifestyle-routine activity framework. *Crime & Delinquency*. Advanced online publication. doi: 0011128717714794.

Scherer, H. L., Snyder, J. A., & Fisher, B. S. (2016). Intimate partner victimization among college students with and without disabilities: Prevalence of and relationship to emotional well-being. *Journal of Interpersonal Violence, 31*(1), 49–80.

Sween, M. & Reyns, B. W. (2017). An empirical test of target congruence theory on intimate partner violence. *Deviant Behavior, 38*(1), 61–73.

Wilcox, P. & Cullen, F. T. (2017). Situational opportunity theories of crime. *Annual Review of Criminology*. Advanced online publication. www.annualreviews.org/journal/criminol.

Remarkably Unique Human Appearance

Scary Clowns and Freaks

Bonnie Berry

We can address scary clowns and freak show exhibits in tandem as exotic-in-appearance criminals, in the case of the former, and criminal victims, in the case of the latter. Moreover, Benjamin Radford (2016), mostly attending to "bad clowns" (his preferred term), reminds us that clowns can be offenders as well as victims, as when clowns are beaten up for being clowns. He also remarks on the overlap between clowns and the disabled (hunchbacks, those with acromegaly or enlarged proportions of the face, and so on), the latter of which, as the reader will see, were once exhibited as "freaks."

SCARY CLOWNS

First, let me address "scary clowns." The name itself is puzzling since clowns are supposed to be funny rather than scary. Yet, they are scary to some people and in some circumstances. As to circumstances, when clowns are out of context, for instance not in a circus or some other entertainment venue that commonly contains clowns, they are scary. Clowns, appearing individually and in a public area such as a street or a park or showing up at your front door, are confusing and therefore scary. The reason I am discussing them in a text about crime and appearance is that they can be criminal offenders and their appearance is part of their offending (see Image 15).

Clowns are scary because our brains cannot know for certain if they are threatening or not; the confusion itself is scary (McAndrew, 2016). This statement begs the question of why the uncertainty is threatening. My answer is "contrivances." Clowns are humans in disguise and we can't be

IMAGE 15. Scary clown on front porch (Getty Images)

sure what is beneath the disguise, behind the makeup and unusual clothing. In the same way that bank robbers are anonymous when wearing a mask, we are automatically on alert when we can't see the real person, bare-faced. The only reason, we suppose, that a person would hide her or his true identity is to fool us or hurt us. Clowns are disturbing because they are humans who don't look like humans but instead have exaggerated features or outlandish clothing and makeup (Radford, p. 23).

Frank McAndrew, a psychologist, says as much in his studies of creepiness. He finds that we are creeped out by clowns because of the inherent ambiguity surrounding clowns, most importantly, their makeup and clothing. We experience ambiguity, which by itself is an uncomfortable feeling, and the uncertainty about clowns is the uncertainty of the threat posed by them since their identity is shielded and the motivations unknown. Especially relevant to this text, McAndrew's study of creepiness found that unusual or strange physical traits (bulging eyes, creepy smile, inordinately long digits) do not necessarily creep people out but *in combination with* odd behavior can definitely frighten the observer.

Criminally bad clowns comprise only a very small minority of clowns, engaging in stalking, molestation, assault, and homicide. Only about a dozen professional clowns have been accused of serious crimes (Radford, pp. 3, 99).

History

Radford claims that clowns were never really good. Clowns and clown-like characters are nothing new; they have been noted over thousands of years, for example as jesters satirizing and making fun of powerful people and getting away with their ridicule. They got away with their behavior so long as they were entertaining and funny. "Persons of ridicule" date back to ancient Egypt, much like court jesters in England (see Shakespearian plays of Tudor England) who made fun of others including royalty (McAndrew, 2016). The evil clowns, bad clowns, or scary clowns that we are encountering today are evolutions of the earlier jesters who have progressed or digressed into present-day unpredictable and menacing creatures (McAndrew).

Lovejoy (2016) finds that early antecedents of scary clowns, deriving from the sixteenth century in the form of Harlequin, who wore brightly colored tattered clothes, were more irritating than bad. Nonetheless from early times such as these, we read stories of traveling scary clowns leading troupes of "comic demons." Things got bad or creepy when Grimaldi came along. Although not especially scary, Grimaldi was a sad and self-destructive clown, a pantomime player wearing garish makeup. Definitely scary was "Punch," the baby-abusing and wife-beating serial killer not unlike the murderous clown Pagliacci, from the nineteenth-century opera of the same name (Lovejoy, 2016).

So scary clowns are not new. We have had waves of clown sightings over the decades. The "Phantom Slasher" of Taipei, Taiwan in the 1950s and the "Mad Gasser" of 1944 Illinois, US (a time when gassing was a horrifying occurrence in the battlefields of World War II) are examples. A more recent wave has been the creepy or "phantom" clown sightings beginning in the United States in 1981 when children began reporting seeing them, with other waves of clown sightings occurring in 1985 and 1991. The police have issued APBs (all points bulletins) and conducted searches during these waves but no clowns were captured (Lovejoy, 2016, p. 5). Was it imagination, hysteria? Probably not.

The Reason for Recent Scary Clowns

The year 2016 seemed to be a big year in creepy clowns, for good reason as we will see. In 2016, scary clowns had been terrorizing communities in the United States; they were reported trying to lure women and children into wooded areas, threatening people with knives and machetes, and yelling at people. Reporting on the 2016 scary clown phenomenon, Christine Clarridge (2016) writes of scattered sightings of men (most scary clowns are men) wearing clown clothes and clown makeup menacing the public throughout the United States in small and large towns. Sinister clowns appeared in at least twenty states, leading to arrests and a school closing.

In explanation, a social psychologist at Washington State University, Craig D. Parks, cited in Clarridge, agrees with Lovejoy (2016) that these disguised and deviant jesters engage in this frightening behavior owing to distress, anxiety, and a desire to stand out and be noticed. They feel de-individualized and anonymous. This phenomenon occurs more commonly when there is a lot of social conflict, tension, and societal-wide anxiety, Parks says. Sure, some of the reports have turned out to be hoaxes but not all: many truly threatening acts have been perpetrated and arrests have been made.

So it seems that the best explanation for recent and perhaps past waves of scary clown appearance is one of social contagion in the form of deindividuation. Lovejoy (2016), in her editorial about clowns as offenders, remarks that, "Most of those [scary clowns] who have been arrested in clown costumes during the Great Clown Panic of 2016 have been disaffected young men who donned the attire to cause public distress" (p. 5). Scary clowns appear, disappear, and reappear coincident with varying social and political times. Thus, anxious times bring about "disenfranchised men in makeup" presenting themselves as scary clowns.

The year 2016 was a rough year in the United States because of the highly unusual presidential election that was in play, with the winning candidate capitalizing on the sense (accurate or not) of disenfranchisement expressed by white men. US citizens were subjected to wild, off-the-scale lying by a number of significant people who could and later did pose danger to the United States as a society and to the world. It was (is) a time of "low levels of trust in official institutions and sources of information" (Lovejoy, p. 5). In 2018 as I write this, we are still in anxious, "post-truth" times.

Fashionable Scary Clowns

One would think that it's the end of the latest scary clowns panic when the New York fashion world imitates them. In the *New York Times* fashion pages, runway models have donned clown clothes and applied clown makeup. Depicted are models wearing baggy clothes of mismatched colors, harlequin outfits and masks, and outsized bright orange hats such as Bozo the Clown might be proud to wear. Friedman, reporting on these fashions, remarked that, "Nowadays, not looking like a clown may be easier said than done" (2016: D2). This tells us that, if clowns are commonplace, they lose their scariness.

Lovejoy would disagree with me about the transitory nature of the scary clown phenomenon because, as she says with good reason, disenfranchised young men/scary clowns feel cut off from power and opportunity, and that is why they haunt parking lots and apartment complexes. (I would add a caveat about alienated young men: women and the not-so-young are also feeling alienated. Why they are not engaging in the scary clown phenomenon deserves examination.) Even in mass hysteria, urban legends, social media gone viral, whatever phrase one prefers to address a phenomenon such as this, there is some reality at its kernel. People are disaffected and are acting out, inappropriately and frighteningly, in a way that is disturbing yet interpretable. In this unusual way, alienated people alter their physical appearance to make a statement.

FREAKS

In the United States and other nations, human oddities were once exhibited for viewing by the paying public in circuses, sideshows, and other venues; and the reason I am discussing them here is that they were commonly criminally victimized. The practice died out in the first decade of the twentieth century owing to discontent over displaying people with physical and mental differences for profit (Bogdan, 1988). The eugenics movement, beginning in 1904 and mostly ending after World War II, "promulgated the idea that physically and mentally inferior people were far from being benign and interesting; rather, they were a danger" and needed to be sterilized and thus weeded out of the population (Bogdan, 1988: 62; see also Black, 2003, for a history of the eugenics movement aimed at creating a "master race"). This supremacist philosophy has become viewed as repugnant, although it has not entirely disappeared from some segments of the population; there are those who feel that the disabled should not be properly cared for, should not have rights equal to the abled, and certainly should not procreate.

By the late 1930s, those with mental and physical differences were less considered curiosities than diseased or disabled. Moreover, the sheer number of freaks was reduced in a real as well as a visual way owing to scientific discovery that shifted the meaning of abnormality, medical discoveries that explained variations in human appearance, and interventions such as institutionalization. As to the latter, "the incarceration of human oddities in asylums and a declining interest in freak show careers on the part of potential exhibits probably had more to do with the scarcity than did any cures" (Bogdan, 1988: 66).

Some freaks were not really freaks but people whose appearance represented a social interest; this appearance could have been congenitally odd or artificially altered. Recall the discussion of early criminology in the Introduction to this text, when early scholars explained criminals as atavistic and primitive throwbacks. Some freak exhibits were also incorrectly portrayed this way, as for example "missing links," a fascination at the time. Their primitive appearance was not uncommonly aided by contrivances to make ordinary people look unevolved even when they were just ordinary-looking people.

Definition and History

According to Wikipedia, a freak show is "an exhibition of biological rarities, referred to as 'freaks of nature.'" Typical features would be physically unusual humans, such as those "uncommonly large or small, those with both male and female secondary sexual characteristics, people with ... extraordinary diseases and conditions ... Heavily tattooed or pierced people have sometimes been seen in freak shows, as have attention-getting physical performers such as fire-eating and sword-swallowing acts" (Wikipedia, 2016, see Image 16).

IMAGE 16. Circus performer (Getty Images)

Freak shows became popular in England in the mid-sixteenth century, where humans with deformities, conjoined twins, and the like were exhibited. In the nineteenth century, freak shows reached maturity in England and the United States, as commercially successful industries. Modern freak shows (circa 2000–2010) are rare today and exist(ed) only in a changed format, as in the Los Angeles Circus Congress of Freaks and Exotics and Cirque Du Soleil.

Freak shows have fallen out of favor because of the debate about exploitation, much as the circus had ended its tours in 2017 because of the exploitation of nonhuman animals. The Ringling Brothers and Barnum and Bailey Circus closed in May 2017, having been in business since 1871 (146 years), owing to falling ticket sales (Nir & Schweber, 2017). Animal rights organizations had targeted the circus for its cruelty to nonhuman animals, thus driving down attendance. One wonders if human animals in the form of oddities and freaks, had they continued to be exhibited, would also have led to protest and reduced ticket sales. Both nonhuman animals and human animals in the entertainment world have been objectified. On the whole, we have become somewhat more sensitive to the plights of vulnerable beings.

Terminology

Every time I type the words "freak" or "freaks," I feel uncomfortable. I suppose I shouldn't since people who study freaks, few though they are and scholarly though they are, use these words. I don't want to be insulting, and the words sound that way to me. "Human oddities" doesn't sound any better. But I must get over my reluctance to use these words, and I am comforted by the fact that such respected scholars include Robert Bogdan, who studies freaks and with whom I have had the pleasure of communicating, uses this terminology.

There is some disagreement about the most appropriate term for extraordinarily short people. "Dwarves" seems to be the accurate term, according to Bogdan. However, Sheila Black (2017), herself not quite five feet tall owing to a disease KRN 23 (X-linked hypophosphastemia), reminds us that the preferred term for uncommonly short people is Little People (or LPs). She says that this is the term that most people with dwarfism prefer.

Did the freak exhibits care about what they were called? In a word, no.

They did, but not the way our present sentimentality would have us think. A few might have been sensitive to such words as *freak*. ... As the eugenics movement clouded the scene and human differences became medicalized, the status of human oddities declined, and some exhibits began to resent what they were called. ... Robert Wadlow, an extremely tall young man who lived in the 1920s and 1930s, avoided being associated with the word *freak*. But other than a few isolated cases, there is no evidence that exhibits took the nouns used to refer to them seriously.

(Bogdan, 1988: 271)

Indeed, the term "freak" was not so deeply stigmatizing and discrediting in the past as it is today.

Freaks as Victims and Offenders

I asked Professor Bogdan if freaks, as he understood them, ever committed crimes. He replied that of course they could commit crimes and may have done so, but there is no record of them doing so with one partial exception. I say "partial" because the offenses they committed would be taking advantage of "rubes," members of the public who paid money to view the freaks. Often, the freaks themselves did not profit from exhibiting themselves but they were part of the scheme to defraud the public:

Life was about tricking the rube, and making money. The exotic [...] presentations of the freak show were abundantly fraudulent. The most important criterion for judging the appropriateness of the word *freak* was, most likely, whether it was good for business. ... What [freaks] were called is an issue for us; it was not one for them. As freaks sat on the platform, most looked down on the audience with contempt – not because they felt angry at being gawked at or at being called freaks, but simply because the amusement world looked down on "rubes" in general. Their contempt was that of insiders toward the uninitiated. For those in the amusement world it was the sucker who was on the outside, not the exhibit.

(Bogdan, 1988: 271–272)

In Bodgan's book on visualizing disability (2012), which also includes stories about freaks (since many freaks are differently abled), he reminds us that some freaks made a great deal of money and had comfortable lives. These would be the celebrity freaks who were able to capitalize on their differences. Some of the stories are about the disabled who embellished their disabilities to bilk the public for money; some are about people who aren't disabled at all but who pose as such.

So, while freaks were and are mostly seen as victims, they can be viewed as criminals or as representatives of criminals who dupe rubes; both may engage in lying, dishonesty, and misrepresentation in order to exploit the public. To the extent that freaks are offenders, it is in this light of cheating the public rather than committing violent offenses. Only in movies is there a common theme portraying the disabled and the deformed as violent offenders (Bogdan, 2012: 116–117).

In Beth Macy's (2016) treatment of freaks, the freaks were no better than slaves with the industry management reaping in all the profit. Macy wrote a history of two albino Black men, the Muse Brothers, who were badly exploited by the sideshow and circus industries.

As Macy has recorded, some freaks were actually sold into virtual slavery, even though slavery had officially ended as an institution in the United States in 1865. They were sometimes sold by their parents who were in dire need of money. Such was the case with "Zip," a Black microcephalic ("pinhead") man who was sold and made to perform on stage shows. He was fiercely controlled by his "owner" on and off stage, and was considered exotic not only because of his microcephaly but because he was Black. Blacks were not uncommonly at that time (the 1860s) considered to be subhuman, and the remnants of such prejudice linger today. Like the Muse brothers, Zip was "paid" only in food and board, and was treated as a trained dog. Not dissimilarly, George Bell, "the colored giant" and minstrel, was illiterate and badly exploited. Indeed, it has been recorded that White giants were paid more than Black giants, often twice as much.

As with much else in life, stratification rules. There was segregation and a strict hierarchy across carnival workers with freaks being at the bottom, performers (e.g., aerialists) higher up the stratum with better pay and better accommodations. Perhaps the physical appearance itself is a strong explanation for the difference in pay and working conditions (Macy, 2016: 120).

Exploitation and a Functionalist Explanation

This discussion of freaks and their obvious exploitation brings me to a question I had not considered before reading about this topic. The transparent assumption would be that exhibited human oddities would abhor their lives, and I suspect that this is true for many or most of them. But not all freaks would agree with me, as I learned. Early justifications reason that it was okay to use freaks in this way, applying what a sociologist would call functionalist theory. Who else would employ the freaks? At least being employed in this manner offered them a means to be self-sufficient and have a sense of worth. Well, not really since at least some of them were exploited and enslaved. This line of reasoning is reliant upon Davis and Moore's functions of poverty (1945); for example, the poor fill the ranks of the US military, the poor buy used cars that better-off people wouldn't buy, etc. The functionalist explanation is understandable intellectually but it seems to excuse social phenomena, such as exploitation and poverty, as appropriate and right.

Today's View of Freaks

Some humans who have a notable physical difference are still treated unfairly and are criminally victimized. The albino Black men featured in Beth Macy's book were basically slaves for a large part of their career as sideshow freaks, from 1899 (the year they were kidnapped as youngsters by a sideshow promoter) until they were middle-aged men. Yet albino Blacks are still in danger, as we see in the case of the albino Tanzanian sisters who were granted asylum in the United States for fear of being murdered (Do, 2016). They were taunted and attacked as "ghosts" in their home country, where it is believed that their albinism is related to witchcraft and that their body parts carried magical powers and thus could be sold for profit. In Mozambique, albino Blacks are kidnapped and murdered, sometimes by family members, for their body parts (skin, bone, etc.) because "if you have a piece of albinism on you . . . you'll have luck and money" (Rodriguez, 2017: 7). Dead albinos are not safe either: their graves are robbed of body parts, with the deceased albino worth up to $75,000 in parts that can be sold. Those albinos who are not killed live in fear and face enormous discrimination. They do not want to leave their homes, albino children avoid school and avoid walking alone, they cannot trust anyone. The Tanzanian government has made some head-way in discouraging the trafficking of albino body parts and has started a public information campaign to explain to the public that albinos are not magical and that they are people just like everyone else.

A New View: Acceptance

In current times, and part of an anti-bullying campaign, fashion photog-rapher Rick Guidotti "launched a campaign to show the beauty of people with albinism and to include positive messages about children with all kinds of genetic differences, including left palates and mobility issues" (Macy, 2016: 72). It is way past time to accept physiological difference. We may be approaching "a sociology of acceptance," in Bogdan's terms (1988: 269), in which we recognize and accept differences.

Outside the boundaries of the freak show, many so-called human oddities had neighbors and family; they loved and were loved, were accommodating and accommodated, were respectful and respected. In addition, while freak show participants were not on the highest rung of the amusement world's own stratification system, they were a welcomed and taken-for-granted part of the culture. Indeed, from the life histories of freak show exhibits we might learn more about how blatantly different human beings are included into the human community, while knowledge could, if taken to heart, call forth a new direction in the study of human differences: a sociology of acceptance.

(Bogdan, 1988: 269)

The same could be said of all of us, including the criminally victimized and criminal offenders. Even though many of us engage in poor behavior and deserve some means of control or assistance, the fact of appearance difference need not play a role in discriminating against us.

References

Black, E. (2003). *War against the weak: Eugenics and America's campaign to create a master race*. New York, NY: Four Walls Eight Windows.

Black, S. (2017, June 4). Trying to embrace a "cure." *New York Times* Sunday Review, p. 6.

Bogdan, R. (1988). *Freak show: Presenting human oddities for amusement and profit*. Chicago, IL: University of Chicago Press.

Bogdan, R. (with M. Elks and J. A. Knoll). (2012). *Picturing disability: Beggar, freak, citizen, and other photographic rhetoric*. Syracuse, NY: Syracuse University Press.

Clarridge, C. (2016, October 24). What's up with these creepy clowns? *Seattle Times*. Retrieved from www.seattletimes.com/life.

Davis, K. & Moore, W. E. (1945). Some principles of stratification. *American Sociological Review*, 10, 242–249.

Do, A. (2016, August 27). Facing threats, albino Tanzanian sisters granted asylum in U.S. *Seattle Times*. Retrieved from www.seattletimes.com/nation-world.

Friedman, V. (2016, October 27). The creepy clown in your closet. *New York Times*, p. D2.

Lovejoy, B. (2016, October 16). What do the scary clowns want? *New York Times* Sunday Review, p. 5.

Macy, B. (2016). *Truevine: Two brothers, a kidnapping, and a mother's quest: A true story of the Jim Crow South*. New York, NY: Little Brown and Company.

McAndrew, F. T. (2016, October 27). Why clowns creep us out. *The Washington Post*. Retrieved from www.washingtonpost.com/posteverything/wp/2016/10/27.

Nir, S. M. & Schweber, N. (2017, May 22). A final bow for the greatest show on Earth. *New York Times*, p. A22.

Radford, B. (2016). *Bad clowns*. Albuquerque, NM: University of New Mexico Press.

Rodriguez, D. (2017, May 7). The hunted. *New York Times* Sunday Review, pp. 6–7.

Wikipedia. (2016, October 2). Freak show. Retrieved from http://en.wikipedia .org/wiki/freak.show.

CONCLUSION

Appearance Criminology

A New Approach toward Equitable Treatment

Bonnie Berry

This Conclusion is centered mainly on solutions. Solutions may entail adopting a new attitude about physical appearance, a revision of legislation, development of new policies, and proposing a new subdiscipline of criminology. Some of the discussion below refers to the specific appearance differences as the contributing authors have described them, such as skin color, while other points of discussion refer to the specific problems that some groups of people face because of their appearance, such as victim blameworthiness. Still other topics are unresolved, but the writings herein have offered unique and new views on these topics, for instance whether it is better to be hidden or to be visible to the public and the criminal justice system, if one has a stigmatized appearance.

What I mean to say, as I hope that I have throughout this text is this: physical appearance is a difference. And that is all it is or all it should be. Our appearance says nothing about our abilities, our capacities for kindness, our intelligence, our criminal tendencies or our deservedness to be criminally victimized. Some of us, depending on our appearance, are treated unfairly in life, in all manner of social opportunities (employment, health care, education, romance, social networks, and so on), yet this process of bias is based on the most superficial of human variables. Beauty is skin deep. So are plainness, unattractiveness, skin color, size, and the myriad features that have been addressed here.

Besides a summation of the main themes of this text, I recommend, as hinted above, practices and policies to reduce bias based on their physical appearance. I recommend against race-denying alterations and beautifying strategies for the singular purpose of fitting the mold of socially dictated standards, although it is understandable why people do engage in these practices. Instead, I suggest the development of social awareness programs that encourage social acceptance of a wide array of appearance traits.

In particular, societies would benefit from legislative reform, equality and human rights commissions, research, education and training of first-responders, among other broad societal changes. As well, narrower control system changes are in need of questioning, such as reducing the militarized police presence when it serves to intimidate the local community against lawful protest. Relatedly, improving the manner in which immigration personnel identify and respond to suspected but yet-to-be determined suspects would be globally helpful in the name of fairness and justice.

Whole societies benefit from social movements that increase awareness and acceptance of physical differences, notably the Black Lives Matter movement, fat-acceptance movements, the Idle No More movement grounded in Indigenous rights, and disability-rights movements. Individuals caught up in the criminal justice system, as offenders and as victims, would obviously benefit from increased awareness and acceptance. Finally, the criminal justice system itself would benefit since improved, accurate pinpointing of criminal intent and criminal behavior would prevail, if freed from the bias of appearance.

ALTERING LOOKS, ALTERING SOCIETY

If appearance is related to criminal behavior, as Agnew (1984, Chapter 1 in this text) proposes, one admittedly fraught avenue to eliminating this relationship would be to provide programs to alter the appearance of delinquents and adult offenders. It would be preferable to alter social bias against unattractive people but this route would be the far greater challenge. As to the former, cosmetic surgery, which has been tried with limited success on prison populations, may be applied to correct defects or to simply improve looks (see, e.g., Kurtzberg, Mondell, Lewin, Lipton, & Shuster, 1978). There is a small amount of research indicating that adult offenders who have had their physical appearance surgically enhanced are less likely to return to prison (Lewison, 1974).

Of course, this route implies informed consent in a highly coerced population thereby calling into question how consensual the consent really is. A second barrier would be the cost. Given our current environment in the United States, it is difficult to imagine governmental programs agreeing to pay for enhancing the appearance of criminal offenders.

Moreover, as has been argued elsewhere, there are numerous and important social questions about the wisdom of altering appearance when oftentimes these alterations play into the hands of racist, ageist, sizeist, and sexist social attitudes (Berry, 2008). However, in her useful analysis *Dubious Equalities*, Kathy Davis (2003) reminds us that cosmetic changes, including surgery, do advance us as individuals in our quest for equal treatment. If we need to change our appearance to gain employment or for other social advantages, there is nothing "wrong" with doing so in the sense that this endeavor levels the playing field. The same argument could be expanded to the context of crime: if offenders and victims need cosmetic alterations to be successfully (re)integrated into society, then they should be afforded them.

Agnew's second suggestion, to somehow reduce discrimination via sensitizing society, and specifically law enforcement and other criminal justice personnel, is the preferred, while also being the more utopian, route. This same idea has been reexamined in my work (2007, 2008) with the conclusion being that it is possible through social movement mechanisms to change social attitudes regarding appearance bias, but the degree of success remains in question.

However, while slow and incremental, awareness and rights movements have made some headway in various arenas such as women's rights, civil rights, animal rights, and other movements that recognize the equal worth of beings. The movement forward is almost maddeningly slow and there are constant setbacks. And, yes, equality pertaining to physical appearance faces more intractable barriers than other rights movements, as I mentioned in the Introduction, with appearance equality having more than once been referred to as the last bastion of equal rights movements. This doesn't mean that we, as a society, should not try to engage the public in understanding the basic points that the contributing authors have made here and that I and other authors on the topic of general appearance bias have made: people are people, good and bad, regardless of what they look like.

Improvements in Physical Health

Aside from the idealistic suggestions of consciousness-raising, I recommend at least a consideration of improving the physical health and therefore physical appearance of those involved in crime as offenders or as victims. On this topic, I suggest dental care, hygiene (notably skin care), removal of deformities where possible, and healthy weight maintenance. Surgeries and other alterations to correct painful deformities or to make those with obvious disfigurements are advisable *if the recipients want them and are not coerced.* I would also include weight loss under this caveat. I am wary of recommending weight loss programs across the board because there is significant literature, including my own work, arguing that people can be "healthy at any size" unless they are suffering from weight-related ailments such as diabetes. In other words, heavy people are not necessarily unhealthy and weight loss programs have a high failure rate that has little or nothing to do with the reducing food intake.

In sum, if unattractive people are victimized disproportionately or if they are more commonly associated with criminal peers *because* of their unattractiveness, then we may want to consider appearance alterations such as dental care, deformity correction, and any means to make them less targeted as victims or criminal associates. If victims are targeted because of their attractiveness, on the other hand, we need to alter crime controllers' attitudes that they "had it coming" because of their attractive appearance.

Many of the solutions that I propose are stalled by an absence of funding for improved health care and thus appearance. In the United States, health care and dental care (which should not be considered separable) are unavailable to large swaths pf the population. I cannot think of a delicate way to explain this phenomenon so I will explain it openly as cruelty and greed on the part of segments of our present-day society that refuse to offer health care to the less fortunate. Nonetheless, we must prepare for a day when solutions may be more likely. While not addressing the relationship between poor dentition and criminal involvement specifically, Mary Otto (2017) proposes several solutions to poor dentition, among them the provision of better government insurance.

A good example of programs that can repair appearance, particularly appearance that has been ruined by criminal victimization or criminal activity, is the *Give Back a Smile* program, which is sponsored by the American Academy of Cosmetic Dentistry Charitable Foundation. This program provides free care to abuse victims with broken or damaged teeth. About 75 percent of victims of domestic assault have injuries to the head, neck, and mouth, with knocked-out teeth being preeminent (Raymond, 2011). We need more such programs. I argue as well that we need more such programs for the criminal offenders whose appearance is not optimal, having lived a life of poverty, neglect, and absent health care. Commonly, crime victims and offenders do not have the financial resources to reclaim their before-crime appearance.

In short, criminal offenders and crime victims are often in need of cosmetic repair with victims being the more sympathetic of the two groups. Physical damage, such as missing teeth and destroyed faces, is a secondary form of abuse. That is, victims are physically and psychologically harmed by the abuse itself and additionally are socially harmed, as when social and economic opportunities are blocked, because of the physical evidence of abuse. If we can improve appearance, we can improve abuse victims' social opportunities. Assuming that it is true that offenders or victims are more likely to be unattractive than nonoffenders and nonvictims, improved appearance can thus improve social opportunities, educational, employment, and other life options. Thus, crime would be reduced.

As I have written elsewhere and herein, there are numerous and important social questions about the wisdom of altering socially bounded appearance traits when oftentimes these alterations play into the hands of racist, ageist, ableist, sizeist, and sexist social attitudes. Apart from -ist issues, though, improving health-related traits is an easy argument to make.

Policy and Legislation: A Recognition of Bias

If we are subject to differential treatment because of our appearance, as victims or as offenders, we are in a realm of unfair victim compensation, false accusations, false convictions, and an entire range of injustices because of what we look like. Although I, generally, am not in favor of criminalization and instead am generally more on the side of decriminalization, I tentatively suggest that we increase hate crime legislation and enforcement for crimes against the appearance-challenged. For example, a case of a man in Mississippi who killed his transgender ex-girlfriend resulted in a 49-year sentence under the US hate crime law (Stack, 2017). The length of the sentence is unusually long but the Federal Hate Crimes Act serves to point up the importance of bias in criminal behavior. Hate crime legislation is also used to up the ante in crimes against Blacks, Jews, the disabled, and other disadvantaged minorities. If we could raise awareness by increasing criminal penalties against appearance-bias crimes, we might, through this means, clarify the relationship between appearance and crime and, thus, reduce criminal justice unfairness against those who don't fit the socially desirable appearance mold.

Likewise, if people (for example children) are bullied because of their appearance (for example because they are overweight or disabled), we need to strengthen legislation against such abuse. Better still, to strike at the core of bias-based bullying, we need to enlighten school authorities, neighborhoods, employers, families, and school mates' recognition of bullying and arrive at strategies to reduce it. This reasoning and recommendation holds true at the college level, as shown by Scherer and Reyns (Chapter 13), when people are bullied for invisible and visible disabilities. University administrations, faculty, and staff need enlightenment as to disability bullying and strategies to counteract it.

Recognition is a good starting point, especially if it is followed by constraints imposed on subjugating minorities, including the visibly different such as racial minorities, the disabled, and the unattractive. What this means for the science of criminology is that it would be most helpful, in advancing scholarly thinking and therefore advancing solutions to unfair crime control treatment, to adopt a framework to better understand cultural differences and cultural needs. Cunneen and Tauri (2016) advise recognition of the destructive role played by colonialism (also referred to as colonization) as a means of treating Indigenous peoples fairly in the crime control process. Cunneen and Tauri commend the United Nations General Assembly's adoption of the *Declaration on the Rights of Indigenous People* (2007), which aims to guarantee self-determination, equality, protection of the Indigenous culture, and the like. Such declarations, framed in the appearance-bias-and-crime-control context, could have significance for all of the appearance facets that have been discussed in this text to ensure fair treatment of suspects, offenders, victims, and all who are caught up in the crime control system.

In sum, it would be well to develop global strategies to legislate against appearance discrimination, not only in the realm of crime control as my contributors and I have discussed here, but also in general society, as I have argued elsewhere. True, it can be disheartening to watch, as the centuries go by, anti-discrimination efforts that seem to go nowhere, as Wotherspoon and Hansen have remarked in this text (Chapter 3). But it is possible to legislate against discrimination and it is not helpful to do nothing.

While it would be easier if legislation were not required to change our discriminatory behaviors, Dayna Bowen Matthew (2015) ably points out that law is required to confront implicit, covert bias. In her enlightening treatise on racial inequality and US health care, Matthew speaks specifically to inequalities in the US health care system due to *unconscious* discrimination as a structural malady in search of a systemic cure. This work hearkens back to my recitation of the findings by Sommers and colleagues (2006, 2008, 2009), which showed that health care workers can inadvertently reach incorrect conclusions about whether dark-skinned women have been injured, since bruises and abrasions do not appear as readily on dark skin as they do on light skin.

Matthew provides quantitative and qualitative evidence that African, Asian, Hispanic, and Native American peoples are not provided with the same degree and quality of health care as provided to White people. This is not surprising given that the United States and other societies continue to exercise biased treatment of non-whites regarding health care as well as many other necessary resources such as education, housing, and employment. However, where Matthew's work breaks new ground is to point out that traditional civil rights laws only punish *obvious* racism.

These antidiscrimination laws punish only outright bigotry and the most virulent forms of racism. Now that these forms of overt racism are out of vogue and mostly absent from the health care system, the rule of law has been neutralized and no longer controls racial discrimination. Therefore, the great American tradition of running two separate and unequal medical systems for white and non-white patients is back.

(p. 3)

In other words, while probably unintentional, unequal health care exists and can be relieved by the Matthew's proposed "Biased Care Model" that takes into account this implicit bias. This model is more of a game-changer than we might think since it implies that implicit racial and ethnic bias is not inevitable and is changeable; however, it requires a *morally and legally* responsibility on the part of society to make these changes. In short, we need laws to deal with implicit bias because, while well-intentioned, political efforts have failed to equalize disparities.

Forgive my meandering on health care disparities and race, but this side journey does apply to the question at hand about appearance bias and crime. Matthew reminds us that underlying the health care disparity is economic disparity. I have said the same thing as relevant to physical appearance, and developed my own model as described in the Introduction. Changing laws can but do not necessarily solve disparities of various kinds (health care, crime control, etc.). Leveling economic opportunities can go farther to remove disparities. Socioeconomic status affects physical appearance, physical appearance affects socioeconomic status, and both affect involvement in crime. In sum, Matthew declares, and I agree, that we must face facts that bias occurs and that legislation to remedy these biases must be based on empirically founded facts. Even though our biases may be unconscious, we need not be paralyzed into ignoring them and doing nothing about them.

Education, Training, and Acceptance

Given the importance of this question about the relationship between physical appearance and denial of fair treatment, I advise, some might say unrealistically, that we become accepting of appearance differences. It would be socially functional to recognize and accept that appearance is a superficial trait and that, for the most part, is irrelevant for judgments about character, intelligence, capability, social worth, and so on. Ideally, this awareness would take place on a large social scale as well as on more micro levels such as individual (for instance, bully-victim) and organizational (such as, police department-suspect) levels.

Some of the source of appearance bias is ignorance or inattention. Appearance bias is not well-understood and mainly unacknowledged by the public. It is acknowledged on a superficial level: when people find out that I study appearance bias, they usually say that they have been subject to such bias or that they know of someone who has. When appearance bias is brought to our attention, we recognize its existence. We may recognize it as a social problem, but we do not ordinarily think of it as a means of severe discrimination as it occurs in the crime control process. Social movements centered on social awareness of appearance bias as a form of inequality would reduce the ignorance about this significant social problem.

Given that physical appearance is largely a matter of genetics, poverty, and other uncontrollable factors rather than choice, I advise sensitivity training for criminal justice personnel, juvenile justice systems, victim advocates, and school employees. Overall, the public, our educational systems, and our social control systems need greater awareness about the occurrence of appearance bias, the many forms that appearance bias takes, and the consequences of appearance bias. This may take a similar form to the extant training programs around racial sensitivity. For example, as I stated earlier in the Comments to Part II, better training for forensic medical staff is warranted to determine the impact of skin color differences on assessments about assault (sexual and other): if we cannot determine with our own eyesight that an assault took place or didn't, we need more minute ways to determine the evidence.

Besides empirically verifiable evidence, another means to educate is to engage in discussions about microaggressions, most easily facilitated in college classrooms, that can readily be spread to other audiences. The students who engage in these discussions tell other students, their own families, their co-workers and others about these conversations. Sue (2010) and others have addressed microaggressions along many dimensions (race, gender, disability, orientation, etc.), which are helpful discussion points; overlooked and much-needed, however, are addresses of microaggressions along an appearance dimension.

SUMMARY OF TOPICS: NEW VIEWS AND NEW RESPONSES

A Chicken-and-Egg Question: Does Unattractiveness Lead to Criminal Behavior and Victimization or Does It Follow Criminal Behavior and Victimization?

Here, I would point the reader to Brent Teasdale's and my study (Chapter 2) showing that unattractive young people are more likely to be victimized, more likely to engage in criminal offenses, and more likely to be shut out of legitimate employment opportunities and continue in criminal activities. Recall also Brenda Chaney's work (Chapter 6) showing that the appearance of women on trial can be a consequence of an abusive past and a criminogenic environment, with their subsequent appearance in court determining whether they are incarcerated, which then affects what happens to them for the remainder of their lives. Unfortunately and obviously, their having been incarcerated lessens their chances of successful community reintegration. These two studies as well as many others cited herein show that unattractiveness can lead to victimization *and* criminal involvement in a downward spiral.

Crime Control Intervention and Race Relations

We saw in Comments to Part II that racialized features attract the attention of police and are more likely to lead to arrest compared to White features and less-exaggerated Black features. The literature has shown that being Black is a signal for police intervention, convictions, and harsh sentences, but being Blacker is even more so. What is less known is whether other racial features of the Indigenous, Asians, and Latinos/as operate as do Black features, with the more racialized features leading to more frequent and more severe public and criminal justice intervention.

It is established that there is racial bias in crime control, resulting, for example, in racial minorities' lives being ruined and ended for the exact same acts that Whites commit and for which Whites are not apprehended, convicted, and sentenced. Racial targeting of Black people and other minorities suggests that a deep-seated approach is needed to open the public eye to the blatant facts of racism, to force a recognition of racial unfairness through public messaging.

The management of Indigenous populations is complicated by the bivariate crime control systems, both fraught with injustices. Terry Wotherspoon and John Hansen (Chapter 3) suggest updated and intensified inquiries as well as governmental commissions to finally and effectively eliminate systemic exclusion and racial discrimination. Yet these inquiries have been ongoing for decades, with little effect and continued criminalization and criminal victimization of the Indigenous populations, which brings us back to the need not just for recognition of these injustices but, additionally, for other means to reduce bias. Scrimshaw says much the same, that, until systemic racism against the Indigenous is recognized, there will be only limited progress to reduce inequality (2018). Perhaps improved monitoring and serious investigations of appearance-relevant unfairness practiced by police, courts, and corrections would ensure needed changes. Another enlightened approach to reducing unfairness in the criminal justice treatment of Indigenous peoples would be movements such as the Idle No More movement in Canada. Like the Black Lives Matter movement, Idle No More and similar movements force an awareness of unfairness against those with highly visible racial features; with awareness, the hope is, we may approach equal treatment.

Steve Bishopp (Chapter 9) offers a possible change in methodology when he illustrates that police presence can be merely a presence or it can exist in an extreme and provocative form. We saw the latter especially after the Ferguson, Missouri incident, in which an unarmed Black man was shot and killed by a police officer who was then acquitted of wrongdoing. The locals of Ferguson felt that the acquittal was unfair and served as an undeniable indication that Black Lives Do Not Matter. As a result, rioting occurred. Consequently and coincidentally, the police showed up in riot gear, carrying heavy weaponry, looking very militaristic, complete with tanks. This seemed to make matters worse because, as a result, the locals felt as though the police were viewing their community as a war zone, with the locals totally powerless against a "police state." In contrast, as Bishopp describes, the Dallas, Texas Police Department sports an array of clothing styles and a range of weaponry (from light to heavy), which are designed to correspond to the level of threat posed by the community *and* the level of threat posed by the police. We might conclude that a functional policy for the police to adopt would be to accurately measure the level of threat and not automatically move toward an intimidating appearance.

Some of the other chapters focus more on courts and corrections and the attention that criminologists as well as criminal justice personnel need to pay to biased interpretations of demeanor, behavior, and physical appearance. Because someone looks a certain way does not mean that she or he is guilty.

Being Pretty: Does it Help?

Well, yes, mostly being attractive helps, but it is complicated. I have already mentioned, as have other authors, that being attractive is not always helpful depending upon the type of crime for which one is suspected. The Wareham, Berry, Blackwell, and Boots study (Chapter 7) shows that attractive sexual assault victims are viewed as less blameworthy and that the offenders accused of violating attractive victims are viewed as deserving of harsher punishment. The study by Teasdale, Gann, and Dabney (Chapter 8) found an interaction among several variables only one of which is attractiveness: attractive Black female traffic violators are treated more harshly than attractive Black male violators, showing an interaction between attractiveness, gender, and race. Being attractive, Black, and female does not pay off in these instances as much as being attractive, Black, and male. Both of these chapters list and explain the wide array of studies showing contradictory findings about attractiveness and leniency.

Disability

Thorneycroft and Asquith (2015) offer an extensive list of solutions and recommendations to improve the situation for the visibly disabled as crime victims. In general, we might view victimization of the disabled in the same way as we view all hate crime victimization. We need better policing strategies and better reporting mechanisms. As to policing improvements, better education and training are called for as well as specialist policing units to manage interventions in cases of disablist violence. As to reporting, we need to open channels for reporting disablist violence to encourage victims and third-party reporting. As to third-party reporting, because of the disabled's distrust of the police, the disabled may be more likely to report to a third party instead of the police; since that is the case, we need to formalize third-party mechanisms to ensure that crimes are reported and recorded. Such third-party organizations may benefit from input from advocacy organizations, which can then strengthen referral and connections to strategic policing units trained to assist in disablist violence.

While the above are short-term strategies, the long-term strategies entail a "fundamental reframing of disability" such that we as a society can "change the meanings, attitudes and perceptions of disability in the criminal justice system" (Thorneycroft & Asquith, p. 503). This last recommendation is one that I have repeatedly encouraged over the years of writing about appearance bias. Without a fundamental change in attitudes about people, based on what they look like, it would be difficult or impossible to improve the lot of the appearance-challenged.

Using national and international samples, Scherer and Reyns (Chapter 13) document that the disabled are far more likely to experience interpersonal violence (sexual violence, stalking, physical assault, and verbal threat) than the nondisabled. They find, significantly for this text, that the visibly disabled, those with visual signs of vulnerability (such as wheelchairs, canes, and crutches) are even more at risk than the abled or the disabled with no invisible disabilities. Whether visibly disabled or not, sensitive policing and open channels to reporting are necessary to reduce the disabled's vulnerability to crime.

Integration, Assimilation ... or Maybe Not: Visibly Ethnic, Visibly Terrorist, and Visibly Different

Chapter 5 by Billy Ulibarrí remarks on the hazards of public exposure for the victims of human trafficking. Yes, they need jobs, health care, protection, education, and all the other benefits of being visible members of society. However, especially since 2017 as trafficking pertains to Latinos/as, to be exposed is to risk deportation at worst and, at minimum, crime control intervention on the assumption that Latino/a appearance is indicative of criminal involvement. Victims of human trafficking, regardless of race and ethnicity, are fearful of reporting abuse for the same reasons: visible involvement in society makes one vulnerable to secondary abuse by a crime control system. Yet, one of Ulibarrí's main points is that a social construction of human trafficking as ubiquitous, even when it is not ubiquitous but rather is highly targeted, brings forward the false social message that we are all, regardless of appearance or other traits, potential victims and potential offenders.

As to the revisited question about Indigenous peoples, I had asked Heather Valdez Freeman, Program Director at the Tribal Law and Policy Institute, if it would be better for US Indigenous people to be more integrated into the majority society in order to gain more and better resources and fairer crime control. Recall in the editorial comments to Part II that I had raised this question given the fact that Indigenous people in the United States, Canada, and Australia are isolated from the broader White culture. Given that they are isolated, their offenses and their victimizations may go unattended. They are out of sight and out of mind. True, but my reasoning was faulty and Ms Freeman clarified the problems with integration:

> ... sounds way too much like assimilation. Assimilation was yet another low point in federal Indian policy which failed, but did wreak havoc with Native culture for many tribes. The current movement supported by many tribal nations focuses on sovereignty, self-government, cultural continuity, etc. Crime control, in this view, is best handled by tribal police, who are enforcing tribal law, founded in tribal culture and values. Outsiders (state/federal) are the ultimate in non-community oriented policing. The answer is not to move Native people into the "broader society" but to move control into the hands of tribal government.
>
> (Freeman, personal communication, May 30, 2017)

One area of appearance bias that has been reduced via increased visibility is the greater exposure of highly unusual human appearance, once referred to as "freaks." In Chapter 14, I address extraordinary human appearance in the forms of scary clowns and "freaks." The clowns may be with us for a while given that they are apparently a manifestation of alienation, but the freak exhibits are a rarity nowadays. However, those with extremely obvious human differences, such as albinism in Black Africans, are still bullied and murdered. Society is getting smarter about odd human appearance and some of our increased smartness is about visibility. With visibility, we become accustomed to seeing human oddities as normal. As normalized people, they are less likely to be victimized but simply recognized as ... people.

It's the Interpretation of Terrorism, Not the Terrorist Appearance

Switching to the visibility of terrorists, it is well-documented that White US citizens are far less suspect in US terrorism cases even though their involvement in terrorism is far greater. Indeed, terrorist markers, such as Muslim clothing, are mainly false identifiers of actual terrorism identity. Here, as with all the other features associated falsely with crime, public messaging is needed to explain how wrong we, the public and the crime control system, are in using physical features as evidence that people are innocent or guilty. The 1995 bombing of a federal building in Oklahoma City, perpetrated by two native-born White men, resulted in 168 people killed and more than 680 people injured. This staggering bloodshed carried out by very ordinary-looking White men is in strong contrast to far fewer numbers of people being killed in the 2015 San Bernadino, California shootings and the 2013 Boston, Massachusetts bombings. The United States as a people and as represented by the government, had a strong reaction to the San Bernadino killings of 14 people and the Boston killings of 3 people possibly because these acts were carried out by a Pakistani and her husband, both clothed in Islamic attire and both known to be committed to jihadism in the former case and by two brothers who identified as Muslim Chechens. The San Bernadino and Boston attacks inspired a severe backlash toward foreign-born, non-Christian outsiders even though far fewer people were killed and injured compared to the Oklahoma attack.

Mark Hamm (Chapter 11) and Daniela Pisoiu (Chapter 10) remark, in different ways, about our fallacious targeting of terrorists, real or not real, based on their appearance. Hamm, as he has written consistently over the decades, has pointed out that White men are usually to blame for terrorist acts in the United States. Pisoiu travels a very different route in explaining terrorist appearance by showing that it can be a fashion statement more than a religious and cultural statement. Who knew that terrorist attire could be "cool." Nevertheless, such terrorism markers as Pisoiu describes them, can rightly or wrongly target adherents to clothing styles as terrorists.

Multiplicity Effects in Appearance and Crime

Pascoe (2012) recommends fair treatment of gender-nonconforming students through research and social activism: new research has reframed LGBTQ and "gender-variant youths not just as victims, but as activists who see themselves as agents of social change …" (p. xiv). She further advises that researchers provide "road maps for transforming schools into less heteronormative, sexist, and homophobic spaces …" (p. xiv). This is good advice. Moreover, I think Meyer (2015), in his book on queer violence, is on to something when he says we should concentrate intently on the issue of *combined* oppressed traits of queer status, race status, class status, and gender status. He remarks,

... attempts to reduce anti-queer violence that ignore race, class, and gender do so at their own peril, as such approaches are likely to aid only the most privileged gay subjects. Instead, by emphasizing marginalized queer people's perspectives, scholarly and advocacy work can dispel the myth that LGBT people experience violence uniformly and aid a broad range of queer people, including those who experience racism, classism, and sexism, rather than simply attending to the needs of white and middle-class gay men.

(p. 13)

Related to the socioeconomic stratification that I remark upon throughout this text and the "oppression Olympics" that Meyer writes about, refer to the chapter by Elicka Peterson Sparks and Ian Skinner (Chapter 12) and to Meyer's recommendation that we not construct "differently marginalized groups as rivals [since] that prevents them from working together toward challenging inequality. Indeed, what keeps marginalized groups from forming coalitions with one another is not necessarily their differences per se, but rather how those differences are used to divide them" (Meyer, 2015: 33).

Meyer maintains that the violence visited upon the LGBTQ community is

better understood by focusing not only on homophobia and heteronormativity but also on the dimension of inequality. By perpetually emphasizing sexuality, we continue to favor the experiences of the most privileged LGBT people – those who need the least help – and marginalize the experiences of the most disadvantaged.

(p. 157)

What is needed is a focus on *all* inequality, Meyer remarks, and I agree. In fact, that is the main point of this text, to recognize that appearance bias, like homophobia, racism, sexism, disablism, classism, and all the other "isms" are forms of social inequality that needlessly lead to individual and social harm. Bear this multiplicity argument in mind for the discussion below about future research. Based on what we have been able to glean so far in this relatively unexplored area of criminological research is the probable fact that multiple variables interact with each other to create appearance bias in crime control. Untangling these many variables involves knowing about them and weighing their varying impacts on criminality, criminal victimization, and social control response to crime and victimization. If, for instance, being attractive *and* queer increases or decreases victimization, we need to know that. If being wealthy, educated, *and* unattractive affects criminality and victimization, we need to know that. You get the idea: many variables interact to enhance or detract from risk of crime, victimization, and crime control intervention.

We need a recognition of *intersectionality*. Here I must express gratitude to an anonymous reviewer of this text who noticed the intersectionality of the topics presented herein. Of course I must have thought of intersectionality, meaning the interrelatedness or the causal and correlational relationships between the variables associated with appearance and crime, but it took an outside observer to see it in obvious, out-in-the-open terms. The recognition of intersectionality is absolutely essential to understanding the phenomena (yes, plural) of appearance bias and crime and, just as importantly, to offer solutions to the life-affecting, life-threatening, and society-damaging effects of appearance bias in the crime context.

FINAL WORDS: APPEARANCE CRIMINOLOGY

Since, as my contributors and I have suggested, physical appearance is an integral part of the crime control process, it is reasonable for the field of criminology to adopt a new subdiscipline focused on appearance. This new research area might be called appearance criminology or, perhaps more broadly, visual criminology.

Understanding how appearance affects the criminal justice process and the decisions made at each level of the process would be one venue to study appearance criminology. The mere but important fact that appearance changes after a lifetime of abuse or an incident of abuse has not been attended to in a scientific fashion. The criminal justice system, victims' advocacy, and general society would benefit from minute documentation of such appearance changes. For example, if crime victims appear in court with their bruises and cuts healed, the court is not getting a full picture of the abuse and the culpability of the offender.

To do things right, appearance criminology could investigate the entire crime control process as influenced by the appearance of the victims and the suspected offenders, from initial police contact to application of the death penalty. Just looking at one slice of the process is helpful and, per my editorial comments to Part III, it is inescapable that one slice is significant as a make-or-break part of the entire process. In mugshots, for instance, we see that the appearance of people in booking photos greatly influences court decisions to convict and imprison. But because the initial encounter with the criminal justice process can affect the rest of the process, up to and including imposing the death penalty, we need to look at how appearance bias influences the entire process.

Future Research

Clearly, there is much that we do not know about appearance bias and crime that needs empirical verification. Think back to the hypothesized model proposed in the Introduction. While the data do not presently exist, it would be helpful to the sciences of criminology and sociology and to the pursuit of justice if these variables could be measured empirically, especially as pertaining to each other. Recall that the independent variables (IVs) are demographic traits (race, age, gender, socioeconomic status) and appearance traits. These IVs are correlated and may be causal, with demographic traits influencing appearance. Both types of IVs affect the dependent variable (DV), case outcome. That much is known. But how are the IVs weighted? Does, for example, being poor affect justice-related appearance more than, say, race? Do demographic traits weigh more than appearance traits to affect justice outcomes? These independent measures may be difficult to tease apart because they are, in fact, correlated. Yet it is crucial that we do measure them – as correlated, causal, or independent – if we are to understand the role of physical appearance on crime, criminal victimization, and crime control.

This model is important to understand because many of the IVs that define us are beyond our control. We have limited or no control over our age, our race, our gender, disability, socioeconomic status, and thus our appearance. And it is important to try to understand how much each of these variables weighs in contributing to our appearance and, importantly, to the way in which we are treated by the public and by the criminal justice system. For instance, if being Black is closely related to poverty, these variables may operate in a multiplicative way to almost ensure involvement in crime as a victim or as an offender; in both cases (being a victim or an offender), being poor and Black speaks to unfair treatment.

Stratification abounds in these studies of appearance bias (see Berry, 2008; Bogdan, 1988; Meyer, 2015). This text is an early inroad to becoming aware that appearance is one way in which we as humans are stratified. Stratification along appearance lines is pertinent to the crime control picture in that, even in criminal justice settings (courts, prisons, streets and other public venues), victims and offenders are placed hierarchically. Better-looking prisoners, controlling for conviction, may be offered parole sooner or may be placed under less onerous conditions, may be offered work release or better rehabilitation programs, etc. I write "may be" because we don't know these things. We need to know the answers to these questions as well as many crime control-appearance questions.

Gratitude and Farewell for Now

I will end this work with an expression of gratitude. I thank you, dear reader, for your interest in this topic and your willingness to grasp this material. I thank the contributing authors for their hard work and their attempts to make this project understandable and meaningful. With your willingness to grasp this new topic and the authors' willingness to help explain this phenomenon, we embark on the first step in making life fairer.

References

Agnew, R. (1984). Appearance and delinquency. *Criminology*, 22, 421–440.
Berry, B. (2007). *Beauty bias: Discrimination and social power*. Westport, CT: Praeger.
   (2008). *The power of looks: Social stratification of physical appearance*. Hampshire, UK: Ashgate.
Bogdan, R. (1988). *Freak show: Presenting human oddities for amusement and profit*. Chicago, IL: University of Chicago Press.
Cunneen, C. & Tauri, J. (2016). *Indigenous criminology*. Chicago, IL: Policy Press.
Dabney, D., Teasdale, B., Ishoy, G. A., Gann, T., & Berry, B. (2017). Policing in a largely minority jurisdiction: The influence of appearance characteristics associated with contemporary hip-hop culture on police decision-making. *Justice Quarterly*, 34, 1310–1338.
Davis, K. (2003). *Dubious inequalities and embodied differences: Cultural studies on cosmetic surgery*. Lanham, MD: Rowman and Littlefield.
Freeman, Heather Valdez. (2017, May 30). Personal communication.
Kurtzberg, R., Mondell, W., Lewin, M., Lipton, D., & Shuster, M. (1978). Plastic surgery on offenders. In N. Johnston and L. Savitz (Eds.), *Justice and corrections* (pp. 688–700). New York, NY: John Wiley.
Lewison, E. (1974). Twenty years of prison surgery: An evaluation. *Canadian Journal of Otolaryngology*, 3, 42–50.
Matthew, D. M. (2015). *Just medicine: A cure for racial inequality in American health care*. New York, NY: New York University Press.
Meyer, D. (2015). *Violence against queer people: Race, class, gender, and the persistence of anti-LGBT discrimination*. New Brunswick, NJ: Rutgers University Press.

Otto, M. (2017). *Teeth: The story of beauty, inequality, and the struggle for oral health in America.* New York, NY: The New Press.

Pascoe, C. J. (2012). *Dude, you're a fag: Masculinity and sexuality in high school.* Berkeley, CA: University of California Press.

Raymond, J. (2011, September 28). After abuse, shattered smiles bring shame, stigma. Retrieved from www.msnbc.msn.com/id/44678589.

Scrimshaw, G. (2018, February 16). A killing in Saskatchewan. *New York Times*, p. A29.

Sommers, M. S., Zink, T., Baker, R., Fargo, J., Porter, J., Weybright, D., & Shafer, J. (2006). Effects of age and ethnicity on physical injury from rape. *Journal of Obstetrics, Gynecology, and Neonatal Nursing, 35*, 199–207.

Sommers, M. S., Zink, T. M., Fargo, J. D., Baker, R. B., Buschur, C., Shambley-Ebron, D. Z., & Fisher, B. S. (2008). Forensic sexual assault examination and genital injury: Is skin color a source of health disparity? *American Journal of Emergency Medicine, 26*, 857–866.

Sommers, M. S., Fargo, J. D., Baker, R. B., Fisher, B. S., Buschur, C., & Zink, T. M. (2009). Health disparities in the forensic sexual assault examination related to skin color. *Journal of Forensic Nursing, 5*, 191–200.

Stack, L. (2017, May 17). Killer of transgender woman is sentenced under U.S. hate crime law. *New York Times*, p. A21.

Sue, D. W. (2010). *Microaggresssions and marginality: Manifestation, dynamics, and impact.* Hoboken, NJ: John Wiley and Sons, Inc.

Thorneycroft, R. & Asquith, N. L. (2015). The dark figure of disablist violence. *The Howard Journal of Criminal Justice, 54*, 489–507.

Index